Sanctifying Art

art for faith's sake series

SERIES EDITORS:

Clayton J. Schmit
J. Frederick Davison

This series of publications is designed to promote the creation of resources for the church at worship. It promotes the creation of two types of material, what we are calling primary and secondary liturgical art.

Like primary liturgical theology, classically understood as the actual prayer and practice of people at worship, primary liturgical art is that which is produced to give voice to God's people in public prayer or private devotion and art that is created as the expression of prayerful people. Secondary art, like secondary theology, is written reflection on material that is created for the sake of the prayer, praise, and meditation of God's people.

The series presents both worship art and theological and pedagogical reflection on the arts of worship. The series title, *Art for Faith's Sake*,* indicates that, while some art may be created for its own sake, a higher purpose exists for arts that are created for use in prayer and praise.

OTHER VOLUMES IN THIS SERIES:

Senses of the Soul by William A. Dyrness
Dust and Prayers by Charles L. Bartow
Dust and Ashes by James L. Crenshaw
Preaching Master Class by William H. Willimon
Praying the Hours in Ordinary Life by Clayton J. Schmit and Lauralee Farrer
Mending a Tattered Faith: Devotions with Dickinson by Susan VanZanten
Blessed: Monologues for Mary by Jerusha Matsen Neal
Senses of Devotion: Interfaith Aesthetics in Buddhist and Muslim Communities by William A. Dyrness

FORTHCOMING VOLUMES IN THIS SERIES:

Dance in Scripture: How Biblical Dancers Can Revolutionize Worship Today by Angela M. Yarber
ReVisioning: Critical Methods of Seeing Christianity in the History of Art edited by James Romaine and Linda Stratford

* *Art for Faith's Sake* is a phrase coined by art collector and church musician, Jerry Evenrud, to whom we are indebted.

Sanctifying Art

Inviting Conversation between Artists,
Theologians, and the Church

Deborah Sokolove

CASCADE *Books* • Eugene, Oregon

SANCTIFYING ART
Inviting Conversation between Artists, Theologians, and the Church

Art for Faith's Sake 9

Cascade Books
An Imprint of Wipf and Stock Publishers
199 W. 8th Ave., Suite 3
Eugene, OR 97401

www.wipfandstock.com

ISBN 13: 978-1-62032-633-6

Cataloging-in-Publication data:

Sokolove, Deborah

Sanctifying art : inviting conversation between artists, theologians, and the church / Deborah Sokolove.

xii + 190 p. ; 23 cm. — Includes bibliographical references and index(es).

Art for Faith's Sake 9

ISBN 13: 978-1-62032-633-6

1. Subject. 2. I. Series. II. Title.

CALL NUMBER 2013

Manufactured in the U.S.A.

Contents

Foreword

I am certain that I met Deborah Sokolove when she became Artist-in-Residence and Curator of the Dadian Gallery at Wesley Theological Seminary in 1994, but she didn't fully register on my radar screen until she registered for my course. The course was The Hebrew Bible and the Arts. I believe this was the third time I had taught the course.

Now, I had been Professor of Hebrew Bible at Wesley for twenty-three years at that point, and this was not a course I imagined teaching when I first finished my graduate work. But I happened to come to Wesley in time for the beginning of an unusual romance between theological education and the arts. Due to the persistence and vision of an artist named Catherine Kapikian, a program bringing the arts into the life of a theological school had been founded and was flourishing by the early 1990s at Wesley. One aspect of that program, encouraged by a Luce Foundation grant, was to integrate the arts into the full curriculum of theological education. Wesley had quality courses in the arts, but this was an effort to use the arts as a resource in many other disciplines of theological education, and I was an enthusiastic participant in this enterprise.

Except for some early education and participation in theater arts and a lifetime of singing regularly with groups, I had no formal training in the arts. I knew, however, as a Bible teacher that artists of every artistic medium had been interacting with biblical stories and texts in a serious way for centuries. Many people have been as influenced by artistic interactions with the Bible as they have by sermons or formal Bible study. I wanted my students as future pastors and church leaders to know something about that, and to draw on the arts as a resource in their ministries. I began to use the arts in my introductory Hebrew Bible classes, and students responded to this, so I thought a course focused entirely on the interaction of the Hebrew Bible and the arts would be a good idea. I designed the course syllabus to provide interaction with artists' biblical encounters in all the arts: visual arts, music, drama, film, literature, poetry. (I couldn't get dance in there although some student projects did.) I taught the course a couple of times and felt pretty good about it.

Then, in 1994, a program of our Center for the Arts and Religion to bring practicing artists to campus, to work in our studio and interact with our entire community, brought Deborah Sokolove to campus and into my class. Deborah is a trained and accomplished artist. She has degrees in art education and in computer graphics. She is a painter and a sculptor as well as a computer graphic artist and designer. But she is also from a Jewish background but had become a leader in an unusual congregation called Seekers Church, affiliated with Church of the Saviour in Washington, DC. It was wonderful to have her in the class. She made wise and insightful contributions to class discussions. The sharing of her own class project was a highlight for everyone. We often interacted on Wesley's campus and in the Dadian Gallery where she began to curate outstanding shows.

At the end of the course she came to my office to thank me for the course and tell me how much she enjoyed it. But the rest of our conversation I can really translate in only one way. In the gentle but persistent style she naturally uses she said "It's really too bad you don't know more about art."

Well, I actually agreed with this. So when she completed her Master of Theological Studies degree at Wesley in 1998 I invited her to begin team teaching the course on The Hebrew Bible and the Arts with me. We did so through several offerings of the course until I retired in 2009. I had become the dean at Wesley so I actually hired her to do this, and it was my joy that in my final year as dean before retirement I hired her as the second Director of the Henry Luce III Center for the Arts and Religion at Wesley Theological Seminary.

In the years we taught together I did become Deborah's student in many ways as we created in our teaching team the very dialog between Hebrew Scripture and the arts that we were examining in the work of artists in every medium. Many times during those years I can remember saying to Deborah (as friend, colleague, and dean) that I hoped she was going to find a way to publish and share the insights she gave to us in class. Now she has given us a volume that does this, and in a wonderfully readable way.

Before I turn you loose to sample the treasures of these pages I do want to say something further about the author and then something about the volume.

Deborah Sokolove doesn't seem capable of doing anything halfway. She was already a trained and successful artist when I first met her, but she was restless. She found at Wesley a context that valued the intersection of arts and theology. But neither of these were just disciplinary subjects to her. Deborah is a deeply passionate artist and a deeply spiritual person of faith.

In her congregation she is one of the leaders and has used her artistic talents to great effect in the life of that community. At Wesley she could relate art and theology together in a community that valued the deep way she sought to do that. She had even completed an MTS degree and begun to do some teaching but she didn't want to be considered an artist teaching about connections to theology and church. She wanted to be an artist and a theologian and therefore able to speak from the inside of both of these disciplinary worlds. She became a doctoral student in liturgical studies at Drew University and commuted from Wesley to Madison, NJ to complete the work for this degree. There are few in the world of theological education who have prepared themselves so thoroughly to invite, as her volume subtitle does, *Conversation Between Artists, Theologians, and the Church*. She invites each group as one of their own. Few volumes available in the field achieve this intimacy of invitation into conversation. She knows and anticipates the hesitancies, the stumbling blocks, the misperceptions, and the blind spots from each side of the dialogue because to some degree she inhabits both sides of the conversation.

Over the years I have read many volumes on the relationship of art to theology. The questions get shaped and reshaped, but you can almost always tell which side of the dialogue the author inhabits. The reviews then are predictable. Valuable insights but the author doesn't fully understand *my* world (depending on whether the reviewer is an artist or a theologian). That will not be possible with Deborah Sokolove's volume.

Sanctifying Art is a volume with gifts on many levels. It is written in a readable and accessible style and addresses issues in a way that will find audiences among theologians, artists, church people, and students alike. This is a rare quality and it does this with the intention that these communities might fruitfully find things to talk about together. She punctures pretensions, misconceptions, and narrowed vision that exist on both sides of the dialogue. She tackles deep philosophical issues long debated by both artists and theologians, like truth and beauty, and leaves the reader feeling like these debates have become fresh and worth pondering once again.

I cannot remember finding in any volume on art and religion a chapter that is the parallel of Deborah Sokolove's chapter on "Art and the Need of the World." She told me in a recent conversation that it was the hardest chapter to write, and I can believe that. It is filled with the passion of a woman who believes that both art and religion have failed in their purpose if their endeavors cannot positively effect the needs of the world. That introverted art or religion are not worthy of the calling they profess. This chapter alone is worth the price of this book.

But I am not writing a review. This is merely a foreword. It is a word that comes before from someone privileged to journey alongside a remarkable woman named Deborah Sokolove. She became my friend even while she became a trusted colleague and a valued teacher. We had adventures together in our teaching, and she even shares some of this in the volume. Having taken my own journey with her, and having read this volume now, I can tell you that you have a great journey ahead of you as you read on past this foreword.

Bruce C. Birch
Wesley Theological Seminary
Fall 2012

Acknowledgments

There are so many people to thank for the existence of this book that noting them all would take another volume of equal size. However, there are a few people deserving of special thanks, beginning with John Morris, whose careful reading and rereading have made this a better book; Denise Domkowski Hopkins, who read early drafts of the first few chapters and cheered me on through the rewrites; and Kendall Soulen, who disagreed with my conclusions about beauty but encouraged me to keep writing. Thanks also to Peggy Parker and to Ginger Geyer, with each of whom I have shared much laughter about our lives as artists sojourning among theologians and who have both been urging me to write for as long as I have been a member of this odd fellowship of artists in theology-land. I am grateful for Wilson Yates, Robin Jensen, Don Saliers, Frank Burch Brown, and the many others who have given so much of their lives to exploring the intersection of theology and the arts, and who have taught me and befriended me as a latecomer to their company. I am particularly grateful to Carole Grunberg and the late Kate Cudlipp, who gave me a place to stay where I could hear the ocean as I began the writing; to the members of my mission groups and many other members of Seekers Church, who have been praying for this project all along the way; and to my faculty colleagues in the Monday lunchtime prayer group, who soothed my fears and worries with wisdom gained from their own experiences as writers. Thanks also to research librarian James Estes, whose divine calling was repeatedly affirmed as he pointed me in the right direction in my quests for century-old journals and other obscure materials; to Bruce Birch, who introduced me to the ways of theological education and continues to mentor and encourage me; to Catherine Kapikian, without whose vision and energy the Center for the Arts and Religion at Wesley Theological Seminary would not exist; to Amy Gray, Alexandra Sherman, and Trudi Ludwig Johnson, who made sure that everything was running smoothly in the Center office even when I was too distracted to notice; and to our graduate assistant, Vanya Mullinax, who checked quotations and footnotes and asked good questions. Most of all, I thank my husband, Glen

Yakushiji, who not only finds extra spaces and missing commas and points out when I've lapsed into incomprehensible jargon, but also brings me sandwiches when I forget to eat and invites me on bike rides when I've been at the computer too long; and my grown-up children, who have little interest in this subject but seem to be proud of me anyway. To everyone else who is equally deserving of thanks but whom I have neglected to note, please accept my apologies and silent gratitude. It takes a community to write a book.

1.

Prologue

A theologian friend recently asked me, Why does art matter to you? It was late, and I was tired, so I said that it simply does, and that I didn't feel the need to enquire any more deeply into that particular question. The next morning, I found an email in which my friend said that, while my answer was all very well, the real question was, "Why should art matter to anyone else?" My friend went on,

> I've done a little art and I like it. I've looked at some art and felt stirred by it, and not just beautiful art but also [disturbing] art . . . Still art clearly does not matter to me in the same way it matters to you. Are you writing just for yourself or are you writing for people like me? If for me, then I need some windows into your world.

This book is an attempt to open up those windows, not just for my friend and me, but for others—especially others in church communities—who are, like us, trying to find a way to talk about art that doesn't pit experts against neophytes, or lovers of high art against those who never step foot in a gallery, museum, or concert hall.

One of the problems in conversations like this is that artists are often tongue-tied when asked to explain what seems self-evident to them. So, it took a while for me to find the right words, but eventually I was able to say to my friend two, quite different things.

First, my answer to the question, "Why should the art in a museum or gallery matter as much to other people as it does to me?" is, "Maybe it shouldn't." Because of my life experience, or simply because of how my mind works, or how my body responds to color and form, I happen to have a taste for certain kinds of high art, much as I have a taste for chocolate. Just as I wouldn't try to argue my husband into liking chocolate when he prefers vanilla, I have no need to convince anyone to spend time in an art museum when they would prefer to walk on the beach or listen to rap.

On the other hand, an awareness of what is in museums, concert halls, and theaters, and the ways that certain paintings, pieces of music, poems, stories, and other artworks have affected the overall cultural, theological, and spiritual discourse, is part of being an educated human being. Much of what can be known about the church, as well as society at large, in earlier eras is available only through the medium of the arts. To ignore that evidence is to ignore a large part of human experience.

The second thing that I said is that, despite the statement to the contrary, I am aware that art—defined more broadly, at least—does matter to my friend the theologian, as well as to most other churchgoers. To take the most obvious example, the music used in worship is a matter of passionate debate in many congregations. Whether the congregation should sing hymns, praise choruses, or chants from the Taizé community is not simply a matter of taste, but is profoundly formative on individual piety as well as how (or whether) worshippers understand themselves as interdependent members of the Body of Christ. Somewhat less obvious, but nonetheless real, is how the quality, presence, or absence of various kinds of arts within the worship space and the church building overall affects people's relationship to one another, to the church, and to God.

Beauty and Theology

While my friend was aware that not all art is beautiful, many theologians tend to talk about art and beauty in the same breath. For them, of course, God is both the source and the measure of all Beauty—which they tend to capitalize along with those other transcendental virtues, Truth and Goodness. But it is often a short step for theological aestheticians to move from assertions of the absolute beauty of God to declare that this or that piece of art, or this or that type of art, is not only beautiful, but a sanctified manifestation of the beauty of God.

It wasn't always so. For nearly 500 years, visual art was suspect in most Protestant churches; drama was largely absent; and dance was considered virtually synonymous with seduction and sin. Music (mostly in the form of hymnody) and poetry (mostly in the form of prayer) were the only arts that were encouraged. Even in those churches that commissioned expensive stained glass windows or elaborate furnishings and decorations, the imagery was largely conventional and the artistry subordinated to the message. Although Roman Catholic churches continued to use statues and paintings as the focus of devotional and worship practices, by the late nineteenth century these had become mostly mass-produced plaster copies of a few accepted forms. While there were, of course, exceptions, by and large Christian worship offered no place for contemporary art by living artists. In the late twentieth century, that began to change.

For a variety of reasons, including but not limited to an experimental attitude toward worship sparked by the Second Vatican Council and the liturgical renewals that followed in both Roman Catholic and Protestant worlds, the arts began to find a new—if still somewhat uneasy—acceptance in Christian life. Much has been written in the last few years about this renewed relationship. Nearly as many books have been written on theological aesthetics in each of the last ten years as in the previous 100 years taken together. Theological seminaries are adding courses on the integration of the arts into Christian education and worship, as well as rewriting courses on Scripture and church history to include the use of the arts as evidence of attitudes and understandings in a variety of historical periods. At the same time, many Christian artists have found a new boldness in using their faith as the basis of their work, seeing their artistic process as spiritual journey and their product as evangelical witness.

What is missing from this growing attention to the arts in Christian circles has been a critical discussion of what art does and does not do, and why we think so. Art has been lauded as a means of apprehending the holy; as a form of prayer; even as revelation, however imperfect, of God's own beauty and truth. In many ways, the arts, once vilified, are now sanctified; what was once feared as a tool of the devil is now embraced as a means of grace. This volume is an attempt to look at these and other claims that have been made about art, identify the sources of these claims, and consider them in the context of Christian devotion, corporate worship, and theological study so that both artists and the church may take one another seriously as partners in conversation.

Art and Aesthetics

For a variety of historical reasons, the fields of philosophical and theological aesthetics have come to center on the notion of *beauty*. This is especially true in much current writing on theological aesthetics, which (as I read it) seems to center on the understanding that God is the source of beauty and that any standard of beauty ultimately derives from God. While I have no dispute with these formulations, my own understanding of aesthetics comes less from philosophy and theology than from my practice and education as a visual artist.

When artists speak of aesthetics, they are not usually speaking about beauty, but of the relationships (harmonious or otherwise) among the various elements of an artwork, and of how those relationships express ideas or emotions. The root of the word, *aesthetic*, after all, derives from a Greek word meaning "perceptible to the senses." In the singular, an aesthetic is a particular attitude, or set of values, which affects such diverse qualities as color palette, subject matter, medium, attitude, and more. Aesthetics, for artists, is about what can be perceived with the senses, and the effect that such perception has on both emotion and meaning.

A Life in Art

So this book grows out of my life history. While many of the details are quite ordinary, certain particulars will illuminate the source of the concerns that this volume addresses. I have been an artist in my own right for over thirty years. For ten years before I claimed that identity, I was married to a painter. I have worked at various times as craftsperson, fashion designer, graphic designer, and seamstress. I come from a family of musicians, dancers, actors, screen-writers, and artisans. One grandfather designed embroidered skirts for starlets and sequined shirts for Hollywood cowboys; the other was a clarinetist who left the Borscht Belt Klezmer circuit to found the first music store in Southern California. My mother's mother worked as a mill girl in Poland and became a milliner in the Bronx. I have always made things with my hands. One way or another, my life has always been connected with the arts. For the last thirty years or so, I have been a working artist with an active exhibition schedule and occasional liturgical commissions,

In 1965, the year that I turned eighteen, the Los Angeles County Museum of Art opened its new building on Wilshire Boulevard, not far from where I was living. The first exhibition that I recall was of large, flat planes of color; canvases full of splashed and poured paint; and the silk-screened repetition of giant soup cans. It was all a very long time ago, and my memory may be conflating this with one or more later shows, but what I recall was that I was transfixed by my first sight of works by such artists as Barnett Newman, Kenneth Noland, Willem de Kooning, and Brice Marden. The Andy Warhol works probably came later, some time after the scandalous *Back Seat Dodge '38* by Edward Kienholz, shown to much controversy in 1966. The precise chronology doesn't really matter. What does matter is the effect these works had on me and my subsequent understanding of what art is, what art does, and why so many people care.

Up until those shows, I probably had a rather conventional under-standing of art. To the extent that I thought about it at all, I thought that art was about representation, about drawing things as convincingly as possible. I was never singled out at school or anywhere else as "the artistic one," even though I was always making things. But sewing up gypsy outfits for my parents to wear to a costume ball, carefully lettering a ten-foot banner for a science project, inventing new plaiting patterns for lanyards at summer camp, or even helping to lay out the junior high school yearbook were not considered "art," either by me or by anyone else that I knew. Artists were people who drew and painted, effortlessly, with no instruction, as naturally as birds sing.

Drawing wasn't effortless for me. It was, however, a challenge that I was determined to overcome. In my sophomore year in high school, I nearly failed all my classes because I was drawing, incessantly and obsessively. Mostly, I drew hands. Since it was always available, I would draw my own left hand, over and over, in a variety of poses, trying to make the result as lifelike as possible. Sometimes, if they would agree to sit still long enough, I would draw someone else's hands. Hands seemed to me somehow more revealing than faces. A face could lie, but a hand was honest, no more and no less than itself. In drawing the same subject repetitively, I was training myself to see, to make may own hand record the small irregularities, the minute, yet infinitely differing relationships of knuckle and nail, of joint and ligament, of palm and finger that make one hand clearly belong to me, and another belong to you. Thinking back on this period now, I think that I was trying to understand both the difference and the connection between self and other. It was a way of knowing something that could not be known in any other way.

Yet even in this year of compulsive drawing, I never thought that I was, or could be, or even wanted to be, an artist. The only art class I had ever taken was one that was required in the seventh grade. Although I secretly longed to know the mysteries taught in the studio, I could not allow myself to admit it. Instead, I filled my schedule with the heavy academics that would lead to college. I worked hard at the things I was interested in, like Latin and geom-etry, and skated by with low Bs in the subjects that bored me, like biology and civics. Although I knew that I liked to make things, girls weren't allowed to take drafting or print shop, and somehow I had internalized the message that art classes were for slow learners, those who couldn't make it through the college prep curriculum. I listened with longing to other students' tales of what they were learning in art appreciation class, but never could allow myself to admit that that was where I wanted to be. It was only in my thirties that I was able to confess that I wanted to go to art school.

What I learned when I finally got there, besides the technical mysteries of watercolor and lithography; of stretching canvas and kneading clay; of color theory and the elements and principles of design; was that art is a form of discourse, a means of communication, and a record of what humans believe about the nature of the world. Art, the historians in the department taught me, is visual philosophy. Today, I would add that is also visual theology, a way of thinking about the nature of God and the relationship of that God to humankind and to all creation.

Eventually, I earned an MFA and went on to teach art at a state university. Later, I also earned a master's degree in Theology, and a doctorate in Liturgical Studies. For fifteen years, I was the Curator of the Dadian Gallery at Wesley Theological Seminary, where I now teach and serve as the Director of the Henry Luce III Center for the Arts and Religion. In addition, I am an active member of a small, local church where the arts are an integral part of our worship life.

A Few Definitions

It is this immersion in both the world of art and the world of faith that leads me to question the ways that art is thought about in the church and its related institutions. As I read what theologians, liturgical scholars, church historians, and even self-professed Christian artists have been writing about art, I am frequently struck by the disjuncture between what Christian authors claim as the virtues of art, and how the art world itself views and values its own products and processes.

In saying that, I realize I need to provide some definitions. First, I need to clarify that when I say "the church." I do not mean any particular church or congregation, or even denomination. Rather, I am referring generically to Christians and their institutions, primarily in the United States. I realize that such a generalization skates over a great many particular differences, but the arguments for and against the arts in worship and other moments in Christian life tend to transcend denominational lines. Influential writers from a variety of disciplines and denominational backgrounds who write about the arts and the church include Frank Burch Brown, Don Saliers, William Dyrness, Jeremy Begbie, Robin Jensen, and the late Doug Adams, just to name a few. While each of them has a particular viewpoint growing out of their experience of both the arts and the church, their writings like mine are generally addressed to the church at large, rather than any particular denomination.

Next, I must define what I mean by *art, the arts*, and *the art world*. By *art*, I mean primarily what are often called the visual or plastic arts[1]—painting, drawing, sculpture, photography, and the like. Sometimes, however, when I say art, I mean it more generally, including dance, drama, music, cinema, and poetry, as well as the visual arts. I hope that the context will make clear which I mean.

While my perspective is shaped primarily by the visual arts, much of what I have to say is equally true of all the arts. For instance, any artwork, whether visual or not, whether as solid and lasting as a Greek kouros or a medieval cathedral, or as ephemeral as a single performance of John Cage's "4'33'," is an expression of its time and place. An artwork, regardless of medium, is, among other things, a record of the social, political, and historical context within which the artist functions. It is only in relatively modern times that art, regardless of medium, began to be understood as the idiosyncratic expression of the individual artist, or even (as is sometimes claimed) as divinely-inspired revelation.

When I say *the arts*, I am referring to a fairly elastic group of activities and products that includes painting, sculpture, music, literature, concert music, ballet, and other high arts, but may also be understood as stretching to include such applied arts as movies, interior decorating, and graphic design. Although there are many commonalities among the arts, it must be noted that there are very real differences as well. The technical processes and problems facing the printmaker are quite different than those facing the musician, actor, or writer. Nevertheless, regardless of medium, artists tend to recognize similarities that transcend technique, such as the difficulty of translating an interior vision into an external form that an audience can grasp.

Finally, when I talk about *the art world*, I am referring to museums, galleries, art schools, and journals devoted to the dissemination of ideas about art; and the artists, critics, patrons, and art historians who define themselves in relationship to these institutions. In fact, however, there is no longer anything that may be monolithically called "the art world," in the sense that this was meant in the middle of the twentieth century. In the 1950s and 60s, that world was centered in New York, where contemporary, serious, important art of the Modernist persuasion was defined as what was shown in the Museum of Modern Art, and the art of other times and places was exhibited in the Metropolitan Museum of Art.

1. *Plastic*, in this context, means malleable, or able to be shaped or formed. Materials as diverse as clay, bronze, or fabric may be described as plastic in this sense.

Today there are several art worlds, each with its own set of critical principles, standards, sources, and markets. While superficially similar as venues for the display of exemplary artwork, the National Gallery of Art in Washington, DC, the Museum of Visionary Art in nearby Baltimore, MD, and the American Folk Art Museum in New York City, for example, define art in very different ways. The art world, like so many other fields in this postmodern era, has splintered into many sub-specialties, each claiming the authority to decide what it values and promotes, or even to challenge the very concept of *value*. To make things more complicated, similar networks and distinctions exist in other artistic fields, such as music, film, and dance.

Despite this disclaimer, there is a field of human endeavor—however unclear its boundaries—that may be identified as art, and particular people and institutions—however loosely organized—that are principally involved in and concerned with that field. And within that field, those who make, critique, collect, exhibit, teach, and theorize about art as a form of intellectual or academic discourse are what I mean by "the art world." And, until I found myself working and studying in a theological seminary, it was in that world that I had my primary professional identity.

Bridging the Gap

My theological study challenged many of the assumptions that I had taken for granted since art school. For instance, in most art schools, when the standard survey course on the history of Western art gets to the sixteenth century, Michelangelo is a hero who is mistreated by a succession of popes, whose refusal to pay him on time is matched only by their desire to multiply magnificent buildings, sculptures, and paintings throughout the city of Rome. Meanwhile, the leaders of the Reformation are portrayed as uncultured barbarians, who destroyed important artworks out of an overwrought religious sensibility.

When the same period is covered in a Protestant seminary course on the history of the Western church, the Reformers are the heroes, desiring nothing more than to purge the ecclesiastical hierarchy of its wretched excesses. Chief among these excesses were the Pope's penchant for luxury and sensuousness, as exemplified by Michelangelo's magnificent nudes. It is somewhat startling to someone from the art world to discover that the sale of indulgences—a major point in Martin Luther's critique of Rome—was intended (at least in part) to finance the Pope's art patronage. In both cases, the Pope is the villain, but it is not clear how to reconcile my admiration for the work of the Reformers with my delight in Michelangelo's painting on the ceiling of the Sistine Chapel. I imagine that when this period is taught in a Roman Catholic seminary, the tensions are described somewhat differently.

However, the real issue that underlies this story is the question of by what criteria the church is to evaluate art. For the Pope in the story above, Michelangelo's painting was good, both because it conformed to current Catholic doctrine, and because Michelangelo was celebrated as an artist by other artists and patrons—the art world of his day. For at least some of the Reformers, his painting was bad because it could lead to idolatry, regardless of what the art experts of the time might think. Should the criteria for art that is good for the church be defined by the art establishment? That is, shall the church simply accept as good whatever art is currently being bought by major museums or being hailed by well-known critics? Or, should the church develop its own criteria, such as adhering to certain theological positions or exemplifying certain virtues? This question of what is good art, who decides, on what basis, and in what situations, runs throughout this volume.

So, too, does the question of the relationship between art, spirit, and matter. About twenty years ago, I was installing a rather complicated piece of art in a small church. There I was, teetering on a ladder, trying to reach a pole across a six-foot gap without dropping the linked pieces of copper that were suspended from it. Suddenly, a member of the congregation walked by, saying, "Oh, I had no idea that art was so physical!" For my part, I had no idea that anyone could have thought otherwise.

From the prehistoric painters drawing by uncertain firelight deep in the caves at Alta Mira to Michelangelo aiming hammer blows at blocks of marble to force them to release the sculpture held captive within, every printmaker who ends each day with cramping hands and aching back after endless hours of bending over a work table, painstakingly chiseling fine lines into a hardwood block; every potter who stays up all night to tend the kiln, every muralist who scrambles up and down scaffolding to get a better view of the day's work, every dancer who comes to the final act of a ballet with bleeding toes, and every guitarist who practices for hours despite the blistered fingers and throbbing shoulders, artists have always grappled with the sheer physicality of what they do.

For the church member who marveled at my balancing act, however, art was not physical, but spiritual. Art, she believed, was something ethereal, mysterious, sacred, a way of apprehending the holy. Art, she seemed to think, was made in an instant, a painting breathed onto the canvas, a sculpture formed by thought alone, with no effort or compromise between the moment of inspiration and its realization as object. Art, for her, was something set apart, an experience outside of normal life, a divine gift unsullied by human labor.

Although this book is addressed primarily to theologians and pastors, I am writing largely in response to that church member from long ago. In her offhand comment, she embodies the unexamined attitudes and assumptions that the church holds about art and artists. In investigating these attitudes and perceptions, and tying them to concrete situations and examples, I hope to demystify art, to bring art down to earth, where theologians, pastors, and ordinary Christians can wrestle with its meanings, participate in its processes, and understand its uses in a variety of situations.

In showing the commonalities and distinctions among the various ways that artists themselves approach their work, I hope to change the conversation, to help the church talk about the arts in ways that artists will recognize. The church needs to learn the language of art, so that it can understand the artists in its midst as well as the ideas, processes, and practices that inform their work and, in turn, help them to talk about God in ways that the church can recognize. In this way, I believe, the church will realize that the Word of God is more than words. The arts embody the Word as a living, breathing reality constantly transforming our lives through our senses as well as our minds. Like the Pope who believed that a beautiful church filled with great artworks would bring the people to faith, but didn't pay the artist who clambered over the scaffolding in order to decorate the church ceiling, the church today often sanctifies art as an idea but ignores the hard realities of actual artworks made by actual artists. As a member of both the church and the art world, I want to bridge the gap between the habits of thought that inform the intellectual discourse of the art world, and those quite different ideas about art that are taken for granted by many Christians.

When we make clear distinctions between art as spiritual practice and art as scriptural interpretation; between the benefits of art to the artist and its benefits to the audience; and between art for its own sake and art for the worship of God, we will make better decisions about the role of art and artists in our seminaries, our churches, our lives. When art is understood as intellectual, technical and physical as well as ethereal, mysterious and sacred, we will see it as an integral part of our life together in Christ, fully human and fully divine.

2.

The Problem of Art

Art is art. Everything else is everything else.
　　—Ad Reinhardt[1]

Works of art are instruments by which we perform such diverse actions as praising our great men and expressing our grief, evoking emotion and communicating knowledge.
　　—Nicholas Wolterstorff[2]

The world is full of problems: war, homelessness, global warming, domestic violence, AIDS, hunger, drug abuse. The list goes on and on. In a world that seems to be always on the brink of disaster, there is an endless amount of work to do to help the earth heal from pollution of every kind; to insure adequate nutrition, housing, education, and health care to every person; to bring peace among the nations and in every city and village and home. And yet, if all of this is done, and there is no art, then the world will still be a sad, sorry, joyless place.

Still, in most of the developed world, and especially in those parts of the world most influenced by the Protestant churches, art is often treated as suspect, as Jeremy Begbie puts it "a luxurious ornament,"[3] a frivolous frill that is easily discarded whenever resources are stretched and other needs seem more pressing. In the face of diminishing budgets and continual insistence on raising test scores, public schools in the United States are consistently pressured to reduce or eliminate time spent on music, dance, and drawing; the National Endowment for the Arts is repeatedly threatened

1. Reinhardt, "25 Lines," 90.
2. Wolterstorff, *Art in Action*, 5.
3. Begbie, *Voicing Creation's Praise*, xvi.

with losing its funding; and local arts organizations constantly operate on the edge of budget disaster.

Some of the sources for this attitude may be found in the complex relationship that Christianity has had with the arts at least from Augustine onward, describing them at once as a good gift from God and as a distraction from true worship. Other sources are deeper, dating back to early Greek philosophers who posited a dualistic universe in which the physical, material world apprehended through the senses was understood as an unreal shadow of true reality, which could only be apprehended through reason.

The church, broadly speaking, both influences and is influenced by the attitudes of the society around it. Because of our collective discomfort with the arts, both the church and the world tend to think about them in ways that are problematic for artists as well as, ultimately, for society at large and the church in particular. Sometimes, we *instrumentalize* art, turning it into a means to achieve didactic, propagandistic, or other pragmatic ends. At other times, we *commercialize* art, turning it into a commodity to be bought and sold, with little or no regard to its intrinsic worth. In other circumstances, we *demonize* art, seeing only its potential as the object of idolatrous worship, on the one hand, or as the tempting purveyor of other illicit thrills, on the other. Too often, we *trivialize* art, seeing it as the province of children or as a recreational activity for adults with both time and money to spare from what are regarded as more important pursuits. Finally, we may *spiritualize* art, ignoring its sources in the concrete materiality of life while believing that art will somehow save us from ourselves, or that artists have a better pathway to God than everyone else.

Too rarely, we see art as an answer to a real—though hard to define—human need, as a legitimate response to God's call on all our lives to love and serve the world. Many of the ways in which art has been characterized are misunderstandings about the nature and function of art, or address some kinds of art while ignoring others. These mischaracterizations divert us from recognizing how the arts actually help us to understand, interpret, and communicate our experience of the world around us. Instead, they either strip the arts of their genuine power or elevate them to a status that they do not deserve. Such ideas also tend to alienate artists, who think about an artwork in terms of how it operates on the senses; how it fits into its historical, physical, and spiritual context; or how subtle changes to visual, auditory, or physical configurations can shape our experience and touch us at the deepest places of our being. In this chapter, we will consider the ways that churches and artists tend to talk past one another when they think about and use art, and begin to sketch the outlines of a deeper conversation.

Instrumentalizing Art: Reducing Art to a Single Meaning

Art speaks to the senses in ways that are too complex and subtle to be able to fully define in words. We respond physically and emotionally to the colors, shapes, textures, rhythms, timbres, pitch, or other aspects of a painting, a song, a poem, a film in ways that are difficult to describe, but still very real. These responses contribute to our sense of the meaning of the piece, frequently below our conscious awareness, even more than any overt subject matter that might be implied or overtly stated.

Too often, however, art is reduced to its supposed message, as though an artwork were simply a kind of shorthand or diagram for an intellectual idea. While it could be argued that even diagrams are a type of artwork, these tend to be dry, simplistic, and as unambiguous as possible. When a multivalent, well-wrought artwork is treated as a diagram, the very sensory qualities that the artist labored to create are ignored. This happens, for instance, when the words to a hymn are changed for didactic reasons and without equal regard to how they sound or the ease with which they can be pronounced near one another. Too often, such changes alter the aesthetic integrity of the hymn to the extent that people find it impossible to sing.

Too often, artists and theologians seem to talk past one another. My theologian friend who had wondered why anyone should care about art continued to think about the question, responding to my reply with another idea:

> I asked myself, What is art? I answered myself, Art is a human construction. What kind of human construction? Communication. What kind of communication? Communication about what matters in itself and thus distinct from illustration, which points to something *else* that matters. So what matters in and of itself?

On one level, my friend was trying to make an important distinction that artists, themselves, are often at pains to figure out how to explain. Why is illustration often considered to be something less than real art? What is the difference between the kind of art that is seen in museums and the kind of art that is seen in most churches? Why does the art world often disdain Christian art, dismissing it as mere illustration?

One answer to these questions has to do with the observation that illustration relies on its connection to a verbal description or story outside itself, while contemporary museum art is expected to say something profound without an external narrative. This distinction is, in part, what my church friend meant when speaking of "what matters in and of itself."

However, while what art has to say may correctly be understood as communication, it can be misleading to define art in that way. The problem is that when art is defined solely as communication, it is too easy to reduce any given artwork to its supposed message. This kind of oversimplification is rampant in the church, which too often rejects complex, multivalent artworks in favor of tendentious, single-message lessons. As soon as we say that art is communication, and leave it there, we omit all the other things that art also is and that other forms of communication are not.

Many of the roots of equating art with communication may be found in the Reformation. Although there is a popular conception that the Reformation was an iconoclastic movement, that is only partially true. Many Reformers did reject the use of religious images, especially those that they understood to be used in idolatrous ways, but others accepted or even encouraged their use. Both visual art and hymnody, for example, were permitted in many places. However, these arts were accepted primarily as didactic tools rather than for their emotive or symbolic qualities. This bent towards didacticism tended to strip art of all of its affective qualities, reducing it to a visual analogue, a one-for-one translation of discursive language. This is exactly what my friend describes as "illustration."

A comparison of the spare woodcuts that accompany many Reformation texts with the lush, heavily emotive contemporaneous art of the Roman Catholic Counter-Reformation will reveal not merely stylistic difference, but distinctive theological difference as well. The Reformation images are often black-and-white woodcuts accompanying texts. Made with the explicit intention of minimizing their ability to evoke emotion, they simply underline the point already made in words. As William Dyrness points out, for instance, regarding Zwingli's vernacular work on the Lord's Supper,

> which would have been read in many homes, the title page is adorned with simple images . . . These images portray and elaborate this special meal in a clear and simple way that would have been accessible to all who participated in the worship experience. It was teaching by pictures the narrative connections between these miracles and the communion meal . . . . Clearly the images here play the role of helping people envision the theological meaning proclaimed in the preached word and in the sacrament.[4]

For the Reformers, images were not expected to point to any reality beyond the narrative that was depicted, much less participate in such a reality sacramentally. Instead, they were meant to be memory aids for the

4. Dyrness, *Reformed Theology and Visual Culture*, 59.

marginally literate, somewhat like the schematic a-is-for-apple images in picture books for young children.

Hymnody, too, was enlisted in a program of inculcating specific creedal and historical understandings. As theologian, musicologist, and liturgical scholar Robin Leaver notes, Martin Luther insisted that "unison congregational song was a powerful demonstration of the doctrine of universal priesthood, since every member of the congregation was involved in the activity."[5] Leaver quotes from a 1523 letter from Luther to fellow reformer George Spalatin in which Luther praises Spalatin for his skillful and eloquent use of the German language, and asks him to turn psalms into songs suitable for congregational singing. However, Luther cautions,

> I would like you to avoid new-fangled, fancied words and to use expressions simple and common enough for the people to understand yet pure and fitting. The meaning should also be clear and as close as possible to the psalm. Irrespective of the exact wording, one must freely render the sense by suitable words.[6]

Such singable psalm texts, or metrical psalms, quickly became the primary musical form used in worship throughout the churches of the Reformation. While both the poetic quality and the musical settings of such metrical psalms could be of high artistic quality, this was not always the case, and even when it was, such excellence was not always appreciated. Indeed, the primary value for the Reformers was that such songs allowed congregations to more easily memorize and internalize the psalms. This insistence on simplicity and accessibility continues to be an important criterion by which all the arts are evaluated in the church, often to the exclusion of any other value. Too often, the sensory elements through which meaning is also conveyed are completely ignored, as when exultant words are set to somber melodies.

A strict adherence to the psalms, however, was not the only didactic use of hymnody. Luther, in "Ein feste Burg," and later Isaac Watts, in his volume *The Psalms of David Imitated*, interpreted the psalms through a New Testament lens. As Leaver points out, "The revolution that Watts brought about was his insistence that Christian congregational song cannot be confined to the Old Testament psalms, but must embrace the totality of Scripture."[7]

---

5. Leaver, "Liturgical Music," 283.

6. Ibid., 284.

7. Ibid., 295.

Beyond Scripture, hymn texts were used to teach both doctrine and history. The martyr hymns of the various Anabaptist groups, such as the Mennonites, Hutterites, and Swiss Brethren, exemplify another didactic use of music. Persecuted by both Catholics and Protestants, the sufferings and faith of many executed Anabaptists were recounted in narrative songs intended to inspire their co-religionists to similar levels of commitment.[8]

This emphasis on using art to instruct does not mean that all Reformation hymns and images were artistically worthless. Indeed, many hymn texts from the Reformation onward were poetically well-crafted and much of the music similarly excellent. When Martin Luther published his German translation of Scripture, he enlisted the eminent artist Lucas Cranach the Elder—best known for his Isenheim altarpiece—to provide the illustrations. However, this tendency to instrumentalize art, to see it as simply illustrative or a way to make a didactic point rather than to lead to new understandings through metaphoric and sensory qualities, has permeated the Protestant churches.

By the late nineteenth century, the Roman Catholic Church had fallen into similar habits. As Colleen McDannel has shown, both Protestant and Catholic visual materials became increasingly bland and instructional in this period. As may be seen throughout McDannel's lavishly illustrated volume, *Material Christianity*, the visual materials used by American Protestants and Catholics were virtually indistinguishable, and, indeed, often shared. In her discussion of the institutional and cultural structures surrounding the distribution of water from Lourdes following the miraculous appearance of the Virgin Mary to the young peasant girl, Bernadette Soubirous, McDannel notes

> Marian piety with the Lourdes water and replica grottoes flourished in the United States because its themes resonated not only with Catholic traditions but also with Victorian culture. Protestants and Catholics both acknowledged the healing capacities of water and sought to articulate religious and aesthetic values by creating Christian landscapes . . . . Although Catholics understood their Marian piety to be truly "Catholic," the expressions of that piety drew from the culture of the time.[9]

An examination of some visual materials from the late nineteenth century that McDannel shows will demonstrate the point. For example, an illustration of the church and shrine of Our Lady of Lourdes from the *Catholic Herald*, April 24, 1880, which McDannel reproduces as illustration

8. Ibid., 292.

9. McDannell, *Material Christianity*, 133.

88 on page 134, and the print of visitors at the grave of David W. Gihon at the Laurel Hill Cemetery, printed in 1852 and reproduced as illustration 70 on page 112 in the same volume, exhibit similar visual devices, such as exaggerated poses, unequivocal directional cues, and sentimental references.

Prayer cards and other devotional materials featured rotogravure prints of images inspired by late Renaissance and Baroque prototypes. Such derivative images continually recycled visual ideas from the past rather than risking new interpretations that took into account current realities. When contemporary situations were included, they were usually sentimentalized or sensationalized, depending, again, on the didactic point that was intended. By the 1950s, this often took the form of clean-cut young people dressed in contemporary clothing in the presence of rather innocuous Jesus. Although Jesus was depicted dressed in robes, rather than the T-shirts and jeans of the young people, he somehow managed to look like a modern white American.[10]

Such images often moved easily and without comment between Protestants and Catholics. As just one example, a 1946 advertisement for a children's coloring book from a Catholic goods house, reproduced by McDannel,[11] juxtaposes simplified outlines of the popular Roman Catholic devotional figures, the Infant of Prague and Saint Anthony, with nineteenth-century Protestant artworks such as Holman Hunt's *Christ Knocking at Heart's Door* and Heinrich Hoffmann's *Christ in the Garden of Gethsemane*.

Similarly, images of the Virgin Mary and the Sacred Heart of Jesus often found their way into Protestant households.[12] In an article about domestic shrines maintained by Protestant women in Pennsylvania, folklorist Yvonne Milspaw describes her Methodist grandmother's shrine, which

> held a variety of religious objects . . . [including] a glossy framed print of Christ crowned with thorns. Next to that were a votive candle in a broad green glass container, a small, golden glass brick with an intaglio of the crucifixion, and a small aluminum bottle (which had once contained Holy Water) decorated with a lithograph of Our Lady of Lourdes.[13]

This denominational eclecticism continues into the present day. Having spoken about art in a wide variety of church-related venues and conversed with priests and pastors from all over the country, I have observed that today there is an even greater openness to a wider selection of visual

10. Ibid., 52, illustration 33.

11. Ibid., 56, illustration 40.

12. Ibid., 17–66 passim.

13. Milspaw, "Protestant Home Shrines," 119.

materials in many Christian churches, both Protestant and Roman Catholic. However, all too often even excellent, evocative, multivalent artistic materials are subverted into didactic readings as congregations are encouraged to look for the one, true meaning of an artwork. This is parallel to a method of biblical interpretation that insists on a single, correct meaning for each chapter and verse, rather than a hermeneutic of questioning the text. Rather than allowing the arts to open conversations that lead to exploration of multiple ideas, artworks are overexplained, reduced to sermon illustrations rather than allowed to stand on their own as biblical interpretations or analogues of spiritual experience.

Such single-message interpretations lead, too often, to a preacher or Sunday School teacher showing a Renaissance painting that depicts some scriptural narrative with no regard to the intrinsic meanings of the painting itself. Instead of attending to the specific ways that this painting tells the story in color, spatial emphasis, the visual relationships among the various characters, and any other telling details, the preacher will simply say, in effect, "I'm preaching on the Prodigal, so here's a picture of that story," while completely disregarding any potential conflict between the preacher's interpretation and that of the artist. Equally disregarded is the potential for the image to illuminate the understanding of the text by either the preacher or the congregation through attention to the exegesis offered by the artist.

This attitude devalues good art by refusing to recognize that anything other than its subject matter might contribute to its meaning. It also leads to joyless felt banners with the word "Joy" stitched across them; moralistic children's stories that are so predictable that even the children are bored by them; and hymns of praise that are sung like dirges, more out of duty than any sense of delight in the presence of the living God.

Commercializing Art: Making Art a Commodity

There is a certain kind of art that is created solely for the purpose of aesthetic contemplation. Such works have no other purpose than to delight, to elicit the particular thrill that is felt by many in their presence. This is often termed high art, and is considered by many to be the pinnacle of the artistic enterprise. In music, this is sometimes referred to as concert music, and generally takes the form of symphonies, concertos, chamber music, opera, and the like. In the world of literature, a distinction is often made between the literary novel and all other forms of fiction. Serious poetry, drama, and certain films also fall into this category.

In the world of visual art, it is the kind of work that Daniel A. Siedell calls museum art, in his book, *God in the Gallery: A Christian Embrace of Modern Art*.[14] As Siedell points out, the high arts are both a cultural and an institutional practice, a living tradition that exists

> not only *invisibly* in the hearts and minds of its practitioners and participants but also embodied, mediated in and through its *visible* public institutions. And it is in fact this public or outward manifestation that produces the private and inward experience of art. What art is, then, is defined through a public network and not merely by private assertion or opinion.[15]

In general, Siedell is speaking about modern or contemporary visual art and the structures, critical language, and traditions that surround and support it. According to Siedell, such art operates for the serious viewer in many ways like icons do for the Orthodox Christian. Like an icon, he suggests, a work of art is a kind of hypostatic union "between sensuous material and rational ideas."[16] This union of form and content, he argues, is the source of high art's power. Similar arguments can be made about the effects of serious music, drama, poetry, and other artistic disciplines, as found in such visible public institutions as concert halls, theaters, and literary publishing houses.

Not all art has such lofty goals, however. As Nicholas Wolterstorf helpfully notes, there are many purposes for art.

> Works of art are instruments by which we perform such diverse actions as praising our great men and expressing our grief, evoking emotion and communicating knowledge. Works of art are objects of such actions as contemplation for the sake of delight. Works of art are accompaniments for such actions as hoeing cotton and rocking infants. Works of art are background for such actions as eating meals and walking though airports.[17]

Some art is actually intended for commercial purposes, to participate intentionally in the world of commerce. Art in this category is not just the overt advertising that is ubiquitous in our culture, but also includes such things as mass-market music and movies; most (but not all) architecture; and fashion design, industrial design, and all the other fields that include the word *design* in their titles. Sometimes, the line between commercial art

14. Siedell, *God in the Gallery*, 22.
15. Ibid., 24; emphasis original.
16. Ibid., 28.
17. Wolterstorff, *Art in Action*, 4.

and high art is hard to discern, as when a dancehall poster by Henri de Toulouse-Lautrec becomes more prized than paintings by many less well-known artists, or Igor Stravinsky's *Rite of Spring* is used as the soundtrack for an animated film, or the work of popular musicians like Bob Dylan or the Beatles become the subject of scholarly dissertations.

Generally, however, the commodification of art becomes problematic when works that are created for the purpose of contemplation are treated as simply as objects to be bought and sold in the marketplace. In this situation, discomfort arises in those who value art for reasons that are unconnected with money. Artists whose works sell well, or who allow their works to be used to sell other products, are sometimes accused of selling out, of compromising their principles for monetary gain.

Religious institutions rarely are involved in this kind of overt commodification, but they nonetheless often confuse the true value of the arts with their monetary price. Alternatively, they abuse the notion that art is priceless, expecting artists to donate their time and talents even when that would create an undue hardship. While there are, of course, successful artists who command many thousands of dollars for each of the many works they might sell in a year, most professional artists struggle to get by, taking any commission that comes their way, even if the effective hourly rate is below minimum wage. Asking such artists to donate their time and work can severely compromise their ability to pay their bills. Even Michelangelo was nearly bankrupted when Pope Julius II refused to pay him what he had promised for the Sistine Chapel.

Money, in itself, however, is only a marker for an attitude that sees no intrinsic value in artistic activities or objects. The problem of turning art into a commodity arises in churches when how much it costs, how much revenue it can raise, or how it can serve as a symbol of a congregation's social status, outweighs the emotional, spiritual, and communal values that the arts can bring to a congregation and to the individuals that comprise it. In the church, art becomes a commodity when it is seen as a hook that will bring in new members, as a decorative addition to a worship service, or as a way to communicate the cultural sophistication of a congregation.

Art becomes a commodity when stained glass windows are ordered from a catalog with no sensitivity to the particular building and the congregation that worships there; when a church hires professional singers for the entertainment of the congregation rather than teaching its own members to sing as an offering to God; or when an exhibition series is started with the hopes that commissions on the sale of paintings will generate income for the church rather than for its promise as a ministry to artists. When the value of the arts is connected too closely to their monetary potential or liability, the loss is often the ability to experience an artwork directly. What is lost in the transaction is the experience of allowing an artwork to enter through the senses and illuminate the lives of those who come into contact with it.

Demonizing Art: Art as Idolatry

There has always been an iconoclastic tendency within Christianity, a fear that any image might be or become an idol. Often, the source of this diffidence towards images has been cited as the second commandment, as found in Exodus 20:4–5 and repeated in Deuteronomy 5:8–9, in which the Israelites are told not to make *pselet* for themselves, "whether in the form of anything that is in heaven above, or that is on the earth beneath, or that is in the water under the earth. You shall not bow down to them or worship them." The meaning of *pselet* has been variously rendered as idol, carved or graven image, or simply image. In modern Hebrew, the word means statue. But however we understand *pselet*, the context seems to make it clear that representational images are forbidden.

I say *seems* because—as is true of many things in the biblical record—this ban is not as clear as it may appear on the surface. As the beginning of verse 5, which reads "You shall not bow down to them or worship them," points out, the real issue is not representation in itself, but rather idolatry. At the time that the commandments were recorded, the primary function of statues was to depict the gods and goddesses of the state religion. From the point of view of the Israelites, there may have been no other reason to make a representational object except for purposes of worship.

Further evidence that all representation was not forbidden in the Mosaic code comes in at least two places. The first is the mysterious incident in Numbers 21:4–9, in which God sends poisonous serpents to punish the people for complaining. Moses is then instructed to make a bronze snake and put it on a pole, so "everyone who is bitten shall look at it and live." Whatever other notions may be implicit in this story, it is clear that God explicitly commands the making of something that looks as much like a snake as possible. If we could see it today, we would certainly call it art, just as we do other representational images from that period. And it is clear that the biblical witness does not understand this artful representation of a snake as an idol.

The second piece of evidence against a total ban on visual representation is in God's instructions on the design and construction of the Tent of Meeting in Exodus 25–27. These instructions include sculptural renditions of cherubim on the cover of the Ark of the Covenant; almond flowers of pure gold on the branches of the lamp stands; and images of cherubim worked into the fabric of the curtains. A few chapters later, these descriptions are repeated in a report of what was actually done under the direction of Bezalel and Oholiab, God's chosen leaders of the work.

The issue in the second commandment, then, is not art, as we understand art today, or even representational images, but rather idolatry. It is not the making of images, as such, that is forbidden, but making them for the purpose of bowing down and worshipping them. In the early days of Christianity, as in Moses' day and for the centuries in between, idolatry continued to be a present danger. As the followers of Jesus spread beyond Palestine into the wider Roman empire, many converts came from religious traditions that worshiped a variety of deities. These were understood to be present in their statues. Thus, some writers in the early church period were understandably skittish about representational imagery.

This was not universally true, however. Since the discovery of the early third-century frescoes at Dura Europos, assumptions about a uniform, or even widespread, anti-image bias of the early church have been challenged. Some have pointed out that the lack of images in the first two centuries of Christianity may have had more to do with its status as a persecuted religious body with little money to spend on decoration and few buildings to decorate than with any ideological position. It is certainly true that as soon as Christianity became a state religion, its royal patrons arranged for elaborately embellished buildings, filled with portraits of themselves as well as various biblical and extrabiblical personages and objects.

Nonetheless, the writings of early Christian theologians and preachers repeatedly circle around the issue of images and idolatry. This concern is not restricted to the visual arts, nor even to representation as such. As early as the late fourth century, Augustine of Hippo (354–430) wrote about his own struggles to keep his appreciation of music within proper bounds. Berating himself for loving the sound of the music more than the edifying words, and perhaps even more than God, he wrote,

> at one time I seem to myself to give them more honour than is seemly, feeling our minds to be more holily and fervently raised unto a flame of devotion, by the holy words themselves when thus sung, than when not; and that the several affections of our spirit, by a sweet variety, have their own proper measures in the voice and singing, by some hidden correspondence wherewith they are stirred up. But this contentment of the flesh, to which the soul must not be given over to be enervated, doth oft beguile me, the sense not so waiting upon reason as patiently to follow her; but having been admitted merely for her sake, it strives even

to run before her, and lead her. Thus in these things I unawares
sin, but afterwards am aware of it.[18]

Augustine's concerns were repeatedly echoed by other ancient writers.
Suspicion of the arts, especially of visual art, came to a climax in the iconoclastic controversies of the eighth and ninth centuries. The matter of icons
was settled in the Christian East at what is today celebrated as the Triumph
of Orthodoxy in 843. The Western church continued to vacillate between an
austere asceticism, as exemplified by the writings of the Cistercian monk,
Bernard of Clairvaux, and a sumptuous exuberance reflecting the glory of
God, as exemplified by the church built at St. Denis under the direction
of Bernard's contemporary, Abbot Suger. In his *Apologia*, written in 1125,
Bernard writes disparagingly of the "enormous height, extravagant length
and unnecessary width of the churches, of their costly polishings and curious paintings which catch the worshipper's eye and dry up his devotion."[19]

Abbot Suger extolled precisely the kind of elaboration that Bernard of
Clairvaux deplored. His church at St. Denis is one of the earliest examples
of what came to known as Gothic architecture. Such buildings featured
pointed-arch windows filled with stained glass, ornate embellishments at
every turn, and a lapis sky filled with golden stars on the ceiling over the
altar. In his account of the building process, Suger argued that only the finest materials and workmanship were worthy for the service of God. As he
wrote in his treatise, "De Administratione,"

> If golden pouring vessels, golden vials, golden little mortars used
> to serve, by the word of God or the command of the Prophet, to
> collect the blood of goats or calves or the red heifer: how much
> more must golden vessels, precious stones, and whatever is most
> valued among all created things, be laid out, with continual
> reverence and full devotion, for the reception of the blood of
> Christ! . . . The detractors also object that a saintly mind, a pure
> heart, a faithful intention ought to suffice for this sacred func-
> tion; and we, too, explicitly and especially affirm that it is these
> that principally matter. [But] we profess that we must do hom-
> age also through the outward ornaments of sacred vessels. . . .
> with all inner purity and with all outward splendor.[20]

In response, Bernard somewhat grudgingly accepts that it may be all
right for parish churches and cathedrals to revel in outward splendor. It does

18. Augustine, *Confessions*, book 10, chapter 33.
19. Bernard of Clairvaux, "Bernard of Clairvaux: Apology."
20. Suger, "De Administratione," 65–67.

no harm, he admits, to the simple and devout, whatever problems it may pose for the vain and greedy. However, he points out, for poor, spiritual, cloistered monks such things are at best distractions and at worst invitations to sin. He goes on,

> But in cloisters, where the brothers are reading, what is the point of this ridiculous monstrosity, this shapely misshapenness, this misshapen shapeliness? What is the point of those unclean apes, fierce lions, monstrous centaurs, half-men, striped tigers, fighting soldiers and hunters blowing their horns? . . . In short, so many and so marvelous are the various shapes surrounding us that it is more pleasant to read the marble than the books, and to spend the whole day marveling over these things rather than meditating on the law of God. Good Lord! If we aren't embarrassed by the silliness of it all, shouldn't we at least be disgusted by the expense?[21]

In this short passage, Bernard summarizes an attitude that continues to resound in the church as well as the wider society. For Bernard and his spiritual descendants, art is too frivolous for serious people to fool around with, and much too expensive in both time and money when there are more important needs crying out for our attention. For Suger, however, through art and the light that art could reflect and reveal, God could be apprehended directly.

Three hundred years later, the unresolved tensions over the appropriateness of the arts in Christian worship became evident again in the iconoclastic excesses of certain portions of the Reformation. While stories of whitewashed churches and disfigured statues are familiar, it is important to remember that there were significant differences among the various reformers with respect to the arts. Luther, for example, advocated leaving the churches as they were, converting the use of whatever religious art existed to didactic rather than devotional means. He was horrified to discover that Andreas Karlstadt had encouraged the wholesale destruction of religious statuary during his absence from Wittenburg in 1522. Zwingli, on the other hand, was, like Augustine, all too aware of his own tendency to get so carried away by music that he forgot about God and banned even hymns from the worship of his church.

Despite these differences among the reformers and among the ecclesial traditions that derive from each, effective patronage of the arts was no longer seen as a legitimate role for the Protestant churches. The Roman Catholic Church did continue to commission important artworks for a long time.

---

21. Bernard of Clairvaux, "Bernard of Clairvaux: Apology."

However, the widespread secularization of society in the ensuing centuries led to developments in serious visual art, music, and drama that made the practitioners of each of these art forms less and less interested in providing works that were appropriate for Christian worship and edification.

One strand of development that was particularly important in the divorce of the arts from the church can be traced to the eighteenth century, often referred to as the Age of Reason, or the Enlightenment. In his 1974 Mellon lectures at the National Gallery of Art in Washington, DC, Jacques Barzun notes that the philosopher Jean-Jacques Rousseau "pointed to the spectacle of nature. Its beauty and harmony gave warrant for the feeling of awe which he then said that men experience natively like the promptings of conscience."[22] As Enlightenment rationality removed more and more of the mystery from the Protestant churches, in particular, the Romantics continued the elevation of the artist from humble craftsperson to prophetic visionary and priest that had begun with the Renaissance invention of the idea of artistic genius. Eventually, art—especially music, poetry, and painting, but encompassing other arts, as well—became for many a substitute for religion. Barzun continues,

> Like other religions the religion of art promised the individual not only the peace of harmonized feeling and understanding but also the bliss of spiritual ecstasies. For Wordsworth and Goethe, Beethoven and Berlioz, Turner and Delacroix, great art—including their own work—produced all the effects of religious fervor—enthusiasm, awe-struck admiration, raptures and devoutness. Great artists constituted the Communion of Saints. Walter Scott, hardly an extravagant mind, writes in his *Journal* that love of the great masters is "a religion or it is nothing."[23]

Over the course of the next two centuries, a rebellious persona became associated with artists, as they became increasingly involved with those who believed that organized religion was primarily a tool with which the powerful coerced the powerless to submit in mindless obedience. Barzun goes on to suggest that the French Revolution added to the artists' sense of themselves as the true priests and prophets. He notes, "Artists could no longer think of themselves as entertainers or craftsmen serving the leisured. They were now the interpreters of life."[24] Art and religion, once inextricably bound to one another, had become mutually antagonistic. Art itself, rather

22. Barzun, *Use and Abuse of Art*, 26.

23. Ibid., 27.

24. Ibid.

than any particular art work, became—depending on one's perspective—either the very embodiment of spiritual sensibility or an idol.

By the latter part of the twentieth century, the notion of art as idol seemed so self-evident to many Protestants in the United States that making church buildings harmonious and gracious was frequently considered completely unimportant. Any old cinder-block building was good enough, the simpler the better, as long as it could hold all the worshippers. And among certain segments of Christian society, some kinds of art—especially rock-and-roll music, dancing, and movies—were seen as agents of the Devil.

This demonization of the arts continues. In recent years, it is often couched as controversy over works that seem, at least to some, to be sacrilegious, obscene, or anti-American. Such controversies often also involve concern that the works, or the institutions that exhibit them, are supported through public funds. Examples include the 1989 exhibition of Mapplethorpe's photographs at the Corcoran Gallery of Art, which was partially funded through the National Endowment for the Arts; the NEA grant given to Andres Serrano in 1988, the year that he created his notorious photograph, *Piss Christ*; Chris Ofili's painting *The Holy Virgin Mary*, exhibited at the Brooklyn Museum in 1999; and, more recently, David Wojnarowicz's video, *A Fire in My Belly*, which was removed from an exhibit at the National Portrait Gallery in February, 2011.

Often, the people who object to these artworks identify themselves as Christian, and the nature of their objection is the perception that the works are, in one way or another, offensive to Christian sensibilities. While each of these works is admittedly disturbing, all of them have artistic merit, and all are more complex than the simplistic interpretation offered by their critics. Indeed, at least some of the works condemned as sacrilegious grow out of the sincere, if questioning, faith of the artists who make them. Following such events, the non-Christian art world remains confirmed in its dismissal of Christianity as antithetical to the arts. When Christians demonize the arts by refusing to engage difficult works in a spirit of inquiry, they tell artists that they, along with their efforts, are not welcome in the church.

Trivializing Art: Art as Play

It is both curious and telling that, by and large, when people in the church talk about making art, they tend to use words like *play, self-expression, creativity, fun*, or *release*. All of these are, of course, important factors in healthy development and living a rich, full life. In suggesting that seeing art as play trivializes art, I do not want in turn to trivialize the importance of play as a restorative, healing, explorative, expansive, imaginative activity. However, professional artists tend to feel discounted when church members make no distinction between art as recreation and art as vocation.

Michael Sullivan's *Windows into the Soul: Art as Spiritual Expression*, carefully makes this distinction, unlike many other similar books. Even so, this volume is representative of a popular genre which invites Christians to explore various art media as a way to reconnect with the childhood creativity they let go of in the process of growing up. Sullivan, a pastor, recounts his own discovery that working with clay helps him deal with the unexpected death of a young parishioner:

> I knew that signs, symbols, and metaphors of art could free the soul. Art helped me to explore places within that I had never imagined or acknowledged—creative places where the person in me burst out in new songs with words and phrases only I knew but with melodies that others seemed to understand. Being creative with art allowed me to let go of inhibitions and embrace a radical love of God's creation and my place in it as a beloved creature.[25]

Sullivan goes on to say that his intention is not to teach people to become world-class artists, but rather to connect more deeply with God.

Elsewhere, however, such distinctions are often blurred or, more commonly, simply ignored, implying that the kind of insights gained from long hours of practice in the studio are equally available to everyone in brief, free-form sessions. For instance, a practice called InterPlay was developed in 1989 by Cynthia Winton-Henry and Phil Porter. Incorporating elements of dance, drama, storytelling, and music, InterPlay is a way for people to use non-discursive means for communication and self-expression. The InterPlay web site proclaims,

> InterPlay is a global social movement dedicated to ease, connection, human sustainability and play. Unlock the wisdom of your body!
>
> InterPlay integrates body, mind, heart and spirit. . . . InterPlay is devoted to fun. It teaches the language and ethic of play in a deep and powerful way. If you are convinced that seriousness is the path to inner wisdom, then you might want to look elsewhere. If you would like to become a "recovering serious person," then InterPlay might be for you.[26]

25. Sullivan, *Windows into the Soul*, sec. 53.
26. Winton-Henry and Porter, "InterPlay."

InterPlay is intended for secular as well as religious groups, but it has a great appeal among many people who are affiliated with churches or other religious bodies. Under a heading noting "InterPlay with people where they worship helps spirituality become a whole body experience," their website lists hospice and chaplaincy organizations as well as several churches as places to connect with the wider movement.

The leaders of InterPlay make no claim that what they do is art, and those who participate in its events and ongoing activities report the deep healing and spiritual growth that such participation promotes. However, by combining the experience and practices of various artistic disciplines with the notion of fun and play that is embedded in their very name, the notion that art and fun are somehow synonymous moves even more deeply into the collective understanding, both within and outside the church.

While understanding art as play, as self-expression, as community building, or even as therapy is not incorrect, such notions address only part of what art is for those whose primary vocational identity is artist. When artists talk about making art, they tend to call it *work*. Of course, artists do sometimes say that they are going to "go play in the studio," but often when they say that, they mean that they are going to experiment with something new, do something light or inconsequential, or make something outside of their normal production. Attention to an ongoing project, however, is almost invariably considered work.

It is not accidental that a painting or sculpture is called a *work* of art; or that a musical composition is often given a number preceded by the word *opus*, the Latin word for *work*. For the serious practitioner, for the person whose primary vocational identity is that of artist, time spent in the studio is unequivocally work.

While such linguistic distinction may seem to be, itself, trivial, it leads churches (as well as society at large) to devalue what artists do and know. Unlike most other vocations, the arts can be practiced as a hobby, a spare-time activity done for relaxation and pleasure. Lawyers, doctors, or truck-drivers might pick up a guitar and strum for an hour or two in the evening as a way to unwind; a social worker, file clerk, or auto mechanic might throw paint onto canvas as a way to process a particularly stressful afternoon; a nurse, plumber, or CEO might join a local theater club as a way to make friends. For people who derive their primary vocational identity in non-art ways, their engagement with the arts, even as practitioners, often is not essentially different in character from slowpitch softball or fishing. It may be very important to them, and they may even become quite good at it, but it is understood as a delightful extra to the daily work which pays the bills and often brings a great deal of professional satisfaction of its own.

Artists, on the other hand, see their art-making activities as primary, as central to their understanding of who they are. This is not necessarily a matter of economics or even how many hours each day are spent in making art. Many artists are gainfully employed in some other occupation. But, among artists, this is known as one's day job, done in order to pay the bills. For them, the real work of painting or sculpting or writing or composing is done as a second shift, often late into the night, and to the exclusion of adequate sleep, attention to relationships, or anything that might be a recreational activity. For serious artists, to make art—whether as an economic activity or as largely unpaid second shift—is a vocation in the true sense, a calling from God to work that, like ministry or medicine, is both burden and gift. When others assume that it is simply creative release, rather than real, serious work, artists tend to bristle.

Some artists do use the word *play* to describe what they do. Musicians play instruments; actors may refer to themselves as players; and, of course, what they are acting in is called "a play." However, this understanding of play is not intended to imply some innocent, childish, useless occupation. Rather, it derives from an older sense of the word, which implied not so much frivolity as exercise. This sort of play, like professional sports, is seriously intentional, taking years of daily practice to do even marginally well.

The problem, then, is in equating what artists do with what is done merely for fun, as though they were weekend bowlers, or four-year-olds pretending to be superheroes. While a case can be (and sometimes is) made for the serious nature of this kind of play, as well, especially in connection with the socialization of children or the mental and spiritual health of adults, that is a discussion for another time and place. The point I am making here is that when the disciplined practice of art is trivialized as a childish pursuit, recreational hobby, or therapeutic technique, artists feel marginalized and misunderstood, left out of a conversation in which their own hard-won skill and knowledge is devalued by a culture where how hard one works is the marker of seriousness and commitment.

Spiritualizing Art: Art as Savior

Artists hold a special status in Western culture. Simultaneously revered and dismissed, they are presumed to possess a unique insight into the way the universe works even while they are ignored as irrelevant to the important work of the world. The starving artist is a common cultural trope, as is the artist as revolutionary, outsider, flaky, or weird. These stereotypes are largely the invention of the Romantic poets of the early nineteenth century, and were intensified by the writers, painters, and composers of the late nine-teenth and early twentieth century. Lurid stories of Van Gogh going mad and cutting off his ear, of Cocteau and Baudelaire using cocaine and opium, of the enthusiasm for séances and automatic writing among the adherents of art movements such as Dada, of the general aura of licentiousness and debauchery surrounding the avant-garde, are circulated as evidence that artists are somehow different from ordinary people. Not only do they, them-selves, live dangerously; their very existence is often seen as dangerous, as a threat to the morals and mores of the rest of society. Today, many artists continue to cultivate this aura of edginess, having internalized the role that society has given them.

In this discussion, I am speaking of artists quite broadly, to include not only practitioners of what might be called high art—concert music, op-era, ballet, theater, painting, sculpture, poetry, literature, and the like—but also movie stars, pop singers, designers and others whose work falls under the general label of creative. Society tolerates—and sometimes even cele-brates—the flamboyant clothing, the excessive use of alcohol and drugs, the flaunting of sexually charged extravagance, in part because the presumed reward to society is that the artists will return from their perilous journeys outside the ordinary with something precious to share with everyone else.

The reality may be quite different. Many (or perhaps most, it's hard to know) artists live much more sedate lives. They get married, they worry about their kids' schools, they pay their taxes, they go to church. If you met them on the street, you would not assume that they are any different from accountants, teachers, salesclerks, or waiters. For the most part, at least once they are out of art school, artists live like everybody else.

But the stereotypes persist, perhaps because there is a way in which artists are, in fact, different, and because this difference does sometimes lead to odd behaviors. Having trained their eyes, their ears, their minds to notice things that most other people do not, and to produce things that point to that noticing, they do something that people who are not artists perceive as outside the normal range of abilities. To paint a picture, to compose a tune, to choreograph a dance—these things seem marvelous, magical, the result not of work as it ordinarily understood but rather the product of a divine gift or genius.

I do not deny that some people do seem to have more innate talent than others. However, it is important to recall that even those who are more gifted than most still must work hard to develop that raw talent into some-thing that others will recognize as great. In his memoir, *The Street Where I Live*, Alan Jay Lerner noted that every great star he had ever worked with never rested on talent alone, but worked harder, cared more, and had a greater sense of perfection than anyone else. He wrote,

> I remember when I was doing a film with Fred Astaire, it was nothing for him to work three or four days on two bars of music. One evening in the dark grey hours of dusk, I was walking across the deserted MGM lot when a small, weary figure with a towel around his neck suddenly appeared out of one of the giant cube sound stages. It was Fred. He came over to me, threw a heavy arm around my shoulder and said, "Oh Alan, why doesn't someone tell me I cannot dance?" The tormented illogic of this question made any answer sound insipid, and all I could do was walk with him in silence. Why doesn't someone tell Fred Astaire he cannot dance? Because no one would ever ask that question but Fred Astaire. Which is why he is Fred Astaire.[27]

Such a story might be told of any talented, disciplined artist who strives continually to move towards a vision of perfection. The gift of talent is only a beginning, perhaps a necessary—but never a sufficient—condition of greatness. As someone said in another context, genius is 10 percent inspiration and 90 percent perspiration.

Regardless of the presence or absence of innate talent, in many cultures, everyone is expected to sing, dance, tell stories, and/or make images with some degree of facility. Even in our own culture, until relatively recently every educated person was given some instruction in playing a musical instrument, making watercolor sketches, and singing sufficiently well to carry a tune. It is only in our own time and place that teaching these skills is so neglected that only certain specialists are expected to do them at all, with everyone else serving as passive, adoring audience.

However, even when the practice of art is widespread in a society, rather than the domain of a specialized few, certain pictures, tunes, dances, poems, plays, and other artworks seem—at least some of the time—to convey something that feels like revelation, like an encounter with the holy. It is this experience, even more than the presumed differentness of artists, that suggests that those who make such works have a special access to God. There is something about that access that we perceive as simultaneously dangerous and valuable. The artist is given license to be flamboyant in return for going into the dangerous domain of the hidden and bringing back visible (or audible, or tangible) evidence of what is found there. In the popular imagination, the artist is often understood as a kind of shaman, and flamboyant behavior is seen as evidence of that special status.

27. Lerner, *The Street Where I Live*, 89.

While artists may be given license to be unconventional and simultaneously castigated for doing so, it is the artwork itself that is often seen as salvific. The conflation of aesthetic experience with religious ecstasy is the source of a worshipful attitude towards art that is widespread, especially among the highly educated professionals who make up the bulk of the audience for (and patronage of) opera, ballet, concert music, and art museums. A worshipful attitude towards art as a whole, not simply this or that artwork, is particularly problematic because it denies both the particularity of individual artworks and the particularity of individual responses to them. As Barzun puts it,

> . . . it is fraudulent to pass from a great artistic moment felt by one or more persons at a certain time and place to Art in general. Art does not consist only of masterpieces. Not all masterpieces overwhelm everybody equally, nor do they hold their magic invariably, eternally, and universally as the litany of religious adverbs pretends.[28]

As problematic as this attitude might be for those who profess no other religion, such sanctification of art presents even greater challenges when it is imported unreflectively into the church. Barzun is not addressing the church, but rather society at large. Nevertheless, his admonition regarding how to speak (or, more properly, not speak) about art applies to those within the church who want to advocate for the arts. He continues,

> Because Art is not a singleminded power, it cannot fulfill the requirements of a religion. The priest speaks with authority to all believers, no matter what his personal failings; the artist speaks with authority only to some and only when his happy condition or theirs will permit. I know that each of us, from proprietary feelings, would like to say that *my* chosen artist, *this* divine work moves all mankind. It is simply not so. All the epithets of immortal, timeless, self-sustaining, and autonomous applied to any work are but brave lies, when they are not merely partisan publicity.[29]

John Witvliet notes in his preface to Frank Burch Brown's *Inclusive Yet Discerning* that the values and assumptions about good and bad art, the function that art plays in human life, and how such art may affect our own lives, are formed outside of an institutional Christian context. Witvliet notes that when these assumptions are brought into our worship, they

28. Barzun, *Use and Abuse of Art*, 87–88.
29. Ibid., 88.

. . . may help God's people worship faithfully and vibrantly. They might, for example, help us to appreciate an artwork from a culture other than our own, or to discern the pathos or energy of a given work and its significance for Christian prayer and proclamation. At other times, however, these assumptions can erect barriers to faithful and vital worship. They might tempt us to worship artists or artworks instead of God, for example, or to fall into the kind of elitism or pragmatism that erodes our experience of grateful awe that is inherent in the act of worship. They might even prevent us from discerning how emerging forms of cultural expression might genuinely revitalize and deepen worship practices.[30]

Such assumptions lead to what is often termed the worship wars, in which different groups within a congregation argue over what kind of music is best for worship. Often, such differences of taste and opinion lead to separate services for those who prefer to sing the hymns they have known since childhood and those who find joy and comfort in praise choruses that sound more or less like the popular songs heard on the radio every day.

Elitist notions of what constitutes good music (or good art of any kind) can be especially pernicious, as when an organist or choir director's taste is in conflict with that of the majority of the congregation. In an earlier book, Frank Burch Brown describes Methodist theologian Tex Sample's report on the struggling, hard-living, working-class people, noting that they

relate to songs that other classes tend to scorn . . . . They don't respond favorably to imported organists and choir directors insistent on using Bach and Brahms to "lift" the musical tastes of the congregation. They don't much like musicians who feel compromised by the so-called musical debauchery of contemporary, gospel, and country music.[31]

Such assumptions also carry over into a more generalized notion that art is good for people, without much attention to what is meant by art, or what that good might consist in. Thus, the very real benefits that might accrue to people who practice an instrument, for example, are conflated with the quite different experiences of individuals who attend chamber music concerts, listen to rock-and-roll or rap, go to galleries that exhibit interactive digital art, or participate in a weekend retreat that encourages participants to make collages to explore their understanding of a biblical passage. While any of these activities may, in fact, be of benefit to participants, and

---

30. Witvliet, "Series Preface," viii.
31. Brown, *Good Taste, Bad Taste*, 8.

all of them do fit loosely into the category of art (or the arts), it is not at all clear what either the activities or their benefits have in common.

Such assumptions also lead to the growing practice of designating the church organist or choir director as the Minister of the Arts. While in principle I am glad that such a ministry is recognized at all, it is unlikely that a person who is a proficient musician will also know how to address the issues involved in fostering an art gallery or studio, dance and drama ministries, or poetry workshops, just to name a few possibilities. In *Voicing Creation's Praise*, Jeremy Begbie rightly cautions against allowing the visual to become the paradigm of an understanding of the arts. However, it is equally problematic for the specific concerns of music production and performance to dominate our understanding of the arts generally. Not all arts are equal in congregational life. While the type of music that is appropriate for worship is often a matter of contention, very few contemporary Christians would argue that there ought not to be any music at all. The other arts have varying levels of acceptance, and pose their own, particular production and performance problems.

I am not arguing here that a wide range of art activities have no place in Christian life. Rather, I am asking that those who advocate that the arts are integral to Christian life be more clear about how the various arts and differing levels of participation may lead to a fuller, richer, more authentic life in Christ. Rather than simply lumping all the arts, and all arts activities, together under one banner, I believe that it is important, at some level, at least, to make distinctions.

A Sanctified Art

In this chapter, I have looked at five general ways that the church, and society at large, misunderstands and misuses the arts. Whether we *instrumentalize* art, reducing it to a single meaning; *commercialize* it, turning it into a commodity rather than an experience; *demonize* it, seeing only its potential for idolatry or as an invitation to sin; *trivialize* it as child's play or something to while away a free hour; or *spiritualize* it as a pathway to the Divine regardless of the specific theology or worldview embedded in a particular work, we lose track of the genuine, concrete benefits and dangers inherent in bringing art into our lives.

In the chapters to follow, I will explore the complex relationship between art, beauty, and truth as these terms are understood colloquially, theologically, and in the world of art criticism and theory; propose some ways that the church might speak more constructively about art, inviting both Christian and non-Christian artists into a dialogue that can enrich both our theology and our aesthetic experience; and consider how the arts might genuinely address our aching need for meaning, for communication, and for genuine worship of the One who calls us into relationship with one another and with God.

Finally, I will move towards a theology of art that is both sanctified and sanctifying. John Wesley taught that, while each Christian is justified by faith, we spend our entire lifetime moving towards Christian perfection, which he called sanctification. Art, like any human activity, is not perfect, nor does it have the ability to make us perfect. What it can do is carry the tune when we are off-key and keep the beat when we are out of step. A sanctified art is like a mirror that always tells the truth, even when we would rather it lie. A sanctified art can show us both who we are and who we are meant to be as we journey together towards perfection.

3.

Visions of Beauty

Beauty is truth, truth beauty,—that is all
Ye know on earth, and all ye need to know.
   —John Keats[1]

Aesthetics is for the artist what ornithology is for the birds.
   —attributed to Barnett Newman[2]

Beauty and truth have been linked throughout the history of Western thought, never more succinctly than in the famous couplet from John Keats' "Ode on a Grecian Urn." But while Pontius Pilate is cited in Scripture as having asked "What is truth?" there is more agreement, both historically and today, about the difference between truth and falsehood than there is about the definition of beauty. Aesthetic theories beginning with the ancient Greeks and continuing through much of the twentieth century almost invariably linked beauty and art. Christian theologians describe God as the supreme locus of beauty, from whom all other definitions or examples derive their authority and meaning.

As the arts have become increasingly visible in the church in recent years, there has been an increased interest in discussions of both beauty and

1. Keats, "Ode on a Grecian Urn," lines 49–50.

2. I have been unable to discover the original source of this widely-quoted remark. The entry for 1952 in Barnett Newman Foundation's chronology of Newman's life notes, "In a session with the philosopher Susanne Langer, Newman attacks professional aestheticians, saying: 'I feel that even if aesthetics is established as a science, it doesn't affect me as an artist. I've done quite a bit of work in ornithology; I have never met an ornithologist who ever thought that ornithology was for the birds.' He would later hone this remark into the famous quip, 'Aesthetics is for the artist as ornithology is for the birds'" (Barnett Newman Foundation, "Chronology").

art. Justifications for using art in worship as well as other areas of church life are often couched in the language of beauty. However, once such lofty aspirations are brought down to questions of specific artworks, disagreements over matters of taste and quality begin to appear. As in the secular world, what one person sees as the epitome of beauty, another sees as sentimental, outrageous, or hopelessly misguided. Arguments rage over whether this or that artwork is objectively beautiful, or if beauty is merely in the eye of the beholder.

Sometimes, the concept of beauty is enlisted to encompass artworks that repulse either through their subject matter, the handling of materials, or some other factor, and yet are recognized as genuine contributions to human understanding. In such cases, the very definition of beauty is stretched so far beyond its useful limits that it would be better to use some other measures by which to define quality in the arts. In this chapter, we will look at some of the ways that both beauty and art have been seen by philosophers, theologians, and ordinary Christians; suggest a way to talk about quality in art without resorting to notions of beauty; and consider a new way of talking about beauty that steers a careful path between the dangerous rocks of universalizing absolutes and the chaotic whirlpool of unrestrained relativism.

Defining Beauty

The earliest known definition of artistic beauty is the Canon, or Rule, of Polykleitos, known today only through the report of other ancient writers. This Rule does not concern beauty in a general sense, or even in art broadly defined, but rather specifically addresses beauty as perceived in the proportions of the human figure in sculpture. The second-century-BCE physician, Galen, reports that, according to Polykleitos, beauty in this area was not found in strict symmetry, but rather in the correct, proportional relationships among the various parts of the body.[3] Other ancient writers expanded on this definition, including not only symmetry and proportion, but various combinations of balance, harmony, unity, radiance, and similar qualities.

Today, when people try to define beauty, they often refer to these ideas, along with words like elegance, refinement, or clarity. Beauty is often described as that which gives a deep pleasure or satisfaction, or has a certain rightness, or perfection. For many, beauty is profoundly spiritual, linked to experiences of transcendence or the divine. In classical philosophy, beauty was one of the three transcendental virtues, equal in importance to truth

---

3. Tobin, "The Canon of Polykleitos," 319.

and goodness. In theology, these three find their ultimate source, measure, and value in God.

Aesthetics, Art Theory, and History

Dictionaries typically define the word *aesthetics* with respect to the nature or appreciation of beauty. A look at the Greek root will reveal a meaning that is less about beauty than about sensory awareness or sensation. The opposite of aesthetic, after all, is *anesthetic*: something that puts the senses to sleep. Nevertheless, when philosophers and theologians consider aesthetics, they are almost always talking about beauty.

Alexander Gottleib Baumgarten (1714–1762) is often credited with coining the term in 1735, as the name of a field of study within the more general discipline of philosophy. However, for centuries before that, philosophers and theologians had much to say about beauty, art, the world of the senses, and the relationships among them. Indeed, so many authors have traced the history of philosophical aesthetics from Plato and the ancient Greeks to the modern era that it seems superfluous, as well as presumptuous, for me to cover such well-trodden territory. As I am neither an historian nor a philosopher, any summary that I might make would be certain to be incomplete. More to the point, such a digression would be much too long and distract from the central themes of this volume.

However, it is not possible to write about either art or beauty without any reference to the historical background that informs the current state of the discussion. Perhaps the most important thing to note is that up until relatively recently philosophers and theologians have generally assumed that art and beauty were inextricably bound up in one another. As philosopher and art critic Arthur C. Danto puts it in his influential work, *The Abuse of Beauty*,

> The philosophical conception of aesthetics is almost entirely dominated by the idea of beauty, and this was particularly the case in the eighteenth century—the great age of aesthetics—when apart from the sublime, the beautiful was the only aesthetic quality actively considered by artists and thinkers.[4]

In these discussions, it has often been assumed that beauty (or the lack thereof) was a property of an object, something that anyone with the proper perceptual equipment could recognize as easily as they could its shape or size or acoustical properties. For centuries, philosophical theories about art

---

4. Danto, *Abuse of Beauty*, 7.

tended to rest on the twin notions that the purpose of art was to be beautiful, and that the merit of any artwork, as measured by its beauty, would universally be recognized and acknowledged. By the eighteenth century, however, this presumed universality was in endangered by a move towards subjective relativism in which beauty existed only in the eye of the beholder.

In *Voicing Creation's Praise*, theologian Jeremy Begbie surveys philosophical notions about art and aesthetics in the early modern period. Placing Immanuel Kant (1724–1804) at the apex of the Enlightenment, he points out that in Kant's writings the universality of beauty is one of its hallmarks. For Kant, although the experience of beauty was subjective, it was not idiosyncratic. Everyone, he asserted, should agree that this or that thing was objectively beautiful. Begbie notes that Kant, as well as other philosophers, realizes that beauty is not something that can be known intellectually or objectively, but must be sensed subjectively. He writes,

> . . . it is clearly hard for Kant to provide a convincing account of the universal validity of aesthetic judgements [sic], despite his intention to avoid relativism. The universality of judgements of taste is grounded only in the universality of the subjective conditions for judging objects, and it is not evident that we can ever ascertain whether the subjective conditions necessary for an authentic experience of beauty are actually operative. Not surprisingly, Kant says little about aesthetic disputes and how they might be resolved.[5]

Theological aesthetic theories tend to follow Kant, and like him, give little help towards resolving aesthetic disputes. It is this difficulty that opens the way toward relativism. For David Hume (1711–1776), the nature of aesthetic judgment is entirely subjective, arising from our sense experiences, memories, imagination, and dreams. Begbie asserts that for Hume, beauty is not an *a priori* concept, but an idea arising from a series of impressions, a matter of pleasure and satisfaction rather than some kind of absolute, external reality. For Hume, it is not only beauty, but also "tastes and colours, and all other sensible qualities" which exist not in the object, but merely in the senses.[6]

In these philosophical discussions about beauty, little effort was made to distinguish between theories relating to the beauty of the natural world and those relating to art. Both philosophers and artists seemed to simply assume that beauty was an integral property of art, and that the beauty found in art was no different than the beauty found in the natural world.

5. Begbie, *Voicing Creation's Praise*, 196.
6. Ibid., 188.

This began to change with the *Aesthetics* of Georg Wilhelm Friedrich Hegel (1770–1831), a work based on his lectures throughout the 1820s and published in 1830. Danto notes his own excitement on reading Hegel:

> There were two thoughts on the very first page of his work . . .
> One was the rather radical distinction he drew between natural
> and artistic beauty . . . And the other was his gloss on why ar-
> tistic beauty seemed "superior" to natural beauty. It was because
> it was "born of the Spirit and born again." That was a grand,
> ringing phrase: *Aus den Geistens geborene und wiedergeborene.*
> It meant, as I saw it, that artistic beauty was in some sense an
> intellectual rather than a natural product.[7]

Danto goes on to say that the mimetic theory of art, which held that a picture of a field of daffodils is beautiful in the same way that the field itself is beautiful, does not really account for what we value in art. For Hegel, and for Danto, the painting has an importance, a meaning, lacking in the natural phenomenon.

By the early twentieth century, the very concept of beauty as applied to artworks was seriously challenged. In his seminal work, simply titled *Art*, published in 1913, Clive Bell (1881–1964) made a careful distinction between what he called significant form, which could be a property only of works of art, and beauty, which could only properly be said to apply to things in the natural world. Since what he termed the aesthetic emotion could only be aroused in the presence of significant form, this sensation was different than that which was evoked by the beauty of a flaming sunset or a perfect rose. For Bell, the concept of beauty simply did not apply to artworks at all.

Marcel Duchamp went even further. Rejecting even the notion of significant form as a valid criterion for measuring the worth of an artwork, Duchamp famously entered a common, industrially-produced urinal into the Society of Independent Artists in 1917, signing it "R. Mutt" and calling it *Fountain*. As he had with works like the 1915 *In Advance of a Broken Arm*, which was a snow shovel on which the title was painted; or the 1919 *L.H.O.O.Q.*, in which he drew a mustache on a reproduction of the *Mona Lisa*, Duchamp asked viewers to experience *Fountain* as an artwork by moving it from the realm of the ordinary into the realm of the gallery. Although many have subsequently seen these "readymades" as aesthetic objects, exhibiting a certain visual elegance, Duchamp's own intention seemed to be the total dissociation of aesthetics from art. Danto cites Duchamp's later reflection as evidence:

7. Danto, *Abuse of Beauty*, 12.

"A point which I very much wanted to establish is that the choice of these 'readymades' was never dictated by aesthetic delectation," he declared retrospectively in 1961. "The choice was based on a reaction of visual indifference with at the same time a total absence of good or bad taste . . . in fact a complete anesthesia."[8]

Here, and elsewhere, Duchamp was clear that he was not interested in what he termed "retinal art," artworks that were pleasing to the eye. Like the other artists and writers who collectively referred to themselves as "Dada," Duchamp was interested in art as a concept, or even as a way of life. Leah Dickerman notes in her introduction to the catalog to a major retrospective of Dada shown at the National Gallery of Art in 2006 that the intention of the Dadaists was to reconceptualize artistic practice as a tactic in redefining art. Dada principles and practices

signal an assertive debunking of the ideas of technical skill, virtuoso technique, and expression of individual subjectivity . . . . One effect [of this debunking] . . . is the violation of traditional artistic categories—art and non-art, medium and its domain . . . . In Dada works, language, politics, the machine and the commodity permeate the work of art by way of the detritus, processes, and idioms of a new media and commodity culture.[9]

For Duchamp and the other Dada artists, the specifically aesthetic properties of an artwork were much less interesting than the relationship of that work to society at large and to the history of art and art theory. In this way of thinking about art, the worth of any artwork is not found in its sensory properties, but in what it *means*. The question for most artists, critics, and others who take art seriously today is not whether an artwork is beautiful, but whether it is *true*.

Art, Aesthetics, and Beauty

Following in the footsteps of Bell, Duchamp, and others, art since the early twentieth century is in large part an exploration of the notion that art is about meaning and truth. Several years ago, the Hirshhorn Museum in Washington, DC, an institution known for its commitment to contemporary art and the issues that it raises, mounted an exhibition entitled *Regarding Beauty: A View of the Late Twentieth Century*. The show and its profusely illustrated

8. Ibid., 10.
9. Dickerman et al., *Dada*, 8.

and well-documented catalog addressed both of these issues. In the preface to the catalog, the curators, Neal Benezra and Olga M. Viso wrote,

> While ascribing beauty to art may seem natural and appropriate, in recent decades beauty and contemporary art have been considered virtually incongruous. In an art world increasingly focused on global issues and social concerns, artists and critics alike have questioned beauty's efficacy and relevance for contemporary culture. Suggesting frivolity, the machinations of the art market, and a lack of seriousness and social purpose, beauty has indeed come under severe attack. The assault on beauty by the contemporary art world has left a confused and baffled art-viewing public uncertain about one of the very cornerstones of Western art and culture, namely, the pursuit of beauty.[10]

As the other essays and, more importantly, the artworks in the exhibition, demonstrate, not only notions of what constitutes beauty, but what the word actually means and how that meaning relates to art, have been hotly contested.

Nevertheless, it seems that a majority of theological aestheticians writing today, not to mention countless pastors and ordinary Christians, continue to assume that art and beauty are inextricably linked. For them, if an artwork is not beautiful, it doesn't count as art. There are at least two problems here that complicate the conversation between artists and the church about the relationship between art and beauty. The first is that people's assessments often change over time as to whether any given work of art (or anything else) is beautiful. The second is that, for many artists working today, Christian and non-Christian alike, beauty is an irrelevant category.

Two stories will demonstrate the first problem. In 1874, the Parisian art critic, J. Claretie, declared that in their new works, the painters Claude Monet, Camille Pissarro, Berthe Morisot and others "appear to have declared war on beauty."[11] Today, of course, the very artworks that so horrified Claretie—and many others who attended the 1874 show now known as the First Impressionist exhibition—are so wildly popular as to have become virtually clichés of beauty. To judge by the crowds that accompany any major exhibition of Impressionist works, paintings which employ soft colors and quick dabs of paint to suggest the shifting, shimmering light at dawn, as in Monet's *Impression: Sunrise* from 1872, are today considered by many to be the among the most beautiful ever made.

10. Benezra and Viso, *Regarding Beauty*, 11.
11. Ibid., 7.

Lest we imagine that such radical changes in both critical and popular assessments of beauty occur solely in the realm of visual art, consider the fate of Igor Stravinsky's *Rite of Spring*. When this ballet was first performed in Paris in May of 1913, the audience was so disturbed by its dissonant sounds and the angular movements of the dancers that they began to riot after only few minutes. Less than a year later, in March 1914, another concert was held in Paris in which the same music was played, and both audience and critics received it with enormous praise. Twenty-seven years later, in 1940, Walt Disney used it in his animated film, *Fantasia*, to virtually no comment at all.[12]

What these two stories demonstrate is that not only do individuals disagree on the presence or absence of beauty in any given artwork, but also the perception of beauty in a given work may change over time in the same individual as well as in society at large. Or, perhaps, the point is that beauty is, in fact, an irrelevant category in these cases, equivalent to saying, "Wow!" As Danto puts it,

> [B]eauty had almost entirely disappeared from artistic reality in the twentieth century, as if attractiveness was somehow a stigma, with its crass commercial implications . . . . what made paintings "work" seemed poorly captured by the way beauty had been classically formulated, with reference to balance and proportion and order. "Beautiful!" itself just became an expression of generalized approbation, with as little descriptive content as a whistle someone might emit in the presence of something that especially wowed them. . . . In any case it seemed to have so little to do with what art had become in the latter part of the century that what philosophical interest art had could be addressed without needing to worry overmuch about it—or without needing to worry about it at all.[13]

This brings us to the second problem, which is that for many artists today, beauty is simply irrelevant to the way they approach their work. Differing assumptions between theologians, pastors, and ordinary Christians, on the one hand and artists, critics, and art theorists, on the other, about what art is and how it does or should function in society are at the root of much mutual incomprehension in conversations about the role of art in the church. For the Christian world, largely, art continues to be understood

12. This widely known story was related by Jonah Lehrer on a *Radiolab* broadcast first aired on Tuesday, September 24, 2007 on New York Public Radio station WNYC. The program examined the ways that people respond neurologically to sound and learn to appreciate new kinds of music. Lehrer, "Musical Language."

13. Danto, *Abuse of Beauty*, 7–8.

primarily as a vehicle for beauty, which takes on a variety of guises but ultimately points to the beauty of God. For the secular art world, beauty is only one of a large number of aims and theories about the nature and purpose of art.

While various groups and individual artists have explored many different strategies for making art, what virtually all had in common was an interest in depicting ideas, in investing their paintings or sculptures or poems or symphonies with *meaning*. This was particularly evident in painting and sculpture, which in the twentieth century largely abandoned mimesis—the naturalistic depiction of the visible world—in favor of works that were more theoretical and abstract. In poetry and literature, a similar impulse led to such practices as automatic writing and chance arrangements of words cut out from the newspaper. Examples of this experimental attitude, with its interest in process often more than product, can also be seen in avant-garde music, dance, theater, and other artistic productions. This is not to say that artists previous to that time were not interested in ideas, but that up until that time beauty, often defined as a harmonious unity of parts, was a primary goal in all the arts. Around the turn of the twentieth century, however, the idea of beauty itself came to be suspect, and was replaced by other intellectual ideas.

By this, I do not mean to imply that the artists were intending to illustrate some proposition that could just as easily be put into discursive language. Famously, groups of poets, painters, and musicians gathered in cafes and bars in Paris, Geneva, Zurich, Berlin, and elsewhere, talking about politics and other social issues as well as their latest ideas about art, and issuing manifestos, or statements, setting forth those ideas. Many of them also wrote extensively in letters, journals, and other places about what they were trying to do, so we have a record of their ideas as well as the artworks that grew out of these conversations.

The subsequent works of art, however, did not merely illustrate these ideas, but rather embodied them, trying them out to see what would happen. In some ways, the approach of artists as different as Dadaist Hans Arp and the composer Arnold Schoenberg was similar to that of a scientist who makes a hypothesis about the way something works, and then sets up experiments to test that hypothesis. For Arp, the hypothesis was that the chance arrangement of bits of paper that he allowed to fall to the floor would be more meaningful that any arrangement that he might control. For Schoenberg, it was that music should be composed using a rule-based series of the twelve semitones of the chromatic scale. I am, of course, grossly oversimplifying these ideas, and many other examples could be given, but the point is that in each case the resulting artworks were the working out of those ideas as a long series of experiments, in the one case graphically and in the other musically.

Artists following these approaches typically do not ask themselves if an artwork is beautiful, but rather if it works or if it is true. That is, does the specific combination of tone, value, harmony, dissonance, size, and other qualities in fact embody the content that the artist wants to convey. These are, of course, aesthetic questions, but only if one understands *aesthetic* as relating to the senses, rather than according to any standard of harmony, unity, or balance. When artists speak of aesthetics, they are not usually speaking about beauty, but of the relationships (harmonious or otherwise) among the various elements of an artwork, and of how those relationships express ideas or emotions.

Artists also use the word "aesthetic" to describe a particular attitude, or set of values, against which a particular artwork might be measured. Thus, one would not expect a work created prior to the twentieth century to exhibit a modernist aesthetic of clean, simple lines; a few, clear colors; and no extraneous decoration. Conversely, a more narrative work made after the 1980s might be said to exhibit a postmodern aesthetic, with ironic or playful references to a multitude of historical and geographical sources. Aesthetics, for artists, is about what can be perceived with the senses, and the effect that such perception has on both emotion and meaning.

This understanding of aesthetics informs the development of serious art throughout the modern and postmodern periods. In the middle of the twentieth century, the New York-based Abstract Expressionists seemed to take Claretie's accusation against the Impressionists as a compliment. Benezra notes,

> As Barnett Newman succinctly stated in 1948, "The impulse of modern art is the desire to destroy beauty." Working at mid-century, Newman and his fellow Abstract Expressionists sought to free themselves from the shackles of centuries of aesthetic tradition and expectation. For Newman as for many others, the pursuit of beauty had become an indication of conservatism and failed nerve, an ignoble ambition to be shunned at all costs.[14]

What Newman sought in his work was not beauty, but the sublime. By this, Newman seemed to mean a striving for union with God, understood as the Absolute. In "The Sublime is Now," he writes,

> The invention of beauty by the Greeks, that is, their postulate of beauty as an ideal, has been the bugbear of European art and

14. Benezra and Viso, *Regarding Beauty*, 11.

European aesthetic philosophies. Man's natural desire in the arts to express his relation to the Absolute became identified and confused with the absolutisms of perfect creations—with the fetish of quality—so that the European artist has been continually involved in the moral struggle between notions of beauty and the desire for sublimity.

. . . I believe that here in America, some of us, free from the weight of European culture, are finding the answer, by completely denying that art has any concern with the problem of beauty and where to find it . . . . We are reasserting man's natural desire for the exalted, for a concern with our relationship to the absolute emotions . . . . We are freeing ourselves of the impediments of memory, association, nostalgia, legend, myth, or what have you, that have been the devices of Western European painting. Instead of making *cathedrals* out of Christ, man, or "life," we are making it out of ourselves, out of our own feelings. The image we produce is the self-evident one of revelation, real and concrete, that can be understood by anyone who will look at it without the nostalgic glasses of history.[15]

Not everyone in the art world was as dismissive of either history or beauty. Nevertheless, the word *beauty* as such disappeared from most art-critical discourse, transformed eventually into a theory that came to be called Formalism.

In the 1950s, much of what was important in the art world was articulated by two highly influential and colorful art critics, Clement Greenberg and Harold Rosenberg. Clement Greenberg was the primary proponent and explanatory voice of Formalism and what came to be called Abstract Expressionism. For Greenberg, painting, in particular, needed to be purged of any notion of illusionism or imitation of the natural world. A painting is simply paint on canvas and should be evaluated according to the relationships among its constituent parts, its formal relationships, rather than by any information external to it.

For Rosenberg, Greenberg's contemporary and professional rival, artworks necessarily embodied the artist's life and context. He is credited with coining the term "Action Painting," particularly as practiced by Willem de Kooning and Franz Kline. For Rosenberg, making art was an heroic, existential struggle, in which the process was at least as important as the eventual product. Formalist concerns were not ignored, but rather subsidiary to the actual act of painting.

15. Newman, "The Sublime Is Now," 173; emphasis original.

By the 1960s, for some artists, the work of art as such became completely dematerialized in favor of the pure idea. The Conceptualists, as they came to be called, followed Rosenberg's ideas to their ultimate conclusion, seeing art more as a process than a product. Conceptualists took the notion of simply seeing how an idea might work out to its farthest possibility.

In music, John Cage's famous (or infamous, depending on one's point of view) 1952 piece for any instrument or combination of instruments, "4'33'," called for an indeterminate number of performers simply to be present, allowing the random noises of those gathered in the concert hall to be all that was heard. One can hardly say that this was a musical composition in the sense of putting notes on paper. However, Cage's set of instructions for one or more musicians is sold in the same way as any other sheet music, and thus can be legitimately called a composition.[16]

This understanding of a composition as "a set of instructions for one or more musicians" seems to me analogous to the kinds of works created by Conceptual artists like Sol Lewitt. Lewitt, like his intellectual forbearer Hans Arp, was more interested in process than product. Like a composer, Lewitt worked out a set of instructions that could be performed by any suitably trained artists. The titles of Lewitt's wall drawings, such as *Wall Drawing #65 / Lines not short, not straight, crossing and touching, drawn at random using four colors, uniformly dispersed with maximum density, covering the entire surface of the wall* from 1971, are, quite literally, the instructions for performing the works, and bear the same relationship to any given instance of that work as the performance of a play does to the script or a concerto does to the score.

For Cage, Lewitt, and many other artists, the working out of such ideas was much more important than any notion of beauty or even formalist critique. It is one of the ironies of history that, in hindsight, despite their insistence on the irrelevancy of a concern for either the art object itself or its formal properties, many of the works created by the Conceptualists, like those of the Dadaists before them, do, in fact, exhibit the kind of formal elegance that is often meant when people speak of beauty.

Conceptualism was only one strand of an increasingly complex art world, in which artists, patrons, and a large proportion of highly educated arts professionals (curators, critics, historians, bureaucrats, and others) defined and redefined art. In the 1980s, when I was in art school, it had become commonplace to say that art was visual philosophy, a way to discuss reality in visual terms. Definitions of art had become completely divorced from

16. Performance notes on the sheet music read, "*For tacet (any instrument or combination of instruments)*" (Cage, "4'33'").

the objects, subsumed into a larger cultural territory of meaning, ethnicity, gender, class, and other political categories.

Today, in a postmodern society, the notion of art has become even more contested. There is no longer a single, unified art world in the sense that it existed in the middle of the twentieth century. Rather, there are multiple art worlds, each with its own standards, objectives, and traditions. Each of these art worlds comprises a community of interest in which technical excellence, cultural connections, historical significance, or some other factor generally tends to define what is considered important. While such communities of interest may speak of the objects that they praise as beautiful, beauty as such is rarely an explicit norm.

Beauty and the Church: A Concrete Example

As the art world has moved away from beauty as a defining characteristic, the church has continued to assume an essential connection between art and beauty. Problems arise with using beauty as an evaluative category for art in the church when the discussion of beauty moves from theology and theory to concrete situations. Too often, the notions of art and beauty are so tightly bound together that any art that is not perceived as beautiful by the speaker is branded as "not art" and certainly not appropriate for the church.

For instance, in her 2010 essay "The Artist: What Exactly is an Artist, and How Do We Shepherd Them?" in *For the Beauty of the Church*, Barbara Nicolosi writes, "I want to lay out a few ideas about the nature of the beautiful, because *beauty is the terrain of real artists, and one way to recognize them is if they dwell in this terrain.*"[17] Nicolosi goes on to cite a definition of the beautiful given by Thomas Aquinas, as that which possesses wholeness, harmony, and radiance. These, she says, define the terrain of the artist.

She continues,

> Wholeness means that nothing is missing. . . .What do we get from wholeness? . . . We yearn to cleave to the One, and when we experience completeness, we have a sense of being at home and at rest. So the beautiful gives us a sense of peace. . .
>
> Harmony means that all of those parts that are present are related to one another in a complementary relationship. Every part brings out the best in all the other parts, and there is no domination or submission. And what do we get from harmony? When we experience harmony, we feel a sense of joy, because we are created to dwell in community. . . .

17. Nicolosi, "The Artist," 106; emphasis original.

Finally, there's radiance. When we experience a beautiful
object, it communicates something profound to us, some kind
of moral, spiritual, or intellectual enlightenment.

The purpose of art, she says, is to elicit feelings similar to those experienced in the presence of a natural vista, the "paradoxical mix of humility
and euphoria" in response to God's unmediated creation. Because urban
people do not have as much access to nature as do those living in an agrar-
ian society, the church needs to patronize beautiful art "that will make us
okay with our creaturehood so that we to can feel a yearning to praise swell
in our spirits."[18]

Art, then, for Nicolosi and for many others, is only legitimate as a vehicle of the beautiful; and the criteria of beauty are found in certain aspects
of the natural world. For Nicolosi and those who share her views, the true
aim of art is to mirror the most beautiful aspects of the natural world.

This mimetic view about the purpose of art is widespread outside of
the art world, but relatively rare within it ever since it was discredited by
Clive Bell over a century ago. Artists may, for instance, want to call attention
to suffering, or to the despoliation of the natural world by human greed;
they may want to consider the nature of sin, or the way that disease wreaks
havoc with the human body; or they may want to explore the workings of
human perception artfully rather than scientifically; and so on. Many of the
results of these sorts of artistic inquiry will not be beautiful according to any
of the classical definitions, because that kind of beauty is not its intention.
Nor will they be beautiful according to the mimetic theory, since they do
not imitate or reflect beautiful aspects of the natural world.

In rejecting beauty as a goal, many artists devote their work to advocacy for a variety of causes. Since the early twentieth century, social justice
has been a particular concern of the *avant-garde*. More recently, much art
has been made lamenting the despoliation of the natural environment. In
contrast, many people in the church, as well as in the wider society, lament
the fact that some art serves political ends rather than beauty. When they
say that, however, what they often mean is that the art in question promotes
values or ideas with which they disagree. If the ideas inherent in the making
of the art are repugnant, the artwork is often dismissed as ugly.

Barbara Nicolosi's essay exemplifies this kind of thinking. In it Nicolosi discusses Robert Graham's statue, *Our Lady of the Angels*, which hov-
ers over the huge, bronze doors of the recently dedicated Roman Catholic
Cathedral of Our Lady of the Angels in Los Angeles, California. This image,
with its simplicity, strength, and presence, took my breath away with delight

18. Ibid., 109.

when I first saw it. Its halo a simple opening through which glows the blue California sky, the statue speaks both of eternity and of the concrete realities of its time and place. This, I thought, was no simpering, domesticated Mary, but rather a strong, stolid, unsentimentalized woman who works with her hands and somehow is also the majestic, welcoming Queen of Heaven. So I was somewhat surprised to read the following description in Nicolosi's essay:

> It's just dreadful. The statue is of completely uncertain gender, with a female torso, but harshly cropped hair and distinctly masculine arms and hands. In fact, my students call her "Man-hands Mary." But it's worse than just androgyny. The image has black lips, Asian eyes, a Latino face, and other scattered Anglo features. When I first went on a tour of the new Cathedral, our guide said "This statue was conceived so that people of all races would see themselves in it and feel welcome in this place." And *I* said, "But it's kind of ugly. I don't know about you but if you saw that kind of freak inviting you into its house . . ."[19]

This kind of criticism about an artwork that someone dislikes is all too common in the church. Based in implicit assumptions that there is only one kind of feminine beauty, and implying that there is something freakish about persons, who, like the model for the statue, are of mixed race, it conveys a dismissive attitude about anything that doesn't accord with the writer's own ideas. She continues,

> My point is that the goal of the statue was not to make something that would deliver the beautiful. The goal of the statue was to communicate a political message. The fact that it is ugly and my students mock it indicates that it has been a failure as a political vehicle too. In politics, you lose wholeness because the political only tells its own side of the story. As a result, people lose a feeling of rest.[20]

This way of thinking about art and beauty is endemic in the church. In its refusal to consider any but a very narrow definition of either art or beauty, it endangers the genuine dialogue between artists and the church that I hope to foster. A dispassionate examination of the history of art will show that every artwork has a point of view, a way of describing the world that both encodes and promotes a particular way of thinking. If we dismiss an artwork because it does not conform to our preconceptions about art or

19. Ibid., 111.
20. Ibid.

beauty or God, or because we disagree with its point of view, then we close off any possibility of experiencing something new in its presence.

Defining Beauty as Relational Experience

A great deal of current writing in theological aesthetics begins and ends with God as the ultimate definition and exemplar of beauty. I cannot disagree with this formulation, as God is the source and ground of all that we do or experience. Beauty is a word that describes a deep and important experience, something that is often akin to the sacred.

As Nicolosi's rejection of Graham's sculpture demonstrates, the experience of beauty is conditioned by one's expectations and beliefs about what is or is not beautiful, and about the relationship of art to beauty. Although the art world in general has rejected beauty as a useful category for at least a hundred years, most people who are not engaged in serious art theory and criticism continue to assume that art and beauty are inextricably linked. Since beauty continues to be of such great importance to discussions of art within the church, I believe it is important to find a new way to define what beauty is and how to discern it.

However, I do not find it helpful to define beauty (or truth or goodness or anything else, for that matter) as a reflection of God's glory when it comes to deciding whether any given thing is beautiful, or true, or good. Once we are faced with that task, we must have some kind of practical standard by which to measure or compare. To posit beauty (or God) as an absolute standard to which particular objects may conform to a greater or lesser extent leaves too great a gap between theological assertion and practical, everyday experience. Into this gap will inevitably fall cultural conventions, personal taste, and conflicting assessments by a variety of authorities with unstated, but nonetheless operative, assumptions about what is and is not beautiful.

I would like to suggest another strategy. Perhaps beauty is a relational experience. Perhaps the notion that God is Beauty is similar to the notion that God is Love. Consider 1 John 4:8, "Whoever does not love does not know God, for God is love." In recent years, it has become commonplace to assert that love is not a noun, but a verb. On the face of it, this assertion is absurd, as it is obvious that the word *love* can be used as a noun. The point, however, is that love is not an object, a static, physical thing which can be put down and picked up at will. Rather, as the scriptural passage makes clear, loving is active. Whether loving is a feeling which arises in relationship to another being, or the loving words, actions, and experiences which communicate that feeling from one person to another is left ambiguous. But where there is no active loving, there is no love. Thus, to say that God is love is to say that God's own actions are the pattern for loving behavior, rather than to assert that love has some independent existence apart from the act of loving.

Similarly, it seems to me that beauty has no independent existence apart from the complex of physiological, psychological, and spiritual experiences that is evoked in the presence of things that are described as beautiful. It is that complex of attitudes, thoughts, and physical sensations that has been called "the aesthetic emotion." In this way of thinking, beauty is an experience, rather than a thing.

Clive Bell tried to define the aesthetic emotion as that which the sensitive, properly educated person would have in the presence of significant form. I believe that his description of the aesthetic emotion may be applicable to what I am calling the experience of beauty. He begins,

> The starting-point for all systems of aesthetics must be the personal experience of a peculiar emotion. The objects that provoke this emotion we call works of art. All sensitive people agree that there is a peculiar emotion provoked by works of art. I do not mean, of course, that all works provoke the same emotion. On the contrary, every work produces a different emotion. But all these emotions are recognisably the same in kind; so far, at any rate, the best opinion is on my side. That there is a particular kind of emotion provoked by works of visual art, and that this emotion is provoked by every kind of visual art, by pictures, sculptures, buildings, pots, carvings, textiles, etc., etc., is not disputed, I think, by anyone capable of feeling it. This emotion is called the aesthetic emotion; and if we can discover some quality common and peculiar to all the objects that provoke it, we shall have solved what I take to be the central problem of aesthetics. We shall have discovered the essential quality in a work of art, the quality that distinguishes works of art from all other classes of objects.[21]

Unfortunately, whether what is to be discerned is beauty or significant form, Bell's reasoning turns out to be circular. If only the sensitive person can discern significant form, and significant form is what arouses the aesthetic emotion in a sensitive person, there can be no way of knowing who is a sensitive person or what is a significant form except for the assertion on the part of the individual who claims to have had an aesthetic emotion. Despite Bell's insistence that only something made by a human can have

21. Bell, *Art*, 131 Kindle location.

significant form, while beauty may be found in natural objects as well, substituting *significant form* for *beauty* does not solve the problem of deciding what works of art ought to elicit the aesthetic emotion.

However, I think that Bell's initial intuition is correct. The personal experience of a peculiar set of physical sensations, emotions, thoughts, and ideas is exactly the right the place to start looking for beauty. What led Bell astray was the ingrained, unquestioned, cultural assumption that beauty (or, in Bell's case, significant form) is a thing with its own, independent existence and that this "thing" that we call "beauty" is a lasting, essential property of some objects and absent in others.

This may have more to do with the grammar of Western languages than with reality. In order to describe an object, we name its properties, such as color, size, shape, or texture. The box is red. The fabric is scratchy. The tree is big. The ball is round. Any object may have a number of properties, and the more specific the list, the more nearly the description will match the object. But just as we say "the ball is round," we may also say "the ball is beautiful." But now we have entered a different order of description. While anyone who has internalized the concept of roundness will agree generally that the ball is round, there will be many opinions about whether or not the ball is beautiful. While one person will be rapturous over its harmonious proportions and delicate coloring, another will find it trite and ordinary, and a third will proclaim it downright ugly. The form of the sentence in each case is identical, but the order of description is different. In the one case, the shape is an intrinsic property of the ball (until someone lets all the air out and it becomes flat). In the other, what appears at first glance to be an intrinsic property on further investigation turns out to be more to be a matter of opinion. But whose opinion should prevail? And on what criteria should we decide?

Historically, the answer has generally been that the opinion of the educated art expert should prevail. However, like Clive Bell's sensitive person who ultimately cannot say how he knows that *this* object has significant form and *that* one does not, except that he has experienced an aesthetic emotion in the presence of one and not the other, so, too the educated expert cannot say exactly why this object seems to be more beautiful than that one.

What experts can talk about are the formal qualities of an object, such as the elements (line, shape, form, texture, color, value) and principles (balance, rhythm, harmony, contrast, directional movement) of design; the skill of the artist in manipulating materials and methods; the place that a particular work of art has in the grand conversation that is the history of art; or the implicit or explicit meaning of the work, taking into account the various relationships between its subject matter, the various formal elements, and its historical relevance. What the art expert cannot say with any integrity is whether the object at hand is objectively beautiful, because the expert's education has shown that standards of beauty are so different in different eras and places that to speak of beauty as having some objective reality is a futile exercise.

On the other hand, the expert, like any other human being, does have experiences of beauty, and may even say that something is beautiful. What is meant is often that it conforms to the classical definition of beauty, which has to do with some of the formal terms I have just mentioned. Something is classically beautiful to the extent that it is harmonious, well-balanced, and sufficiently complex to keep the eye or ear or mind moving. This has some-times been called "unity-in-diversity." But if beauty is simply a matter of harmony, or unity-in-diversity, then beauty becomes a superfluous concept. Clearly, there is something more to beauty than mere formal properties.

In his book, *Voicing Creation's Praise*, Jeremy Begbie makes an admi-rable case for freeing the concept of beauty from what he terms its "Platonic bondage" as well as its chaotic counterpart, unrestrained relativism. Instead, he offers a vision (or perhaps a tune, given his insistence that the visual arts have had too much influence on the development of philosophical and theo-logical aesthetics) which is rooted in a more solidly biblical understanding "that God's very being is constituted by relatedness-in-love, by a commu-nion of Persons-in-relation."[22] Calling on Karl Barth's affirmation that God's beauty embraces death as well as life, and Hans Urs von Balthasar's urging that we understand God's creation together with salvation as the exemplar of true beauty, Begbie wants us to define beauty not as an eternal, unchang-ing property but as a quality that unfolds over time. He writes,

> Beauty, I mentioned earlier, has all too often been abstracted from time and temporal movement, and turned into a static, timeless quality. Suppose, however, we refuse to divorce it from the transformation of the disorder of creation in the history of Jesus Christ. Suppose we begin there. Does this not open up a more dynamic, and more theological paradigm of beauty?[23]

While I agree with Begbie's initial critique, I believe that he does not take this new theological paradigm of beauty to its logical conclusion. Just a few pages earlier, Begbie writes admiringly of the insights of Hans-Georg Gadamer, a twentieth-century-German philosopher who critiqued

22. Begbie, *Voicing Creation's Praise*, 148.
23. Ibid., 224.

Enlightenment approaches to aesthetics and stressed a relational understanding of art. Begbie notes,

> Gadamer is committed to laying great stress on the act of en-
> joying and interpreting art: a work of art is strictly speaking
> only art when it is experienced as such by someone. This is
> no play without players: we are not playing if we are detached
> and disinterested spectators. Likewise, the work of art is not a
> self-contained and self-enclosed object which stands in front of
> a spectator or listener waiting to be contemplated. Just as Ga-
> damer calls attention to the bouyancy, the to-and-fro movement
> that belongs to play, so he does the same in the case of art. There
> is a dynamic interaction or transaction between the work of art
> and the spectator . . . . The meaning of a work of art is not simply
> "there" to be discovered, it comes to realisation only as the work
> is encountered.[24]

Perhaps because I am a practical theologian, a working artist with degrees in both art and liturgy, rather than in systematic theology, I am willing to push the analogy a little further. Bringing together the insight that a
Christian aesthetic must be grounded in the living reality of God's eternally
loving trinitarian dance, and Gadamer's observation that the meaning of
a work of art arises in the relationship between it and the person who is
willing to be in relationship with it, I suggest that beauty is not, in fact, a
property of any work of art, static or temporal, but rather an experience that
arises in the relationship between the object and the audience. That relationship might be called love.

I realize that, in its insistence on relationship, which necessarily has
a subjective component, this notion is similar to the Kantian position that
the aesthetic experience is purely subjective, or Clive Bell's intuition about
the viewer's response to significant form. The difference is that, unlike Bell
and countless others, I cannot accept that any object or event *is* beautiful
(or possessing significant form) in the same way that it is big, or round, or
even red.

Naturally, that doesn't keep me from using the term when I encounter
something that elicits the aesthetic response in me. I am as likely as anyone
to say, "oh, that is very beautiful!" But when I do say it, it is always with the
mental reservation that someone else may not find it beautiful at all. Unlike
Kant or Bell, I am not claiming to make an absolute, universal judgment, but
rather reporting on the fact of my own aesthetic response.

24. Ibid., 200.

Restraining Relativism

Having just admitted that I am making a purely subjective statement when I declare that something is beautiful, what will keep me out of the chaotic pit of relativism? As Augustine put it, "Do beautiful things delight because they are beautiful or are they beautiful because they delight?"[25] In other words, do I love something because it is beautiful, or do I experience it as beautiful because I love it? Let me try to find a way through this puzzle with an example in Elaine Scarry's book, *On Beauty and Being Just*.

Scarry holds that beauty is an intrinsic quality of objects, an objective, fixed property which may be universally apprehended. For her, if we fail to see beauty in an object at one time, yet do see it later; or, conversely, if an object that we once regarded as beautiful no longer seems so, then we are in error. In each case, she says, we are (or have been) simply wrong, as the object is objectively either beautiful or not. [26] To make her point, she writes of the passage in *The Odyssey* in which Odysseus, who has nearly drowned, sees Nausicaa playing on the beach. Struck by her beauty, he compares the sensation to the similar experience of seeing a young palm tree at Delos, also after a long and dangerous time at sea.

In Scarry's extravagant claims for the self-evident beauty of both the girl and the tree, the way she describes the event is as telling as the point she is trying to make. She writes,

> Odysseus's speech makes visible the structure of perception at the moment one stands in the presence of beauty. The beautiful thing seems incomparable, unprecedented; and that sense of being without precedent conveys a sense of the "newness" or "newbornness" of the entire world.

A few paragraphs later, she asserts that beauty is sacred. Odysseus had begun

> with the intuition that in standing before Nausicaa he might be standing in the presence of Artemis, and now he rearrives at that intuition, since the young palm grows beside the altar of Delos, the birthplace of Apollo and Artemis. His speech says this: If you are immortal, I recognize you. You are Artemis. If instead you are mortal, I am puzzled and cannot recognize you, since I can find no precedent. No, wait. I do recognize you. I remember

---

25. Quoted in García-Rivera, *Wounded Innocence*, 112.

26. Scarry, *On Beauty and Being Just*, 12–16.

watching a tree coming up out of the ground of Delos . . . . Nausicaa and the palm each make the world new.[27]

Scarry asserts that the beauty in which Odysseus delights is inherent in both the girl and the palm tree. But perhaps another explanation is possible. Perhaps it is not that either girl or tree is extraordinarily beautiful, but rather that Odysseus, in his extreme exhaustion and delight at simply being alive, is predisposed to see anything and everything in a special light. Perhaps it is not that Nausicaa and the palm made the world new, but that the percieved newness of the world is due to Odysseus' heightened awareness. After nearly drowning, Odysseus is in a new relationship to the world, and thus to them. In that moment of deep relatedness, he is already predisposed to see them—along with everything else—as beautiful.

The revelatory vision of palm tree in Odysseus' story connects to another example, that of Scarry's own change in perception or estimation of palm trees. Earlier in the book, she relates that, having spent most of her life on the East Coast, where trees tend to be great branching affairs, she does not recognize the tree-ness, let alone the beauty of palm trees.[28] Instead, they seem to her to be simply clumsy trunks, topped with branches all stuck together. Then, one day, she is on a balcony, more or less at eye level with the fronds of a palm. For the first time, she can see the striped play of light and shadow that characterizes these trees. Now that she understands this essential characteristic, she can see that palm trees are, in fact, beautiful, and she has been in error.

Scarry describes filling her house with prints of Matisse paintings, allowing herself to become saturated with his vision, asserting that the paintings he did at Nice all reflect and grow out of the striped nature of palm frond light. It is not clear if this explanation of his work comes from Matisse's own testimony or from Scarry's intuitions. Either way, based on her careful observation of the paintings, it seems reasonable to suggest that living with these images has attuned her to that very light that she later sees in her confrontation with the real palm tree. Her serious, intentional relationship with the Matisse images has taught her to see the palm tree in a new way.

Once again, it is possible that Scarry's error is not in her inability to discern a beauty that has always existed , but rather in her assumption about the nature of beauty. Perhaps the beauty she perceives is not an attribute of the object, but rather of her seeing, of her disposition, of her openness to experience, of her relationship with the palm trees.

27. Ibid., 22–25.
28. Ibid., 17.

The author's new way of seeing is analogous to the observation I once read that Turner, Church, and other artists have taught us collectively to perceive picturesque landscapes where previously we had only seen threatening wilderness, or that the Impressionists have taught us all to see that shadows are blue or green, rather than as some undifferentiated darkness. Similarly, we can learn to see even a pile of crushed cars or a garbage bin as beautiful, if only we place it in the correct aesthetic context. So, too, it may be that the beauty Scarry now experiences does not inhere in the palm tree but rather in her relationship with it.

As I see it, beauty is not an inherent property of some given objects, and not of others, in some absolute way. The notion of taste comes closer to what I regard as the truth. If we like something (or even love it!) we are more likely to experience it as beautiful. This is true even of something we have never before come into contact with—a new form of music, a new style of clothing, a person we have just met. We might instantly say that this new thing is beautiful (or ugly), before we have a chance to love it. But, I would argue, this immediate experience of beauty is not in the thing, itself, but rather in how closely it accords with our previous notion of beauty, our inner needs and desires, our toleration or need for novelty, and any other factors that are peculiar to our personal condition. Even our state of physical hunger or satiety, fatigue or rest, ill-health or well-being, contribute to our ability, willingness, openness to see anything (or nothing) as beautiful.

What all of these examples suggest is that, given the right mental, physical, and spiritual conditions, human beings have the ability to experience everything as beautiful, as though through the eyes of God. That "everything is beautiful" experience is well attested in the writings of both mystics and theologians. As Alejandro García-Rivera says,

> Textbook aesthetics tends toward dualisms between the work of art and the beholder, the artist and the community that appreciates his and her art, a work of art and a work of craft, the ugly and the beautiful, natural beauty and artistic beauty, and so on, and so forth. On the other hand, a living aesthetics sees a true continuity in the beautiful. The beautiful encompasses the ugly and the pretty, the work of art and the work of craft, the natural and that made by human hands. Indeed, a living aesthetics is less a disinterested beholding of some alienated object than that which moves the heart.[29]

For García-Rivera, the experience of beauty grows out of loving relationship with the world, with community, with one another. It is a

29. García-Rivera, *Wounded Innocence*, ix.

commonplace observation that every mother sees her baby as beautiful, even when a more objective observer might note that one baby is more harmoniously formed than another. This is why all attempts to formulate a canon of beauty are ultimately doomed to failure. If beauty is not a thing, a static attribute or set of attributes, but rather, an event, a relationship between object and beholder, then the assertion that God is the ultimate source and measure of beauty makes more sense. In the light of God, the entire created order is beautiful. And the more the beholder is willing to invest in really attending to the object of attention, the more it is likely that whatever is seen in this way will be experienced as beautiful.

Human Beauty

Although every created thing and every person is beautiful in the eyes of God, Nicolosi's response to Robert Graham's statue of Mary demonstrates that not everyone agrees about either artistic or human beauty. There are certain attributes, like harmony, symmetry, unity, etc. that more commonly are considered beautiful than others. There is, however, a danger in conflating such ideas about natural or artistic beauty with that of human beings, particularly women. I remember hearing of an experiment which showed that regardless of culture, men seem to prefer young, healthy, wide-eyed women to old, wrinkled, heavy-lidded ones. If that is true, then this particular standard of female beauty may be relatively universal, being tied more to biology than any notion of divine perfection. However, it is also demonstrably true that various times and cultures have ascribed beauty to women with a variety of physical attributes. If descriptions in literature and depictions in painting and sculpture can be believed, at one time and place or another, women who are short, tall, fat, thin, muscled, soft, blond, brunette, pale, or dark-skinned have been called beautiful.

However, such standards of feminine beauty are impersonal, disconnected from notions of loving relationship. Looking with the eyes of love, the loving husband of an old woman often finds her as—or even more—attractive as she was to him when they both were young. Or a painter, sensuously limning every curve and fold of an aged face, not only sees that face as beautiful, but helps us to see it so, as well. These two examples—the loving husband and the portrait painter—return us to love and relationship as a way to avoid the chaos of relativism.

What each of these examples, as well as Scarry's story of the palm tree, show is that the perception of beauty is dependent on willingness of the perceiver to be in relationship with that which is perceived. When we feel most deeply in love with a person, we perceive that person as astonishingly beautiful. Similarly, when we are angry with the same person, we may find that the very attributes which we earlier found attractive are now repugnant to us. The person's features, of course, have not appreciably changed in each of these two moments. Rather, our aesthetic response is activated in the presence of loving feelings, and de-activated in the presence of anger. And these responses are completely independent of whether the person in question might be judged attractive by any other person. Indeed, people who are quite homely in the eyes of the outside world are often described as beautiful by the people who love them.

Art and Truth

Since beauty understood in this way is not an intrinsic property of an object, but rather a matter of relationship, it cannot be a very useful measure for evaluating the worth of any particular instance of art. It is, however, possible to talk about art in a way that goes beyond personal taste.

When artists, critics, and other arts professionals talk seriously about quality in art, there are a number of properties or dimensions that they take into consideration. These dimensions include such things as design, craft, and truth. Each of these dimensions operates independently of the others, and different kinds of art may emphasize one set of dimensions over another. And while it is often hard to articulate how we recognize each of these dimensions, it is possible not only to distinguish them from one another, but to speak of the relative quality or value of an artwork based on its success in exemplifying each these dimensions and the way the various dimensions relate to one another.

Truth is perhaps the most subtle, yet the most important, of these dimensions. In her essay, "The Nature and Aim of Fiction," Flannery O'Connor writes,

> Art is a word that immediately scares people off, as being a little too grand. But all I mean by art is writing something that is valuable in itself and that works in itself. The basis of art is truth, both in matter and in mode. The person who aims after art in his work aims after truth, in an imaginative sense, no more and no less.[30]

Truth in art is ultimately based in our experiences as physical and emotional beings. Although music and visual art can be so abstract as to

---

30. In O'Connor, *Mystery and Manners: Occasional Prose*, 65.

be entirely divorced from narrative, even they depend on certain relationships between their constitutive elements and other human experiences for their affective force. For example, we understand a pointed, jagged line as an expression of aggression or danger, or loud, percussive sounds as unsettling, because of our experience of such things in the physical world. Similarly, a sinuous, curving line or a soft musical passage tends to convey peaceful, calming emotions because we have felt soft pillows and heard loving whispers. The literary and dramatic arts are even more dependent on a fairly high degree of connection with everyday life. Nevertheless, the truth of a novel or story or poem, as that of any form of art, is more in its form than in its conformity to ordinary life. As Flannery O'Connor points out,

> In a strictly naturalistic work the detail is there because it is
> natural to life, not because it is natural to the work. In a work of
> art we can be extremely literal, without being in the least natu-
> ralistic. Art is selective, and its truthfulness is the truthfulness of
> the essential that creates movement.[31]

Since O'Connor is writing about fiction, it is clear that what she means by *truth* is something other than facts. The truth that O'Connor refers to lies in specific word choices, in the overall structure and the internal rhythms and correspondences of the way the story is told, as much as it exists in the narrative as such. This kind of truth is conditional, grounded in the specifics of time and place and dialect, but not verifiably true in the way that a newspaper story might be. Nor is it an eternal verity, unchangeable through time and eternity. Rather, it is the truth of human lives and relationships, a truthfulness that makes attentive readers say, Aha, yes, life is really like that. It is an inner truth, a reflection of reality at its deepest, most mysterious level. This kind of truth is intimately connected with the true value of art. This kind of truth is found in all art that matters, from a Bach concerto to a Jackson Pollock action painting to a poem by Denise Levertov.

The Good, the Bad, and the OK

Of course, most of the art that comes into our homes and churches does not have the lasting, resonant quality of works by Bach or Pollock or Levertov. Much of the art made in our time, as in every other time and place, is of middling quality. It's not bad, but neither is it great. How, then, can we decide whether any given work is worth our time and attention and money?

---

31. Ibid., 70.

In *An Experiment in Criticism*, C. S. Lewis suggests that the quality of a literary work is best discerned by its ability to support what he calls "good reading." This kind of reading includes, among other things, attentiveness to the aural quality of individual words as well as the relationships among them; enjoyment of the detail that brings a field or a building or a character to life; and alertness to the symbolic uses of language. For Lewis, good reading, or, for that matter, good looking or good listening, is essentially receptivity, a willingness to give oneself over to the particularity of the work itself. Genuine appreciation, he writes, demands surrender:

> We must not let loose our own subjectivity upon the pictures and make them its vehicles. We must begin by laying aside as completely as we can all our own preconceptions, interests, and associations. We must make room for Botticelli's Mars and Venus or Cimabue's Crucifixion, by emptying out our own. After the negative effort, the positive. We must use our eyes. We must look, and go on looking till we have certainly seen exactly what is there. We sit down before the picture in order to have something done to us, not that we may do things with it. The first demand any work of art makes upon us is surrender. Look. Listen. Receive. Get yourself out of the way.[32]

Only once we have truly given ourselves over to a work, allowing ourselves to experience what is really there, can we decide if it has any value in and of itself. Turning again to literature, Lewis suggests that we are able to discern what is valuable by contrast with the worthless. He argues,

> The ideally bad book is the one of which a good reading is impossible. The words in which it exists will not bear close attention, and what they communicate offers you nothing unless you are prepared either for mere thrills or for flattering daydreams. But "invitation" comes into our conception of a good book. It is not enough that attentive and obedient reading should be barely possible if we try hard enough. The author must not leave us to do all the work.[33]

Similarly, a good work of visual art will invite close attention to its particular aesthetic qualities, its colors and shapes and internal relationships, as well as the moods and meanings those colors and shapes and internal relationships embody. Similar criteria can be applied to other media, such as drama or music.

32. Lewis, *Experiment*, 19.
33. Ibid., 113–14.

Most works in any medium will fall somewhere between great and ideally bad. There is, then, a continuum, a range of competence in any one or combination of qualities that a given artwork may exhibit. It is much easier to point out a clumsy design, sloppy craftsmanship, or derivative style than it is to decide if a work is worthwhile in an overall sense. Again, C. S. Lewis may point the way. Lewis suggests that the most useful way to evaluate an artwork is by examining the way its audience approaches it. If an artwork can be deeply appreciated, even by one person, then it has at the least some goodness in it. He writes,

> the very fact that people, or even one person, can well and truly read, and love for a lifetime, a book we had thought bad, will raise the suspicion that it cannot really be as bad as we thought. . . . the book [someone] likes may continue to seem so bad that we have to attribute [such] liking to some early association or other psychological accident. But we must, and should, remain uncertain. Always, there may be something in it that we can't see. The prima facie probability that anything which has ever been truly read and obstinately loved by any reader has some virtue in it is overwhelming.[34]

Like the good book which, according to Lewis, permits and invites good reading, a good work of art in any medium permits and invites close, involved attention. It both permits and invites its audience to submit to its formal qualities and inner relationships while being aware of its relationship to the world beyond it. Some works simply do this better than others. We call the ones that do it best, and most reliably, great. Other works do it less well, so we might call them OK. And the works which seem to actively reject such deep, willing submission are the ones that are simply bad. As for beauty, while a person may, indeed, have an experience of beauty while being immersed in a great, or even OK, painting or song or poem or play, I would suggest that this experience of beauty arises because of the person's relationship with the work, rather than because beauty is an intrinsic quality of the work.

A New Vision for Beauty, Truth, and Art

In this chapter, I have reviewed some of the ways that philosophers, theologians, artists, and ordinary people have thought about the entangled questions of art and beauty. Although many artists reject beauty as a useful category for their own art, the world beyond the somewhat rarified

34. Ibid., 110–11.

atmosphere of studio, gallery, museum, concert hall, and conservatory continues to assume that art and beauty are inextricably linked.

This is particularly true of the church, which is beginning to understand that artists have something important to contribute to our understanding of God, the world, and one another. Unfortunately, too often mutual incomprehension stops the conversation before it begins. When theologians and other Christians restrict the definition of aesthetics to questions of beauty, we misunderstand what artists say and how they say it. When we restrict the definition of art to that which conforms to classical ideals of beauty, we reject the insights that can only be known through engagement with the full range of artistic inquiry. When we insist that art must conform to arbitrary and outdated ideals of beauty, we lose the ability to evaluate art on more appropriate and objective grounds.

By enlarging the definition of aesthetics, the church may learn from artists how the physical and symbolic properties of any object or experience address both the senses and the intellect of those who encounter it. By offering more concrete criteria for evaluating and understanding artworks, I hope to disconnect the question of quality in art from questions of beauty. By suggesting that beauty is a relational experience, rather than an intrinsic property of objects, I hope to move the conversation about both art and beauty beyond assertions of taste, on the one hand and the absolute beauty of God on the other. If God is the source and measure of all beauty, we can only experience the beauty of humanly created things through relationship with them, just as relationship is the only way to know God

4.

Good Art

Art is a means of communion among people.
　　　—Leo Tolstoy[1]

Art is a lie that tells the truth.
　　　—attributed to Pablo Picasso

A student challenged me once, saying that there was no such thing as bad art. Art, she said, was an expression of a person's true self, and, as such, cannot be judged. I have been living with that challenge ever since, trying to tease out what it means to say that something is good art, bad art, or not art at all.

The answers to these questions depend largely on the context in which they are asked. Some art works that are considered good in the world of museums and art schools might have no place in a church. Conversely, art that is made to be used in worship may be unable to stand on its own when seen in the clean, well-lighted space of an art gallery or heard in the uncompromising clarity of the concert hall. Artworks made quickly and inexpertly during a workshop or retreat may reveal a deep and important spiritual truth to those who were present during their making, but have no value or appeal for anyone who was not there and did not hear the accompanying story.

People often talk about wanting to preserve certain standards, or quality, in art. But standards that are applicable when we look at art in one way make no sense when we look at it from another perspective. In some cases, the goodness or benefit of art is found primarily in the process, in

---

1. Tolstoy, *What Is Art?*, 37.

the making or doing or participating. In others, it is only the product, the object, the poem, the final performance that brings an audience to its feet or moves the reader to tears that can be judged as good. Even then, a song that is good for singing a baby to sleep may be too simplistic for aesthetic contemplation and too quiet for hoeing a field.

What is good art? What is the relationship between the artwork and the process by which it was made? Can an artwork be good in one context and bad in another? What is the goodness of art? Or, to put it another way, what is good art and what is it good for? If beauty does not help us decide, what standards do we apply, and in what circumstances?

Coal Dust and Glue

I once heard Heather Elkins, Professor of Worship, Preaching, and the Arts at Drew University's Theological School, tell a story of making a pastoral visit to a man in the last stages of black lung disease. After a fit of coughing that ended with a spume of bright, red blood, he struggled to regain his breath. Finally, he said, "That's the way of coal. It goes in black as hell, and comes out red as blood." Saddened at her inability to help him, Elkins went down to the gift store of the hospital, where she saw a figurine on the clearance table.

As Elkins described it, the small figure was made of coal, formed into the shape of a woman with hands outspread, offering a ripe harvest of fruits and vegetables bountifully arrayed on the skirts of her apron. Thinking it must cost more than she could afford, she picked it up to look at the price tag on the bottom, and discovered that the original price had been marked down several times to the latest sale price of $2.50. When the clerk heard her laugh of delight, she said, "You can have it for one dollar, if you want it. It isn't really made of coal. It's just coal dust and glue."[2]

As Elkins speaks, one would think that she was describing a piece of museum-worthy art, rather than a sentimental memento of life in Appalachia. She is moved both by the subject, which connects with her memories of her own upbringing not far away, as well as her adult commitment to feminist images of God as bountiful provider. As a theologian and a poet, she also takes into account the metaphorical power of the materials that went into its making, which remind her of the biblical account in which humans are made of dust as well as connecting with the dying miner's words. For Elkins, and for those who hear her animated telling of the tale, this

---

2. A slightly different version of this story is found in Elkins, *Holy Stuff of Life*, 97–98.

figurine—as well as the cast-off quilts, rustic brooms, and many other hand-made artifacts that have come into her life—carries all the evocative power of Picasso's *Guernica* or a Bellini Madonna.

A less emotionally involved observer, however, might easily note that the object of Elkins' admiration was not, in fact, very good art. Indeed, according to more objective standards, it might be regarded as little more than sentimental kitsch, made for no purpose higher than to capture a tourist's cash.

But Elkins is not interested in using this figurine as an object of pure, aesthetic contemplation. In responding to the subject matter of the figurine, and even the metaphorical connections between its component materials and those of the dying miner, she ignores most of its specifically aesthetic qualities. Its size, its color, the formal relationships among its lines and shapes are irrelevant to her purpose. For her, the little woman made of coal dust and glue speaks to an emotional place that has nothing to do with the objective quality of the piece as art, and everything to do with her own story. For her, as for most people most of the time, the ability to connect with the story is the most important criterion in the definition of good art.

Matters of Taste

In contrast to the above example, aesthetic contemplation—the enjoyment of a work of art because of the particular arrangement of various elements—is a very refined sort of pleasure. This is the pleasure that Clive Bell was trying to describe when he wrote about the aesthetic emotion as the proper response to significant form. Aesthetic contemplation is the process of regarding a work of art for its strictly artistic properties, such as its formal properties—its internal harmonies, rhythms, colors, and shapes, for example— as well as the technical skill of the artist, and the relationship of its formal properties to its narrative or descriptive content. Such contemplation is understood to be disconnected from morality, narrative, personal connection, or any other concern that is not strictly connected with the artistic properties of the work. Any type of artwork—a poem, a painting, a musical composition, even a novel or a film—may become the object of aesthetic contemplation. Works made expressly for this purpose tend to be what is meant when people talk about fine or high art.

As an artist, curator, and teacher, it is my professional task to recognize the difference between visual art that is good for the purpose of aesthetic contemplation, art that is intended to be but does not fulfill that criterion because of some flaw or deficiency, and works that are intended to fulfill some other agenda. This ability to differentiate between these various categories is what is generally meant when someone is said to have "good taste," which is understood as an objective valuation of the quality of a given work of art.

There is another meaning to the word taste which has to do with individual preference. In this sense, there can be no distinction between good taste and bad, but rather a recognition that some things appeal to one person, while other people have different preferences. As an individual with a particular set of life experiences and personal tendencies, I may simply prefer one work to another, regardless of any objective criteria regarding the quality of the works.

However, as Frank Burch Brown points out, good taste is neither as universal or as disinterested as Kant supposed. Rather, it has been used as a marker of status, class, and entitlement. To say that something is in good taste is often to say that it is favored by social elites. Conversely, bad taste is often associated with people who are uneducated, poor, or otherwise disadvantaged. Even among professionally trained observers, subjective preferences may color objective evaluations. Brown notes that it is problematic to simply

> treat judgments of aesthetic taste as "disinterested," and free of all but purely aesthetic concerns. No longer can we trust the Kantian claim that judgments of taste are rooted strictly in individual judgment, uninfluenced by the opinions of others, and yet so representative of what humans share in common that they can claim to be universally applicable—warranting the assent of everyone.[3]

When speaking of taste in the sense of subjective preference, rather than objective evaluation, it is rarely possible to say why someone likes chocolate rather than vanilla ice cream or the other way around. However, despite occasional assertions to the contrary, the fact that one person likes one and another the other does not make either chocolate or vanilla superior in any objective way. Similarly, it is possible to disentangle matters of quality from matters of taste in art. Consider the following four categories:

- Good art that I like
- Good art that I do not like
- Bad art that I do not like
- Bad art that I do like

3. Brown, *Good Taste, Bad Taste*, 7.

Good art that I like is what Kant would say is the norm. No person of good taste will argue if I say that Rembrandt's self-portraits are among the most revealing, intimate, truthful, and skillful depictions of an individual human being ever painted. If I say that I like them, no expert or educated arbiter is likely to try to get me to change my mind. Liking Rembrandt's self-portraits is evidence of my good taste, an alignment of the objectively high quality of the work with my own preference.

Good art that I do not like is a bit more difficult to explain. By way of example, consider the works of the British painter Francis Bacon. Bacon is an artist whose works may be found in the most important museums of contemporary art. When I look at these works, I can admire the brushwork, the composition, the use of color, and many other factors that go into making a painting that coheres visually and conveys meaning. But I also cannot get out of the room fast enough, because these paintings are so disturbing. And that is the point: they are intended to be disturbing, to provoke anxiety. It is precisely because Bacon is such a good painter that they have the effect that they do. It's not just that I disagree with Bacon's worldview as expressed in his paintings (which I do), but that he expresses it so well, so forcefully, that they provoke a sense of disequilibrium in me that is as much physical as emotional. Intellectually, I can acknowledge these as good paintings, but I just don't like them. My subjective preference does not align with my professional judgment.

Bad art that I do not like is almost as easy to defend as good art that I like. The work in question in clumsy, poorly made, the colors clash; or, it is sentimental, silly, idealized, manipulative, or otherwise lacking in artistic value. As an art professional, I am expected not to like it. Once again, my subjective preference is aligned with my estimation of the objective lack of quality of the work.

That there exists bad art that I do like, on the other hand, is even more difficult to justify among my professional peers than good art that is not to my taste. I know that the mass-produced, plaster statue of the Virgin of Guadalupe on a shelf in my office is not well made, that the colors are muddy and run into one another, that edges that should be crisp and well-defined are instead blurred and indistinct. However, like the little woman made of coal dust and glue that so captured Heather Elkins's imagination, the statuette reminds me of a home that is now far away, of friends whose lives have taken a different path than mine, of the faith that sustains me even when I am sad or lonely or scared. I know that it is bad art, but I like it anyway. Just as I dislike the works of Francis Bacon because of the negative emotions and ideas that they provoke, I like my mass-produced, light-up Virgin of Guadalupe because of the positive emotions and ideas that she evokes in me. This is the inverse of the category of good art that I do not like, another instance in which my subjective preference is out of line with my objective judgment.

Judging Art

Putting subjective, personal preference aside, what are the specific, objective qualities that guide the judgments of curators and critics? What do they mean when they say that a work of art is good?

In the discussion on beauty, I noted that one part of the answer lies in what is typically referred to as the elements and principles of design. The elements are the most basic building blocks of any work of visual or plastic art. They are usually listed in the order of their complexity, as line, shape, form, texture, value, and color. The principles pertain to the arrangement of the elements, their overall composition. These principles include such things as balance, harmony, tension, repetition, rhythm, contrast, symmetry, and pattern. Similar sets of elements and principles may be used to describe a play, a musical composition, a poem, or a dance. When these elements and principles work together, an artwork has a certain rightness, a cohesion that is sometimes described as unity-in-diversity.

Another set of criteria by which art may be judged as good or bad lies in the area that might best be termed "craftsmanship." Craftsmanship is the care with which materials are handled, the evidence of skill in manipulating the tools and processes relevant to a given form of art. For a musician, this may be as obvious as hitting the right notes at exactly the right time. For a dancer, it may include the height of a leap or the crispness of a turn or gesture. For a painter, it may lie in the tautness of a stretched canvas or the methodical application of thin, transparent layers of paint.

When these criteria, design and craft, work together, the result is a work that has classically been described as beautiful. Thomas Aquinas seems to have this had in mind when he asked whether art, itself, is a virtue. Positing that art is an intellectual habit, and therefore a virtue because it confers aptness in doing good, he suggests that a good work of art is one that evidences that skillful, practiced ease that is the mark of an experienced carpenter or stonemason or any other master craftsman. Art, for Aquinas, seems to be largely synonymous with skill, or with things produced through skillful means. Carefully distinguishing between the goodness of the crafts-person and the goodness of the thing that is made, he writes,

> The good of an art is to be found, not in the craftsman, but in
> the product of the art, since art is right reason about things to be

made: for since the making of a thing passes into external matter, it is a perfection not of the maker, but of the thing made, even as movement is the act of the thing moved: and art is concerned with the making of things. On the other hand, the good of prudence is in the active principle, whose activity is its perfection: for prudence is right reason about things to be done. . . . Consequently art does not require of the crafts[person] that [the] act be a good act, but that [the] work be good. Rather would it be necessary for the thing made to act well (e.g. that a knife should carve well, or that a saw should cut well), if it were proper to such things to act, rather than to be acted on, because they have not dominion over their actions. Wherefore the crafts[person] needs art, not that [in order to] live well, but [in order to] produce a good work of art, and have it in good keeping.[4]

Like a priest whose lack of moral virtue does not invalidate the sacrament, as long as it is consecrated according to the rules and intention of the church, the moral or spiritual condition of the artist need not affect the value of an artwork. It is enough that the art work serve the purpose for which it is made.

For Aquinas and his contemporaries, however, any discussion of art referred essentially to what we mean today by some combination of design and craft. According to today's standards and understandings, however, neither design nor craft, nor even both together, can fully define a good work of art. Indeed, many works that are very well designed and perfectly crafted are often dismissed as too clean, too perfect, as lacking something important. Musicians whose performances are extremely fine technically are often dismissed as too cold, too mechanical, as lacking in soul or emotion or meaning. By the early twentieth century, art had come to mean something quite different than it did to Aquinas. It had come to mean a particular way of approaching the world, a particular way of apprehending and communicating meaning.

Significant Form

Clive Bell tried to address this issue of the difference between a work of art and other well-crafted, well-designed objects. Restricting the definition of beauty as referring only to objects in the natural world, Bell defined a work of art as something that possessed that quality which he called significant form. Asking what quality is common to Hagia Sophia and the windows

4. Aquinas, *Summa Theologica*, bk. I–II,57.3r.

at Chartres, Mexican sculpture, a Persian bowl, Chinese carpets, Giotto's frescoes at Padua, and the masterpieces of Poussin, Piero della Francesca, and Cézanne, he says,

> The hypothesis that significant form is the essential quality in a work of art has at least one merit . . . it does help to explain things. We are all familiar with pictures that interest us and excite our admiration, but do not move us as works of art. To this class belongs what I call "Descriptive Painting"—that is, painting in which forms are used not as objects of emotion, but as means of suggesting emotion or conveying information. Portraits of psychological and historical value, topographical works, pictures that tell stories and suggest situations, illustrations of all sorts, belong to this class. That we all recognise the distinction is clear, for who has not said that such and such a drawing was excellent as illustration, but as a work of art worthless? Of course many descriptive pictures possess, amongst other qualities, formal significance, and are therefore works of art: but many more do not. They interest us; they may move us too in a hundred different ways, but they do not move us aesthetically. According to my hypothesis they are not works of art. They leave untouched our aesthetic emotions because it is not their forms but the ideas or information suggested or conveyed by their forms that affect us.[5]

While Bell was concerned primarily with works of visual art, his discussion could easily be expanded to include other kinds of art, as well. The sensation that Bell termed the aesthetic emotion is evoked only in the presence of significant form. It is a learned pleasure, unconnected to everyday emotions like fear, happiness, or anger. Likening it to the profound pleasure of a mathematician in the presence of an elegant formula, he writes,

> . . . to appreciate a work of art we need bring with us nothing from life, no knowledge of its ideas and affairs, no familiarity with its emotions. Art transports us from the world of man's activity to a world of aesthetic exaltation. For a moment we are shut off from human interests; our anticipations and memories are arrested; we are lifted above the stream of life. The pure mathematician rapt in his studies knows a state of mind which I take to be similar, if not identical. He feels an emotion for his speculations which arises from no perceived relation between them and the lives of men, but springs, inhuman or super-human, from the heart of an abstract science. . . . [T]he rapt philosopher, and [the

5. Bell, *Art*, 215–23, Kindle location.

one] who contemplates a work of art, inhabit a world with an intense and peculiar significance of its own; that significance is unrelated to the significance of life. In this world the emotions of life find no place. It is a world with emotions of its own.[6]

For Bell, the aesthetic emotion is a response to the abstract elements of a work of art, to the specific interaction of lines, colors, forms, and textures that give a work meaning regardless of what the work seems to be about. His notion of significant form seems to imply a certain kind of rightness in those relationships that, as Flannery O'Connor suggests, should be called truth.

Art and Real Things

In today's world of high art, however, even adding truth to design and craft is insufficient to judge whether an artwork is good, or even a work of art at all. In *The Transfiguration of the Commonplace*, Arthur Danto considers the notion of art as a form of practical philosophy. He begins with a thought experiment in which we are asked to consider several squares of red paint. The first, he says, was described by Sören Kierkegaard as the distilling into a mood, a single color, all the distress of the Israelites crossing the Red Sea and the drowning of the Egyptian forces. The second is another imaginary painting, called *Kierkegaard's Mood*. The next two have the same title, *Red Square*, but one of them refers to a particular place in Moscow, while the other is a minimalist geometric with no connection to anything outside of itself. Other entries in the series include one called *Nirvana* and another called *Red Table Cloth*, purported to be by an embittered disciple of Matisse. Other painted squares include a canvas that has been primed with red paint by a famous artist, but is not intended to be a finished artwork at all. The final entry is a piece of red-painted fence. Why, Danto asks, are some of these things art, and some not?[7]

What follows this thought experiment is an extended meditation on the difference between art and what he terms *mere real things*, and why that matters. Danto uses a word from the language of faith, transfiguration, to describe the difference between art and not-art. For him, to name something as art is to see both the thing itself and art as a concept in a new light. The object in question is no longer simply pedestrian, everyday stuff, but is now infused with meaning, transfigured into something beyond its ordinary self. When an object becomes art, Danto suggests, we see it in its

6. Ibid., 280–97, Kindle location.

7. Danto, *Transfiguration of the Commonplace*, 2–3.

eternal form, as the disciples saw Christ transfigured on the mountain, radiant in the light of eternity.

Ultimately, Danto defines art as a way of understanding, or representing, the world. For him, the aesthetic dimension, whether defined classically in terms of beauty or more recently in terms of the sensuous qualities of a work, is largely irrelevant. Rather, an artwork is "an externalization of the artist's consciousness, as if we could see his way of seeing and not merely what he saw."[8] For Danto, and for the artists, curators, critics, and academics who make up what is commonly referred to as the art world, good art continually redefines what art is and how it works. Art, in this sense, is a form of philosophy, worked out in concrete material rather than discursive words. Through experiencing art, either as maker or as audience, we come to know the difference between art and real things.

Art and Innovation

For the last century or more, innovation has been another important criterion for judging the quality of an artwork. Art history tends to be taught as a series of innovations, each superseding the other in matters of technique, style, and overall approach. Individual artists are celebrated and remembered not only for the truth of their vision, but also for their contribution to what is commonly understood as progress in their chosen field. Thus, Giotto is remembered as the painter who broke from the flatness of the Gothic image into a world of rounded figures with weight and depth. Picasso is revered for breaking the static object into multiple, simultaneous views. In the Modernist era—in the visual arts roughly beginning with the Impressionists and running through the mid-twentieth century—progress was as highly valued in the arts as it was in society as a whole. Modernism, as Danto points out in *After the End of Art*, does not mean the most recent, but rather that which fits a particular mode of describing the world. As he writes,

> While there remains a place in the museum for painting contemporary with modernist art which is not itself modernist—for example, French academic painting, which acted as if Cézanne had never happened . . . there is no room in the great narrative of modernism which swept on past it, into what came to be known as "abstract expressionism" . . . and then color-field abstraction.[9]

8. Ibid., 164.
9. Danto, *After the End of Art*, 8–9.

In the twentieth century, modernist artists not only painted, composed music, and wrote poems and novels, they also wrote letters, articles, and manifestos in which they outlined various theories and agendas by which art would remake society. Such theories included Clive Bell's notion of art for the sake of art as well as a somewhat later idea of art as self-expression. In 1965, Austrian architect, stage designer, and writer Frederick Kiesler argued for a more communal understanding of the purpose of art. In his "Second Manifesto of Correalism," he proclaimed,

> L'art pour l'art[10] of seventy-five years ago and the period of art for the artist's sake of the last twenty-five years are over. Before we can go into new productions, a new objective must be crystallized out of a world consciousness which is the concern of all of us, not of any particular stratum of society. The world events since the last war have grown in turbulence and have thrown us together. Estheticism as a sole criterion for the validity of a work of art is evaporating. The artist will not work any more for . . . glory in museums or galleries but for solidifying the meaning of his [or her] creations on a larger scale without falling into the pitfalls of social realism or anecdotal accounts of events. [The artist] will take active part through . . . forming a new world image.[11]

At some indeterminate point in the late twentieth century, this idealistic Modernist agenda faded into a less polemic, and more amorphous, Postmodernism. While Postmodernism is notoriously difficult to define or pin down, Postmodern works in any medium tend to feature appropriation, an eclectic recycling of elements from the past, often taking an ironic stance towards the source material and even towards the very notion of art. Nonetheless, as in the previous era, innovation, originality, and creativity are highly valued. While serious artists today may quote those from an earlier period, they do it with a certain self-consciousness about both the materials and directions of art. Like their Modernist forerunners, Postmodern artists are expected to say something new, to find their own distinctive voice even as they mine older styles and approaches. To say that an artwork is derivative is to dismiss it as inferior, unworthy of further regard.

10. This is usually translated as "art for art's sake." It was a rallying cry for the *avant-garde* throughout the first half of the twentieth century, which privileged art made for no other purpose than aesthetic contemplation over art made with any practical or moral purpose in mind.

11. Kiesler, "Second Manifesto of Correalism," in Stiles and Selz, *Theories and Documents*, 510.

Innovation, however is still not enough. For something to be considered as good art in today's art world, the artist's awareness of the tradition within which the work exists is in tension with the need to push against that tradition. Good art in this context may be aesthetically pleasing, or may as easily flout aesthetic values deliberately in order to make a point. The more important question for the art world is whether it makes a serious contribution to the ongoing conversation about the nature of art and its relationship to the world of mere things. As in any conversation, an artist who indicates an awareness of where that conversation has already been is taken more seriously than one who does not. If art reveals what the artist is thinking, good art not only invites us into the artist's thoughts, but also suggests new ways of thinking about art and, through art, to think about the world in which we live.

Third Tier Art

When people talk about good art, often they mean the kind of art we have been discussing, the art of museums, concert halls, and important theatrical venues. Names like Giotto, Rembrandt, Van Gogh, and Picasso in painting; or Bach, Mozart, and Schubert in music; or Shakespeare, Ibsen, and Chekov in drama, are so much a part of our cultural currency that they are widely recognized even by people who have no particular interest or expertise in the arts. It is these superstars of the art world who are invoked when people want to make claims about, for instance, the importance of art for the development of spiritual life. While opinions may differ about who should be included in a list of great artists, poets, or composers, there is general agreement that their contributions have not only been important in their own times, but have influenced the practice and appreciation of art in succeeding generations in lasting ways. One might say that such artists, or that certain of their works, are of the first rank, or tier.

There is another group of artists who are not well-known among the general public, but whose works nonetheless grace the walls of many of the same museums, or are sometimes performed in the same concert halls and theaters, as the greats. These artists may not have made major stylistic or technical breakthroughs, but are excellent exemplars of the state of the arts in their time. Such artists go in and out of fashion over time, as scholars evaluate their work in the light of new information and new ideas. Although the names of these second-tier artists are often not widely known beyond a certain of circle of specialists, they, too, continue to influence the practice and appreciation of the arts in many ways. Such artists include the currently fashionable but long-ignored Baroque painter Artemisia Gentileschi, the nineteenth-century English composer Frederick Delius, American poet Robinson Jeffers, and many, many others.

Even less well-known are what might be called third tier art and artists. This is not the same thing as third rate, which implies negligible quality. Rather, by this I mean art that is quite good, perhaps as good as that of artists in the second tier, but that is made by artists who have little public exposure and/or success. Such art is made by artists who have—generally speaking—gone to art school or conservatory or are graduates of serious creative writing programs. Such artists have assiduously developed a coherent individual voice and body of work. In the visual arts, these artists often have a loyal local or niche following, but are not seriously collected or reviewed nationally. Their work tends to be exhibited in local or regional venues, such as university and cooperative galleries, or commercial enterprises that also offer framing, crafts, or coffee.

Many of these artists teach in high schools, university art departments, or independent art schools. Others may work as critics for newspapers, general circulation magazines, or specialized journals; as curators or gallery directors; as designers, art directors, or administrators of arts-related nonprofits; or in other art-related capacities that draw on their specialized skills and knowledge.

However, either because they do not market their work aggressively; or because of geographical or other constraints they are unable to bring their work to the attention of important art critical/art market voices; or because the kind of work they make (whether a matter of subject matter, style, or approach) is currently unfashionable, their work is rarely seen outside of local, parochial, or special-interest venues. These artists may never be famous or listed in anyone's history of art, but their good, solid, thoughtful work has great value to those who encounter it and take it seriously.

Art that addresses Christian or other religious themes often falls into this category. As art historian and cultural commentator James Elkins points out in *On the Strange Place of Religion in Contemporary Art*, art that is explicitly Christian in content frequently gets short shrift from exhibition juries, critics, and art teachers. He writes,

> Contemporary art, I think, is as far from organized religion as Western art has ever been, and that may even be it most singular achievement—or its cardinal failure, depending on your point of view. The separation has become entrenched, Religion is rarely mentioned in art schools and art departments, partly because it is understood to be something private . . . and partly

from a conviction that religious beliefs ought not be brought into the teaching of art. . . . [A]side from the rare exceptions, religion is seldom mentioned in the art world unless it is linked to criticism, ironic distance, or scandal.[12]

In support of this assertion, Elkins recounts his experience as a jurist for an exhibition called *Revelations: Artists Look at Religion*. As he tells the story, the jurors readily accepted works that expressed an enigmatic, private spirituality but rejected out of hand at least two, otherwise interesting, works because they had been done by a monk and a nun, respectively. Elkins continues,

> The only religious work we accepted into the show was an abstract circular pattern done by a Native American. It was a religious symbol of some sort, perhaps related to a Navajo *ikaah* (sand painting) but the artist didn't say. We accepted it, I think, because we didn't know what the religion was. To us, it was an abstract painting.[13]

Elkins goes on to say that the jurors were so nervous about including works that evinced a sincerely held religious conviction, that in the entire show of almost a hundred pieces, none were made by practitioners of major religions.

Although the representatives of the institutions of high art may dismiss intentionally religious work, it does not mean that the work in question is bad art. What it may mean is that such work speaks to a different audience or has a different purpose than the work that tends to find its way onto the walls of museums of contemporary art, the playbills of theaters and concert halls, or the new-book lists of literary publishers. Fame, or the lack thereof, is not a good indicator of good art. Good art, and good, committed, well-trained artists, can be found in many places, helping the communities into which they speak understand the world and their place in it.

Baskets and Brain Surgery

This ability to embody meaning has been the primary function of art throughout most of human history. Every society needs to make sense of the world. In a discussion of the interrelation of making and meaning, philosopher and cultural anthropologist Ellen Dissanayake describes the central place that baskets and basketry have in the daily life and belief system of the

12. Elkins, *On the Strange Place of Religion in Contemporary Art*, 15.

13. Ibid., 47.

Yekuana, an indigenous group that live in the South American rain forest. For a variety of reasons, the Yekuana distinguish between things that they, themselves, make, which they call *tidi'uma*, things made, and meaningless, although often useful, objects that they acquire through chance or trade.

The making of baskets, like all intentional activity among the Yekuana, is not simply manual labor, but is accompanied by ritual actions. The baskets themselves incorporate symbols which, along with the ritual actions, embody the entire story of the group. Dissanayake notes that for the Yekuana, "All functional design participates in a greater cosmic design . . . By making an artifact, one tacitly repeats or restates the message encoded in the story of its origin."[14]

To make a basket among the Yekuana is not simply not simply a matter of eye-hand coordination, skillful manipulation of materials, and aesthetic judgment, but also participation in the most critical and demanding activity of that culture. As Dissanayake casually notes,

> The importance of baskets and basketry among Yekuana *tidi'uma* gives the lie to facile jokes in American popular culture about "basket weaving" being the nadir of intellectual challenge (as opposed to rocket science or brain surgery at the other end of the scale).[15]

Encapsulated in Dissanayake's comment is our culture's almost reflexive disdain for manual labor. It is rooted in the Greek dualism which separates mind and body, exalting the mind or spirit while condemning the body as polluting and worthless. In our culture, we generally accord more status to those who work with their minds than to those who work with their hands. On the other hand, brain surgery, for instance, is considered a high-status, intellectual pursuit. But brain surgery—like basket making among the Yekuana—requires an intricate connection between intellectual knowledge and physical skill. A brain surgeon must hold in mind all the intricate structures and interconnections of the human brain, the idiosyncratic particularities of the brain at hand, the steps of the procedure to be performed along with some number of other procedures in case something goes wrong, as well as being able to manipulate tools in exacting precision.

Similarly, the Yekuana basket maker must hold in mind the entire creation story of the people and the implications of the parts of that story as they pertain to the particular kind of basket that is being made, the songs and rituals that must accompany the making of this particular basket, and

14. Dissanayake, *Art and Intimacy*, 107.
15. Ibid.

the idiosyncrasies of the tools and materials which the work requires, as well as being able to physically manipulate those tools and materials in precisely the right way to obtain the desired result.

Unlike the Yekuana, we tend to dismiss "hand work" as lacking in intellectual rigor, as if what is done with the hands does not involve the intellect. The arts are considered mushy, touchy-feely, disconnected from both the life of the mind and the core requirements of society. We tend to disconnect the body from the mind, to the impoverishment of both. The Yekuana, like artists in our society, know that meaning is embodied in making. Good art in any culture requires both intellectual knowledge and a deep engagement with manipulating the material world. I would suggest that we should think about certain kinds of art, at least, in the same way we regard brain surgery, as rational thinking and manual skill inform one another in an inextricable web.

Art Doesn't Lie

How, then, does art embody meaning? In what sense is a picture is worth a thousand words? How, as is often said, can every portrait be a self-portrait? What do artworks reveal about the artists who make them?

In a standard exercise in beginning drawing classes called blind contour drawing, students are asked to take a large piece of paper and tape it down to the table in front of them so that it won't move. Then, they position themselves so that their dominant hand can easily move around the paper, while keeping their heads turned away. Looking at their non-dominant hand intently, they slowly draw all the curves, wrinkles, and other outlines and inlines of that hand without ever picking the point of their pencil off of the paper and without ever looking at what they are drawing.

The trick, as I tell students, is to picture a small robot walking along the contours of the hand. They are to imagine that this robot is somehow mysteriously connected to both their eyes and the point of their pencil. As the eyes follow the slow steady movement of the robot along the edges of fingers, around fingernails, and along the wrinkles where the skin buckles around the bony joints, the pencil is to move at exactly the same speed in the same direction as the robot and the eyes.

After fifteen or twenty minutes, most of the people in the room will have completed their drawings. When I tell them that they can look at when they have done, there is a ripple of embarrassed laughter. All the drawings do have a certain resemblance to hands, but most are extremely disproportionate, with giant thumbs and tiny index fingers, or fingernails that want to slide off towards the edge of the page.

What these drawings reveal about their makers is the level of attention, or lack thereof, at every instant of the process. One or two are simply schematic, evidence that the person who drew them was working too quickly, not so much looking as mentally saying, "This takes too long. I know what a hand looks like, I'll just draw that." Of the rest, it is as though their eyes and pencils would follow that imaginary robot for a while, and then get impatient and move more quickly, alternately slowing down and speeding up, skipping over details in some places and observing them extremely closely in others.

These drawings reveal more about the person who has done them than they do about the ostensible subject matter. The quality of the line, the disproportionate relationship of thumbnail to finger joint, every squiggle and stray mark, all are the evidence of an inner struggle to attend, to respond to what is before one's eyes rather than simply rely on habitual, schematic ways of knowing. When I point to an area and say, "you got bored here" the students' eyes get wide, and they look at me like I have been somehow able to read their minds. Art does not lie, I tell them.

Lies that Tell the Truth

Art does not lie, but, as Picasso is widely reported to have said, "art is a lie that tells the truth." While he never actually said that, he did, however, make more nuanced statements about the relationship between truth and art. In an interview printed in the May 1923, edition of a journal called *The Arts*, he said,

> We all know that Art is not truth. Art is a lie that makes us realize truth, at least the truth that is given us to understand. The artist must know the manner whereby to convince others of the truthfulness of his lies. If he only shows in his work that he has searched, and re-searched, for the way to put over lies, he would never accomplish anything.[16]

As Picasso understood, a skilled artist can express many moods, ideas, sensations without necessarily feeling them at the moment of expression. The philosopher Suzanne Langer defined a work of art as "an expressive form created for our perception through sense or imagination, and what it

16. Picasso, "Picasso Speaks," in Barr, *Picasso*, 270–71.

expresses is human feeling."[17] For Langer, works of art communicate experiences that cannot be put into discursive form, but are nonetheless knowable. These include

> what it is like to be waking and moving, to be drowsy, slowing down, or to be sociable, or to feel self-sufficient but alone; what it feels like to pursue an elusive thought or to have a big idea. All such directly felt experiences usually have no names—they are named, if at all, for the outward conditions that normally accompany their occurrence. Only the most striking ones have names like "anger," "hate," "love," "fear," and are collectively called "emotions." But we feel many things that never develop into any designable emotion. The ways we are moved are as various as the lights in a forest; and they may intersect, sometimes without cancelling each other, take shape and dissolve, conflict, explode into passion, or be transfigured. All these inseparable elements of subjective reality compose what we call the "inward life" of human beings.[18]

Langer makes the critical, but often ignored, point that while an artwork may communicate such feelings, it does not follow that the artist was actively experiencing those feelings while creating the artwork. This is one part of what Picasso meant when he said that art is a lie. Contrary to certain psychological theories that understand art as unmediated self-expression, as well as to the impression given by quick art experiences in workshop and retreat settings, the serious practice of any art involves a controlled, disciplined activity largely incompatible with the immediate experience of feelings. As Langer points out,

> An artist working on a tragedy need not be in personal despair or violent upheaval; nobody, indeed, could work in such a state of mind. His mind would be occupied with the causes of his emotional upset. Self-expression does not require composition and lucidity; a screaming baby gives his feeling far more release than any musician, but we don't go into a concert hall to hear a baby scream . . .[19]

Nor do we go to a concert hall to hear the musicians sob when performing a sad song, or to the theater to hear actors laugh at Shakespeare's

17. Langer, *Problems of Art*, 15.

18. Ibid., 22.

19. Ibid., 25.

funny lines. When art materials and processes are used to express immediate feelings, the result may be therapeutic, but it is rarely good art.

Langer sees art as a symbolic, metaphoric way of communicating that which is beyond ordinary language. In the sense that what is communicated is not the artist's immediate experience, it is a lie. However, an artist who is skilled in manipulating shape, form, color, sound, tempo, or whatever particular elements and principles are proper to a given discipline, can use these elements and principles to communicate feelings and experiences that ring true both to the artist and to the audience. Unlike beginning drawing students, who are limited in their ability to transcend the immediate, more experienced artists can and do decide when to use a swift, sure line and when a more halting, wavering line will convey an intended feeling. As Langer put it,

> An artist, then, expresses feeling, but not in the way a politician blows off steam or a baby laughs and cries. He formulates that elusive aspect of reality that is commonly taken to be amorphous and chaotic; that is, he objectifies the subjective realm. What he expresses is, therefore, not his own actual feelings, but what he knows about feeling. Once he is in possession of a rich symbolism, that knowledge may actually exceed his entire personal experience. A work of art expresses a conception of life, emotion, inward reality. But it is neither confessional nor a frozen tantrum; it is a developed metaphor, a non-discursive symbol that articulates what is verbally ineffable—the logic of consciousness itself.[20]

With persistence and practice, artists learn to draw recognizable hands, to sing on key, to dance with both precision and grace. These skills can then be used as needed to convey specific feelings, to bring them to conscious awareness in ways that are new, surprising, and true both for the artist and for the audience.

Art and Reality

One of the ways that visual artists convince others of the truthfulness of their lies is a technique called linear perspective. This is a mechanical, mathematical way of representing three-dimensional objects on a two-dimensional plane. While artists in other times and places were able to depict horses and trees and people reasonably accurately through simple observation, the development of linear perspective in early-fifteenth-century Italy allowed

20. Ibid., 26.

artists to show the objects in a scene in their correct sizes and relationships, as if looking at them through a window.

Such artworks are often called realistic, but a more accurate term might be illusionistic or naturalistic. Although works done using linear perspective may appear to be photographically accurate, artists can and do use the technique to create scenes that are completely believable, and completely imaginary. The reality depicted in such works is less a copy of what is in front of the artist's eyes than what is seen in the imagination and rendered onto paper or canvas or wood. It is an illusion, presented to the viewer as an image that is so convincing that it is experienced as real.

Art can convey other kinds of reality, as well. A song or a poem or a painting may accurately describe a vision or a fantasy, rather than anything in the external world. A tune may evoke an emotional state with such force that it brings tears to the eyes. The time in which a novel takes place may be far in the past or the future, but the interactions of the characters ring so true that we come to know something important about ourselves.

In the Eastern Orthodox churches, icons are understood as depictions of reality of a different order. Icons are not expected to look like ordinary human beings; buildings and tables are drawn without reference to linear perspective; and much of what might in another painting depict the garden or the interior in which a person is standing is, instead, simply covered with gold. For the faithful who pray with such images, what they present is much more real than any illusionistic depiction of objects receding in space. Rather, icons are understood to show an eternal reality in which the holy personages are seen as they are in the sight of God. Here, the artist uses paint and wood, not to show things as they appear to the eyes, but as they exist in the eternal reality of heaven, as seen with the eyes of faith.

Art as Religion

In *The Use and Abuse of Art*, cultural historian Jacques Barzun considers the widespread idea that art is a religion. As he notes, "The power of art to evoke the transcendent and bring about . . . unity [between artist and audience] is what has led artists and thinkers in the last two centuries to equate art and religion, and finally to substitute art for religion."[21]

However, for many both within the church as in the wider society, the professional practice and critical discussion of art in the late twentieth and early twenty-first century is often incomprehensible to the uninitiated. Those who go to art museums and galleries in search of spiritual uplift or

21. Barzun, *Use and Abuse of Art*, 26.

revelatory moments are often bitterly disappointed when they come to the contemporary rooms and find what look like piles of discarded paper, paintings that are nothing but drips, or profoundly disturbing images of degraded humanity. They walk away in sadness or in anger, declaring that what they see is junk, pornographic, deeply offensive, or so simple that their two-year-old could do it.

Despite such disappointing experiences, the arts retain an aura of spirituality. As increasing numbers of Christians become interested in the arts, many artists, Christian and non-Christian alike, are invited to give lectures, teach weekend workshops, or offer a series of classes that will open the secrets of the studio to anyone who wants to come and learn. When such lectures, workshops, and classes are given by well-trained artists who are also professing Christians, the connection between art and spiritual growth is strengthened for participants. Understanding that spending an evening in a drumming circle, building found-object sculptures made of rocks and twigs at a weekend retreat, or a few drawing lessons spread out over the course of several weeks will not turn a person into an artist, the artists nonetheless do their best to teach some basic skills in looking and making, or listening and music-making, or writing poetry out of the ordinary epiphanies of daily life.

Such workshops are typically free of the kind of critique and competition that is prevalent in art schools. Instead, the environment is intentionally nurturing and oriented towards spiritual discovery, allowing each person to participate at whatever level he or she feels comfortable. Participants are encouraged to experiment with new materials and ideas without fear of failure, to be immersed in the studio experience without any expectation except to be present to the experience. For those who want a somewhat deeper immersion into art as spiritual practice, retreat centers like Ghost Ranch, the Grunewald Guild, and many others offer residential courses that last a full week or at most a month.

Art on One Foot

It is such short forays into art-making that I have come to think of as art on one foot. The story is told that someone came to the first-century rabbi, Shammai, with the request that he teach him the Torah while standing on one foot. Understandably, Shammai got angry and drove him off with a stick, saying that the Torah is complex and difficult—no one could learn Torah while standing on one foot! The would-be student went away sadly, going to Shammai's rival, Hillel, with the same request. Hillel, being a more peaceable (or perhaps wily) fellow, agreed. He said, "Do not do unto others what is hateful to you. That is the whole Torah."

Hillel's response is often cited as the Jewish version of the Golden Rule, a variant way of expressing what Jesus taught when he said that we should do for others what we would like to have them do for us. But I tell this story not to compare Jesus and Hillel, nor to situate Jesus within his Jewish context (although it is never inappropriate to do just that), but rather to point out that a simple summary, an introduction—however true—is just the beginning of learning.

Hillel did not stop with the Golden Rule. Instead, he followed his summation of Torah with the words, "The rest is commentary. Now, go and learn." For Hillel, "Now, go and learn" was not just a throwaway tag line, but rather the heart of the matter. Like the would-be student of Torah who understood so little of God's Word that he believed it was possible to learn all of it while standing on one foot, many people who feel a new sense of freedom when they participate in art-making for the first time do not understand that there is more to being an artist than this initial moment of grace. They are relieved that, finally, Shammai is not beating them away from art with his shaming stick, and hear Hillel's open-hearted welcome to the studio with gratitude and joy. Too often, that gratitude and joy becomes the conviction that they, too, are already artists, with nothing more to learn.

Every Person an Artist

There is a sign on the door of the studio at Wesley Theological Seminary that declares, "an artist is not a special kind of person, but every person is a special kind of artist." Like many such maxims, this one is both true and false. At its most basic level, the statement expresses the truth that almost all children before the age of four or so like to draw, to sing, to dance. Participation in the arts at this stage is as natural, and as universal, as breathing.

In some cultures, this natural propensity for color, form, rhythm, and harmony is so fully encouraged that virtually every adult sings and dances in public settings, naturally and without inhibition. In *This is Your Brain on Music*, musician and neuroscientist Daniel Levitin relates a story about an anthropologist studying the lives of villagers in Lesotho, a small country in southern Africa. One day, when the anthropologist had gained some trust in the village, he was invited to join the villagers in singing. When he refused, insisting that he couldn't sing, the villagers did not understand. Levitin continues,

Our culture, and indeed our very language, makes a distinction between a class of expert performers—the Arthur Rubinsteins, Ella Fitzgeralds, Paul McCartneys—and the rest of us. The rest of us pay money to hear the experts entertain us. Jim knew that he wasn't much of a singer or dancer, and to him, a public display of singing and dancing implied he thought himself an expert. The villagers just stared at Jim and said, "What do you mean you don't sing?! You talk!" Jim told me later, "It was as odd to them as if I told them that I couldn't walk or dance, even though I have both my legs." Singing and dancing were a natural activity in everybody's lives, seamlessly integrated and involving everyone.[22]

I have heard several friends tell similar stories of being invited to official dinners in places as different as Russia, Turkey, and Viet Nam. After dinner, instead of speeches, each of the hosts stood up and sang a favorite song in honor of their guests. Then, of course, it was the turn of the guests to return the gesture, and sing for the hosts. In each case, the hosts were baffled when their North American guests turned red-faced and flustered, asserting that they did not know what, or even how, to sing. In a culture where everyone sings, unless one cannot even speak, everyone is a singer.

Similarly, the ability to move one's body in more-or-less complex patterns in time to music is an expected part of the social life in most cultures. The embarrassed, "oh, no, I don't dance" is virtually unheard of in India, Greece, most of Africa, or anywhere that a puritanical attitude towards the body has not run dancing underground. Anywhere people gather to celebrate, even in the poorest places, a drumbeat or a handclap gets feet to moving and bodies to swaying, from the youngest children to the oldest grandparents.

It is in this sense that every person is an artist. Even if they have forgotten that childhood freedom, everyone has the potential, if not always the inclination, to reclaim what they once did naturally. Every person who has the ability to walk can, at least potentially, dance; every person who has the ability to speak can learn to sing; every person who can sign their own name could also, given sufficient instruction and encouragement, learn to draw. In cultures or families where such expression is discouraged, however, these potentials are not realized except for those with enough desire to overcome the social and financial obstacles to learning the appropriate skills. It is these highly motivated persons that, in our culture, we call artists.

22. Leviton, *Your Brain on Music*, 7.

This is not to say that people in cultures where everyone sings and dances do not recognize that some people sing or dance better than others. Indeed, often singing and/or dancing becomes the locus of friendly (or not so friendly) competition. In the Greek folk tradition, for instance, the men and the women join hands in separate lines to dance. Everyone dances, but it is clear that the person at the head of each line does so with a special grace. It is this special grace that we call talent.

Talent and Training

Talent, in our society, is generally given too much credit. As most artists know, real freedom in art is found in the skills developed during the long, arduous apprenticeship that is the artist's life. Talent is just a starting point, the initial impetus that draws a person towards that apprenticeship. Talent without training quickly becomes stale, while training, even in the absence of talent, can yield a lifetime of benefits.

It is sadly the case that, in our culture, most people are not given the opportunity to learn basic artistic skills. Instead, children tend to be labeled talented or otherwise as early as the third grade. Those who show particular interest and ability to carry a tune are called musical, while those who can draw a reasonable likeness are called artistic, and those who are particularly graceful become known as dancers. If the parents can afford it, or the school the children happen to attend provides for it, those who are thus singled out as talented receive special instruction in a given kind of art, while the others are given little or no opportunity to improve.

One of the myths of our culture is that singing on key or drawing a reasonable likeness is simply a gift, rather than a skill that can be learned. And so those who are "gifted" or "talented" in the arts get better at what they do, and everyone else is shamed into believing that they cannot sing, cannot draw, and cannot dance. When asked to talk about such early experiences, many adults will say sadly that a teacher told them to stop singing because their voices were so out of key, or that some adult made fun of their drawings. Those thus shamed become adults who are convinced that they are not creative. They are, also, often envious of those who are.

Contrary to the prevailing myth, however, with patient instruction and sufficient practice, virtually anyone can acquire some level of competence in singing, dancing, drawing, acting, or other artistic activities. Certainly, some people will do these things more easily, more naturally, and ultimately more skillfully than others. And, equally certainly, there are some people who, no matter how much they practice, will not hear the difference between B-flat and C, or see the tiny flare of light in the shadow of a drinking glass on a white tablecloth. But, for the majority of people, it is possible to learn at least the basic skills of any art form that they wish to practice.

For the many people who were convinced in early childhood to trade their singing, dancing, drawing, and playing with words for the sober realities of a life without art, the invitation to explore art-making in safe, encouraging, and limited ways often comes as a revelation. When permitted and encouraged to do so, people often experience a sense of freedom from bondage that has held them for so long that they have forgotten it even existed. Allowed to play with color and form, to rediscover their childhood delight in moving rhythmically without fear of judgment, to make whatever sound pleases them in a free-form drumming circle where all are welcome, they experience a moment of grace in which they know for sure that they are a beloved child of God. This is one of the real goods of art.

Oppressing the Glass

The recovery of a childlike freedom in making is often so satisfying that participants have no desire for further exploration or instruction. In others, however, a yearning for greater mastery, a desire to express their ideas with greater complexity and subtlety, is awakened. As people acquire increasing skill in any medium, they also acquire a new appreciation for the physical matter with which they work. This appreciation of the limits and possibilities of matter often spills over into a new vision of both the limits and the possibilities of relationship with others.

For several years, I had the opportunity to team-teach a course called *The Hebrew Scriptures and the Arts* with noted biblical scholar, Bruce Birch. For the final project in this class, students were to exegete a passage of their choice in an artistic medium. One student, who came from a small town in central Pennsylvania, had introduced himself at the beginning of the course as initially having no interest in the arts. Now, his required two-credit introductory class having awakened an unexpected freedom and joy in making, he found himself taking as many arts courses as he could. At the time he was in our class, he was also enrolled in a studio practicum with a stained glass artist.

Because his home church was at that time struggling with state policies and practices that exacerbated the environmental pollution in the area, the student wanted to make something that would speak to the biblical injunction for a just society. As Birch recounts the story,

He announced that he would do a project on Amos 5:24, "but let justice roll down like waters, and righteousness like an ever-flowing stream." He came up with a design that was something like a protest poster in glass. Our stained glass artist told him that glass could not always be made to do what you wanted to do. You had to work with its properties. He tried anyway, but with no success.[23]

The student described how, over and over, he would bring a drawing to the artist, and she would say that it was too complicated, that some shapes simply cannot be cut from glass. So he would go away, and the next week, he would bring another drawing, and she would tell him the same thing. This happened week after week. Finally, he drew something that the artist said could be transferred into glass. As he recounted his struggles and showed the result of his repeated failures and eventual success, his face glowed with the light of discovery.

He said the turning point was when he realized that he was "oppressing the glass." He was trying to make it accept his own agenda. When he worked with the properties of the glass with respect, something else emerged—a remarkable combination of symbols and designs, drawn from Amos but taking a fluid, flowing shape.[24]

This student did not go on to become an artist. When he completed his studies, he went back to his small, rural church not only with a new respect for the physical properties of glass, but with a new vision for how his church could engage with the state over the environment. Birch continues,

He reported that this made him think of Amos's image of justice and righteousness related to water. Water flows around obstacles rather than insisting on moving every obstacle. He decided that this had implications for how the community worked at justice issues in its own backyard. A new committee and a new strategy emerged that was successful in moving around obstacles rather than overpowering them.[25]

The process of making things with our hands, of working with the recalcitrance of tools and materials, can help us understand the inherent character of the created world and lead us into a new relationship with people as well as things. I often tell my students that I am always aware that

23. Birch, "Arts, Theology, and the Church," 119.
24. Ibid.
25. Ibid.

my artwork is a compromise between the perfect, shining idea that exists only in my inner vision; the physical properties of the tools and materials that I am working with; and the skill with which I am able to make my hands follow the contour of that image of perfection.

One of the things that a studio practice teaches is that we can have a vision, and we can hone our skills, but the very otherness of the materials with which we work both limits our ability to make that vision a reality and channels it into certain directions. The use of oppressive tactics to overcome those limits and channels, rather than working with them towards a solution that respects both the materials and our vision, will only result in a simulacrum of the desired good, both in art and in other areas of life.

Art as Practice in Persistence

Like the student who understood that he was oppressing the glass, those who persist beyond the initial enthusiasm of participating in an art form often discover that the goodness of art resides as much in the process of making as in the finished artwork. The initial vision, what we often refer to as inspiration, is only a place to start. It is what carries us through the difficult stages of learning, of trying one thing after another, of learning what works and what does not. As David Bayles and Ted Orlando put it in *Art and Fear: Observations on the Perils (and Rewards) of Artmaking,*

> Consider the story of the young student . . . who began studies with a Master. After a few months' practice, David lamented to his teacher, "But I can hear the music so much better in my head than I can get it out of my fingers."
>
> To which the Master replied, "What makes you think that ever changes?"[26]

The teacher in this story knows that inspiration is always ahead of execution, that artists are always striving after a greater level of expertise, a closer approximation of the perfect, shining vision. Like athletes, who spend hour after hour shooting hoops or swinging at pitches or leaping over hurdles, artists spend hours practicing scales and arpeggios, sketching children at play, or imitating the gait of a tired, old woman as a way of enlarging their aesthetic vocabulary.

But even inspiration and skill are rarely enough to bring an artwork all the way through to completion. Inspiration is what gets us started. It is the initial impetus that allows the painter to put the first mark on the canvas,

---

26. Bayles, *Art and Fear*, 14–15.

the writer to put the first sentence on the page, the pianist to open the score of an unfamiliar concerto. Soon, however, the artist encounters problems. The painting looks like a mud pie. The novel has no plot. The pianist keeps playing the same wrong note in the fifty-first measure.

This is where the arts both teach and require persistence. Many years ago, an older artist friend would talk about "presenting the body" in her studio practice. She would say, "Just go into the studio every day. It doesn't matter what you do there. Even if all you do is clean the floor or rearrange your tubes of paint, it is important to present your body to the body of your work." What my wise friend knew is that when we present our bodies to the body of our work, when we just do the first, easiest thing, we can work our way through even the difficult parts. Tomorrow, we may erase everything we did today, but what we learned in the doing of it will inform the eventual work.

Periods of uncertainty—day after day of erasing, of changing, of making mistakes, of not knowing quite how a work will resolve—are one of the most difficult obstacles to completing any form of art. And yet, it is the persistence to keep working through these passages that ultimately bring the sought-for resolution. As Bayles and Orlando say,

> Most artists keep a well-rehearsed speech close at hand for fielding the familiar request to explain a finished piece. But if asked to describe how it felt *during* the artmaking—well, that often comes out a bit like Dorothy trying to describe the Land of Oz to Auntie Em. Between the initial idea and the finished piece lies a gulf we can see across, but never fully chart. The truly special moment when concept is converted to reality—those moments when the gulf is being crossed. Precise descriptions fail, but it connects to that wonderful condition in which the work seems to make itself and the artist serves only as guide or mediator, allowing all things to be possible.[27]

Despite their awareness that they were fully present every moment during the process of creation; their memory of the often unpleasant drudgery of slowly adding, subtracting, and changing elements, as well as the blissful hours in which time fell away and there was nothing but themselves and the work; their knowledge that it was their own bodies that held the paintbrush, typed the manuscript, performed the play; many artists report surprise when they regard the finished work, as if they were merely a vessel for some creative process outside of themselves.

27. Ibid., 51.

After spending some long number of hours, days, weeks, months, even years peering intently at individual details, solving each problem as it comes up, making decisions based what they perceive as the inner need of the work, the artist finally steps back to discover the full scope of what has been accomplished. The final work may be similar to the original vision, or it may have taken the artist in a completely different direction. In either case, the persistence to keep on going, to try something different, to test new solutions, is what brings the work to a conclusion. This practice of persistence often moves from the studio into everyday life, bringing the possibility of creative solutions to other, equally complicated problems.

Art as Practice in Attending

Another benefit of participation in the arts is the kind of attentiveness that it fosters. Attending to family members, to Scripture, to the world around us, to the quiet promptings of God, are all part of living with integrity and spiritual depth. For a spiritually mature person, attentiveness to what already exists comes prior to taking action, maybe even prior to thought. Attentiveness involves slowing down, looking, listening, opening to the world with all of one's senses. It is a kind of inner silence, in which we experience the essential beauty and holiness of all creation. Jim Kalnin's description of being caught in a rainstorm is an example of this kind of attentiveness. He writes,

> I was standing in the pouring rain on Hastings Street, waiting for a bus, and generally feeling sorry for myself. I stood by the graffiti-covered bus stop bench, wishing for a dry place to sit, staring at the garbage around my feet. I was trying to ignore the drunk across the street who was yelling in my general direction, and the effort focused my attention on a soggy cigarette package and a slowly dissolving newspaper. As I stared at them, something shifted. I was suddenly aware of the raindrops falling past me like little silver rockets. Then they burst on the wet paper and the concrete around it in tiny explosions of light. The rain fell in a steady rhythm, which I now perceived as a pulsing rhythm of tiny explosions of light. This light was bouncing off everything in my field of vision. As I slowly lifted my gaze, I saw light shining everywhere—off the street, the power lines, the sad shops, the other pedestrians, even off the bellowing drunk across the street. I stood transfixed, no longer wet or sad, until the bus came to take me away.[28]

28. Kalnin, "Art as Sacerdos," 58.

Kalnin's experience was in the street, but his regular studio practice predisposed him to attend to the world in ways that someone without such a practice might not. This is not to say that a person who is not an artist cannot have such experiences—there are ample examples in the literature of spirituality that show otherwise—but rather that the training of an artist includes a way of opening oneself to the world that has spiritual, as well as artistic, implications.

This training involves such a deep immersion in the physical, the material, that at first it is hard to understand it as spiritual. Learning to see and mix colors accurately is an important element in the early training of visual artists. Similarly, learning to hear and reproduce pitch is critical for the education of a musician. In both cases, there is some amount of theoretical material that can be learned through discursive explanation. Painters may learn about the spectrum of visible light, the chemical properties of specific pigments, and the definitions of primary, secondary, and tertiary colors, as well as complementary, monochromatic, and analogous color schemes. Similarly, a musician might need to learn about the physics of plucked strings and vibrating columns of air, the mathematical relationships between the notes in a scale, and the definitions of harmony and dissonance. But such theoretical knowledge is always accompanied by a consistent practice in looking or listening, in learning by doing. For painters, such practice consists in repeatedly mixing small batches of color to make an even scale from dark to light, or from red through grey to green, or to match any arbitrary sample. For singers, a similar practice consists in repeatedly singing scales in each key, as the singer's ears and muscles learn to work together to match and produce pitch accurately. Such practice in attentiveness allows visual artists to discern something on the order of two million discrete differences in combinations of hue, value, or intensity, whereas the untrained eye can only see about half that many. Likewise, a musician may hear tiny differences in tuning that are undetectable to the untrained ear.

These are only the basic building blocks of the kind of attentiveness that a studio practice engenders. As they become a kind of second nature, simply part of the artist's overall awareness, this immersion in the material can lead to the kind of experience that Kalnin describes. In the studio, the process of making an artwork is a constant feedback loop of attending to all the minute details as well as the overall effect of what has already been done, assessing whether that effect is what is wanted, and making changes that bring it ever closer to a final form. When the artist leaves the studio to go for a walk in the park, that kind of awareness stays with her, so that she is keenly aware of the many different shades of green, the subtle textures of leaves and grass, the way that shadows alter a color, even when she has no intention of painting that scene.

Participation in the arts as audience can also teach this kind of attentiveness. Since looking at reproductions in the classroom is no substitute for being in the presence of the real thing, I often take my classes to the museum. This is especially important for understanding many abstract works, in which the delicate nuances of color or the physical properties of the paint itself is what makes these paintings so powerful. These details are virtually impossible to see in prints or slides or computer screens, all of which tend to homogenize images into similar sizes and flatten them into nothing but tiny dots of ink or glowing pixels.

During one such field trip, the students milled around, not quite knowing what to make of these large canvases filled with non-representational marks, unnameable colors, and indistinct shapes. They seemed in a hurry to move on from this room filled with works by Jackson Pollock, Franz Kline, and Mark Rothko, to find something that fit their ideas of what a painting should be. They wanted something recognizable, a narrative hook that would tell them what the paintings were about.

The previous day, however, we had spent several minutes chanting together in the style of Taizé. Reminding them that they had professed experiencing a great depth of feeling and spiritual connection in repeating the same simple words and sounds over and over, I asked them to sit down in front of one of the Rothko paintings, labeled simply, *Untitled (1953)*, and look at it for five minutes without speaking. Somewhat uncomfortably, they complied.

After a little while, I could see them relaxing, giving themselves over to the experience. Several minutes later, I quietly asked them to talk about what they saw. Most of them tried to make some association with objects or place that they knew, but one or two gingerly began to talk about the way the edges of color seemed to vibrate, how the various areas seemed sometimes to recede and sometimes to come forward, how the entire picture plane seemed to dissolve into an analog of eternity. They had made the connection between the more familiar experience of breath and sound leading them into a place of connection with the divine and the new sensation of visual contemplation taking them to the same edge of awareness.

The kind of attentiveness that these students experienced is the aesthetic contemplation with which we began this chapter. It is similar to other kinds of contemplation, like following the breath or repeating the Jesus prayer, and has similar benefits. In *God in the Gallery*, curator and art historian Dan Siedell makes a convincing case that this kind of contemplation in front of paintings is profoundly Christian, rooted in ancient liturgical, sacramental, and ascetic practices. Siedell begins his discussion with the assertion, "A Christian faith . . . that is creedal and conciliar has the resources—the very mind of the church at its disposal—to recognize the importance of contemplation as a spiritual discipline that can underwrite and manifest itself as artistic practice."[29]

Comparing the kind of contemplation assumed by a great deal of modern art with that experienced in the liturgical and devotional use of icons, Siedell notes, "Nicene Christian faith offers a broad-based and robust aesthetics . . . that presumes the relevance of aesthetic practice for all human persons."[30] Participation in the arts, whether as maker or as audience, invites us to slow down, to attend to the small nuances, the minute differences between this and that, and in so doing to be open to the eternal Now.

The Goods of Art

Unlike my student of long ago, I do believe that there is such a thing as bad art. Art is a good gift of God, but like any of God's gifts, it can be misused. Art can manipulate: it can be used to sell us things we do not need, to make us believe things that are destructive or false, to indulge selfishness, to uphold oppressive political regimes. And, of course, there is plenty of inexpert, poorly crafted, thoughtless art, made by people who may be unwilling to push beyond easy, familiar, successful formulas or, on the other hand, are just beginning to learn to paint, play an instrument, or write a poem.

Art at its best calls us out of ourselves, asking us to consider the nature of experience, to discern what is really real. Art at its best engages our senses, stretches our notions of what we can see or hear or taste or feel. Art at its best tells us the truth about ourselves, one another, and the world we live in.

But even when art is not at its best, it has many benefits to both maker and audience. Singing and dancing, making a collage, or writing that first poem, however inexpertly, can return us to a childlike playfulness, releasing the joy in making and moving that is inherent in everyone. The compromises and accommodations demanded by the limitations of materials, tools, and skills teach the benefits of collaboration and cooperation over oppression and coercion. Participation in any form of art brings the rewards of persistence, the habit of looking for new ways to solve problems, the surprising satisfaction of bringing something difficult to completion. Artists

29. Siedell, *God in the Gallery*, 15.
30. Ibid., 123–24.

and audience members alike learn to slow down, to pay attention, to notice that the realm of God is already all around them.

Most art, like most things in life, is neither transcendently wonderful nor egregiously evil, neither astonishingly great nor particularly bad. When we talk about good art, we need to ask ourselves by what criteria the art is being measured. We might not buy a recording of a group of random people singing folk songs together on the back porch, but everyone at that party is having a good time. We might not hang the painting done by a five-year-old in a museum, but the child's parents or grandparents will display it proudly on the refrigerator. We might not want to publish every short story shared in a writing workshop, but the students support one another in their learning and form community along the way. There are many kinds of good art, and many things that art is good for. The important question is what standards to apply, and when to apply them.

5.

Art and the Need of the World

When the need for bread is met we discover that we have other hungers, and none so deep as the hunger to be understood.
> —Elizabeth O'Connor[1]

Our lives shall not be sweated from birth until life closes;
Hearts starve as well as bodies; give us bread, but give us roses.
> —James Oppenheim[2]

Too often our society tends to regard the arts as a frill, an elective add-on to make life more pleasant after the basic needs of food, shelter, clothing, and adequate medical care are met. Even those who appreciate and advocate for the arts may contribute to this view, as is evidenced by the words of Elizabeth O'Connor, who herself was a writer and a member of a group of Christian artists who called themselves The Alabaster Jar. She wrote,

> When the need for bread is met we discover that we have other hungers, and none so deep as the hunger to be understood. The artist helps us to interpret, understand and communicate feeling. When the artist is successful we are led into communion with ourselves and with the world, and the solitary work becomes a communal work. For want of this we walk on parched land.[3]

While O'Connor is clear that the work of the artist is an important path for people to enter into communion with themselves and the world,

1. O'Connor, *Servant Leaders, Servant Structures,* 42.
2. Oppenheim, "Bread and Roses," 214.
3. O'Connor, *Servant Leaders, Servant Structures,* 42.

she begins with the assumption that the need for bread is prior. There is much evidence, however, that O'Connor and those who think like her are mistaken. Art, or at least the kind of meaning that art mediates, is a primary human need, without which we lose our sense of self-worth, our dignity, our relationships with one another.

Art fills that human need simply by being itself, by offering delight in a world that is often filled with pain, or a way to transcend that pain through creative expression. John Oppenheim, writing in a time when textile workers and laborers in other industries were fighting for fair pay and safe working conditions, understood that. In his poem, "Bread and Roses," first published in 1911 in *American Magazine*, he wrote:

> As we come marching, marching, unnumbered women dead
> Go crying through our singing their ancient song of Bread;
> Small art and love and beauty their drudging spirits knew—
> Yes, it is Bread we fight for—but we fight for Roses, too![4]

Set to music, Oppenheim's words were taken up by the women who marched on the picket lines in at the American Woolen Company in Lawrence, Massachusetts in 1912. Today, the words continue to ring true for every person, man or woman, who puts up a poster to brighten a prison cell, or writes a poem in a homeless shelter, or sings or hums or whistles or listens to the music of others while doing work that might otherwise be mind-numbing, soul-killing drudgery. In this chapter, we will consider how the arts help us to know what it means to be human, the relationship of the arts to the other needs of the world, and how art makes a difference in the lives of people whose pain would otherwise be too great to bear.

A Basic Hunger

Without art, there would be no cathedrals or skyscrapers; no comic books or movies; no opera or hip-hop; no poetry or party-hats. Without art, our books would all look alike; our buildings would be clumsy cinderblock boxes; and our coins and postage s.tamps would bear only the numbers that indicate their monetary value. Most of our knowledge of the ancient world comes from the art and artifacts that remain. Art is a vehicle of meaning, one of the important ways that we come to understand the world.

In recent years, many churches and theological seminaries have begun to appreciate this simple truth, even as they struggle with its implications. On the one hand, for many people, both in the pews and in the pulpit, the

4. Oppenheim, "Bread and Roses," 214.

Word of God becomes dry and dusty when it becomes an endless stream of didactic talk. On the other, it often seems difficult to explain, even to ourselves, why time and money that could go to feeding the hungry or healing the sick should instead be spent on music, dance, drama, painting, or poems. Isn't art, as O'Connor suggests, just a lovely extra, something to be indulged in only after basic needs are met? Even thinking seriously or theologically about the arts often seems suspect, a frivolous concern best left for after-dinner conversation. As Jeremy Begbie puts it,

> An important question needs to be addressed at the outset, one which it would be all too easy to evade, namely, why should the theologian spend any time on this topic at all? Is there anything particularly reprehensible about modern theologians showing so little interest in the arts? Is art not simply a luxurious ornament to our lives, a distraction for those who have spare time on their hands? After all, in any given society, the number of people who care deeply about the arts is relatively small. Compared to the other pressing issues of our day—the population explosion, the ecological crisis, mass starvation—the arts seem a somewhat trivial concern.[5]

One way out of this quandary is to remember that our humanity is more than the sum of our physical needs. We need wonder, meaning, and connection just as much as—or maybe even more than—we need food and water and air. Recently, I heard Brother Guy Consolmagno relate his own discovery of this truth in another field. Consolmagno is both a Jesuit and an astronomer, serving as the curator of the meteorite collection at the headquarters of the Vatican Observatory at Castel Gandolfo, Italy. In the early 1980s, as a postdoctoral fellow at MIT, he began to question the point of studying stars when people were dying of hunger. Eventually he went to Kenya as a Peace Corps volunteer, where he was assigned to teach physics and astronomy.

While in Kenya, Consolmagno began to understand that there was more to astronomy than looking up at the stars for his own pleasure. He tells the story of setting up a small telescope and a slide projector powered by a car battery in small villages that didn't have any other access to electricity. Everyone in the village would come to see his slides of the stars and planets and look through the telescope.

> And they would show exactly the same "oohs" and "aahhs" looking at the craters of the moon or the rings of Saturn, exactly the same as when I would set this up back in Michigan. And it

5. Begbie, *Voicing Creation's Praise*, xiv.

suddenly dawned on me, well, of course. It's only human beings that have this curiosity to understand: What's that up in the sky? How do we fit into that? Who are we? Where do we come from? And this is a hunger that's as deep and important as a hunger for food because if you starve a person in that sense, you're depriving them of their humanity.[6]

While it could be argued that astronomy, as a scientific pursuit, is more obviously important than art, I do not think that Consolmagno would agree. As his colleague, Father George Coyne, another Jesuit and the former director of the Vatican Observatory, observes "if all we do is feed and clothe people, we're all going to be naked; what really makes us human is music, the arts, science . . ."[7]

Art, like astronomy, feeds a basic hunger to understand how the world works and to find our own place in it. The arts are a way of knowing, a way of observing the world and interacting with it. Like the kind of pure science that simply enlarges human knowledge without any immediate, obvious, practical benefit, art marks us as human. As philosopher Ellen Dissanayake puts it, "To take the arts seriously is to rediscover routes to belonging, meaning, and competence in a world where for many these are no longer part of the human birthright."[8]

Citing studies of non-literate, tribal cultures, as well as the normal development of human infants, Dissanayake shows that what we call "the arts" are an intrinsic mode of communication and learning, an innate propensity common to all human groups. While the specifics differ, every culture uses dramatic storytelling, music, and dance of some kind not as a tacked-on extra, but as an intrinsic part of everyday life. Unlike animals, who seem to have no need to change their appearance or that of their living quarters in symbolic ways, all human groups use clothing, ornaments, hair style, and other alterations to their natural bodily form to indicate their gender, their social status, and their cultural understandings of the nature of the world. Dissanayake says,

> It is important to note that humans do not always simply appropriate the natural world as it is but have everywhere recognized their difference from it as well as their dependence on and interdependence with it. That is . . . they make "cultural" transformation of nature. For example, they do not remain in their birthday suits, as other animals do, but adorn their bodies, sometimes

6. "Asteroids, Stars, and the Love of God."
7. "Two Vatican Astronomers."
8. Dissanayake, *Art and Intimacy*, xv.

with tattoos, piercings, or scarifications and with paint, beads fiber bands, and other ornaments. They do not leave their hair unkempt, like animal fur, but restrain it by braiding, tying, or cutting it and adding leaves or bright feathers. They do not make just a rude nest or den but build regularized environments. They do not eat untreated food but cook and otherwise process it.[9]

Such embellishment extends to the tools and implements that humans make for themselves. Rarely are such objects simply utilitarian. Rather, in virtually every society (except, arguably, our own), spoons, knives, chairs, blankets, and all the other objects that distinguish humans from animals are made to be both meaningful and aesthetically pleasing as well as useful. Often, that has meant embellishment with carving, painting, or other symbolic elaboration. Cup handles are made to resemble animal heads; baskets are patterned to look like coiled snakes; chairs bear the heraldic sign of the king. And even where there is no such embellishment, frequently there is a rightness about the combination of shape, texture, color, weight, and other elements that cannot simply be attributed to mere utility. It matters that a tool not only be suited to its task; it must also feel good in the hand that uses it and please the eye that sees it. Attention to the aesthetic qualities of what we use is an intrinsic part of being human, and we ignore those qualities at our peril.

Art and Meaning

As Father Coyne says of the curiosity to know about stars, the hunger for the arts is as deep as hunger for food, and to deprive people of participation in the arts is to deprive them of their humanity. Indeed, when the need for food and other physical needs is not met, people often turn to the arts to help them cope with the deprivation. In circumstances of where physical sustenance is lacking, the arts often provide spiritual sustenance, a way of finding meaning in what would otherwise be only chaos and terror.

Consider, for instance, the many examples of artistic activity in the concentration camps of Nazi Germany. No one would argue that basic needs of the prisoners of the Third Reich were met in any way. They were systematically deprived of adequate food, shelter, and medical attention as well as simple respect for their humanity. Nonetheless, not only did they engage in a variety of artistic activities, they often risked their lives in order to do so.

9. Ibid., 114–15.

Although much has been written about forced music-making in the camps and its detrimental effects on those who were compelled to be in orchestras for the entertainment of Nazi officers, it is also frequently observed that prisoners played and composed music for themselves and their fellow inmates. Such music was a means of psychological resistance, alleviating terror by allowing them to forget, if only for a few moments, that their lives were in constant danger. Even in solitary confinement, inmates hummed or whistled or scratched drawings on walls as a way to combat fear and loneliness and to preserve their individual identity and collective cultural traditions against the destructive intentions and power of the SS.[10]

In some of the camps, music, lectures, and theatrical performances were allowed or even encouraged, not so much for the pleasure of the captors, but as a means of entertainment for their captives. Keeping them busy and distracted from the terrible conditions in which the prisoners lived was a form of social control as well as a means for the Nazis to show the international community that they treated the imprisoned Jews humanely.

This was particularly true at Theresienstadt. Unlike the concentration camps at Auschwitz, Bergen-Belsen, and other places, Theresienstadt did not have gas chambers or crematoria. Instead, its primary purpose seemed to be as a transit station from which people were deported to more deadly locations. Even so, Theresienstadt was a place of great privation, with little food; less heat in the long, cold winters; and virtually no medical care.[11] As pianist and Holocaust survivor Alice Herz-Sommer recalls,

> Music gave heart to many of the prisoners, if only temporarily. In retrospect I am certain that it was music that strengthened my innate optimism and saved my life and that of my son. It was our food; and it protected us from hate and literally nourished our souls. There in the darkest corners of the world it removed our fears and reminded us of the beauty around us.[12]

As one of the oldest, living survivors of the camps, Herz-Sommer was featured in a documentary 2010, in which the then 106-year-old continued to play Chopin and visit with neighbors over tea. For Herz-Sommer and for countless other people who have been imprisoned, tortured, and deprived of even the most basic of physical comforts, the arts have fed their souls and

---

10. World ORT, "Music in the Nazi Concentration Camps."

11. Descriptions of conditions at Theresienstadt appear throughout Muller and Piechocki, *Alice's Piano*. Similar information may be found at United States Holocaust Memorial Museum, "Theresienstadt."

12. Muller and Piechocki, *Alice's Piano*, x.

kept them sane. Both for practitioner and for audience, the arts have the capacity to give people courage, even in desperate circumstances.

In addition to the ability of the arts to help people find meaning even in their misery, the arts may also be employed as a more practical means of liberation. In some of the concentration camps, artists secretly sketched what they saw, risking their lives in order to document the intolerable conditions. Many of these drawings were smuggled out to agencies like the International Red Cross in Switzerland, who understood them as evidence of the true conditions. Based on such drawings as well as other evidence of the duplicity of the Nazi regime, the Red Cross and other agencies worked for the release of the captives.

Art and Homelessness

While the persistence of the arts in the concentration camps is an extreme example, there are other situations in which the hunger for art does not wait for more obvious bodily needs to be met. Consider, for instance, the evocative poems in *Street Corner Majesty* by David Harris. Harris found his poetic voice when he joined a creative writing group at Miriam's Kitchen, a breakfast program for people who are homeless in Washington, DC. Writing poetry became a means for him to combat the fear, loneliness, and physical privation of life on the streets. In "Small Blue Poem #2," Harris writes of a perfect moment in the midst of life on the street:

> The Sun peeks through layers
> of thick gray clouds and
> bathes me in a warm spotlight.
>
> Says the Sun:
>
> Here is a small blue thing
> lying forgotten in grass and clover.
> Here's a weed
> to be plucked from a lush green lawn.
> Now I've been purged—
> you can gaze upon
> perfection. [13]

Not every person who joins a creative writing group at a homeless shelter will have a book of their original poetry published. But it is not

---

13. Harris, *Street Corner Majesty*, 20.

uncommon for individuals who live on the street to find solace, inspiration, and a place of belonging in such groups even when their physical needs are only being met marginally. One such group is led by Cynthia Dahlin, a chaplain who offers a weekly poetry workshop for the women at N Street Village, another shelter in Washington, DC. Dahlin begins each class by lighting a candle and saying,

> I light this candle in honor of the fact that you have brought your life, your experiences, your emotions, your creativity and your spirituality here today to share, and that is from the deepest part of you, your soul. As the candle flame grows while we are here, I hope your soul will be replenished, and as we share, and create community by your sharing, God is here, and the candle represents God's presence.[14]

Dahlin gives the women a different topic each week, suggesting that they write about their early lives as well as what is going on in the present, and their hopes and fears for the future. She points out that, although the topics may seem pedestrian on the surface, every week the writing brings a surprise. She says that everyone reacts differently to the ideas that she presents, and every session brings a gift in the form of a story, or simply words that stay with them.

At each session, Dahlin gives participants twenty-five or thirty minutes to write, asking the women to allow each other silence by waiting to talk until the last pen is down. When they are done, she invites them to share what they have written, reminding the others to refrain from making comments or asking questions. This, she says, provides the structure and safety that lets the women first write about their pain and then, over time, find their inner strength through the writing. She continues,

> When women first join the class, they do not trust that they might come back again, or know the difficulty of writing a very long piece. They often have trouble keeping silent during the writing, or criticize me—usually trying that first, and then perhaps others. They try to write down their whole lives on one piece of paper.[15]

While the population is transient, many of the women remain long enough to bond with her and others in the group. As they learn to trust one another, the women of N Street Village tell the truth of their lives through poems and stories.

14. Dahlin, "Sermon for May 8, 2011."
15. Ibid.

Life Stories Workshops is another program at N Street Village in which the women learn to find their voices through the arts. Life Stories is a program of the Theater Lab School of the Dramatic Arts, a non-profit institution whose mission is to transform lives through the theater, with summer camps, weekend workshops, and classes in acting, playwriting, and public speaking for children and adults at all levels of experience.[16] At N Street, Theater Lab faculty member Thomas Workman gives the clients basic instruction in improvisation techniques, allowing them to see their stories as something larger than their own, private tales of woe.

At the time of this writing, some of these stories had been gathered into a scripted performance which was presented at the Kennedy Center Terrace Theater. Rehearsals, which had been going on for several months, were recorded by documentary filmmaker Nicole Boxer-Keegan, who hopes to bring *Life Stories* to film festivals when it is completed. She says, "Most of these ladies were born in the 1950s, during an era . . . when there was a political promise that all people would have housing, medical care and education. Somehow, we've lost that over the last 50 years."[17] Boxer-Keegan's hope is that the film will be a window into issues of homelessness and arts advocacy, beyond the project's obvious benefit as art therapy for the women involved.

Art and Education

Art is not just a way to overcome circumstances of extreme deprivation, or a tool for self-improvement for people who are disadvantaged. As a culture, we seem to be constantly forgetting and relearning that the arts are an important part of what it means to be an educated human being. Not only do the arts bind us together through shared metaphor and story; they also teach us important skills that are often not learned in any other way. The habits of mind learned through sustained, disciplined engagement with almost any specific art form help people of all ages to succeed in an increasingly complex world. While this is especially important for impoverished young people who do not have the perspective to see any way out of their seemingly hopeless predicament, it is true for everyone, regardless of social or economic status.

Although many studies seem to find a strong correlation between participation in the arts and higher test scores in reading and math, some researchers point out that the true value of arts education lies in other

16. Boyle, "Life Stories."
17. Ibid.

important kinds of learning. In an article titled "Art for Our Sake" published in the *Boston Globe* in 2007, Harvard Graduate School researchers Ellen Winner, professor of psychology at Boston College, and Lois Hetland, associate professor of art education at Massachusetts College of Art, argue that the current emphasis on test scores tends to eliminate the teaching of important life skills, such as reflection, self-criticism, visual-spatial abilities, and the willingness to experiment and learn from mistakes. These are the very skills that are learned through regular participation in the arts. Reporting on their findings, the authors identified eight habits of mind learned in studio classes in visual arts, music, drama, or dance. In addition to the skills specific to the artistic discipline, students improved in such abilities as persistence, expression, and making clear connections between schoolwork and the world outside the classroom. The authors continue,

> Each of these habits clearly has a role in life and learning, but we were particularly struck by the potentially broad value of four other kinds of thinking being taught in the art classes we documented: observing, envisioning, innovating through exploration, and reflective self-evaluation. Though far more difficult to quantify on a test than reading comprehension or math computation, each has a high value as a learning tool, both in school and elsewhere in life.[18]

Artists seem to know this intuitively. All over the world, art centers and other organizations invite young people to participate in the arts, knowing that while most of them will not become professional artists, all may gain the life-enhancing skills that Winner and Hetland describe.

In the bleak township of Winterveldt, just outside Pretoria in South Africa, participation in the arts gives young people at risk not only a vision for a different future, but the means to get there. The Bokamoso Youth Center grew out of the vision of Steven and Mary Anne Carpenter, who for many years provided health care, nutritional counseling, rape crisis care, and other services. In 1999, the Carpenters were held up at gunpoint by young people whose families they had helped. Rather than leave the community in anger, they looked for a way to address the desperation and hopelessness of young people who had nowhere to go and few productive ways to spend their time.

Today, the Bokamoso Youth Center includes programs in basic life skills development, AIDS awareness, and conflict management; counseling and social services; and a scholarship program which includes scholarship application support, study skills training, and a resource center offering

18. Winner and Hetland, "Art for Our Sake."

textbooks, laptops, peer support, and a place to study. At the time of this writing, over sixty young people had received scholarships that supported them in college or vocational schools.[19]

Such practical programs are undeniably important but are insufficient on their own. Participation in the Bokamoso performing arts program gives the young people a chance to tell their stories artfully through song, dance, and short plays. Taking their performances to other communities, they raise both awareness and money which helps to support the organization that gives them so much. The Bokamoso Youth Foundation website explains,

> Through the efforts of Roy Barber and Leslie Jacobson, two accomplished American playwrights and drama teachers, and talented Bokamoso staff, this program provides Bokamoso youth with the opportunity to develop their talents in music and theater. Performance pieces include traditional song and dance, as well as plays and vignettes emerging directly from their life experience. In Winterveldt, the youth perform at schools and community organizations. Each year, twelve youth are selected for a month-long visit to the US. During their stay, the youth perform . . . to raise funds for their community and share about their lives and the Youth Centre.[20]

While some of the young people who are in the performing group have theatrical aspirations, most do not. Through their participation in the performing arts program, they begin to envision a future in which they can work as engineers, advocates for battered women and children, journalists, nurses, teachers, psychologists, or professionals in other fields. As Pearl Zondo, a member of the group that traveled to the US in 2008, put it,

> In 2007, when I finished my [matriculation exam], I was hit hard by the fact that I couldn't further my studies due to the reality that my mother was the only bread winner, and she struggled to make ends meet. My dream of studying psychology and some day becoming a clinical psychologist began to fade away while I watched loneliness crawl into my future. I knew I had to find something to keep me busy and off the streets, or else I'd end up like most girls in my neighborhood—a mother of two at the age of 20, drug-addicted and probably HIV positive.[21]

19. Bokamoso Youth Foundation, "Bokamoso History."
20. Ibid.
21. Ibid.

Participation in the performing group helped Pearl Zondo regain her dreams and her self-respect. She continues,

> I didn't believe that I could actually sing nicely until they clapped for me, danced with me, and cried when they heard what they call my 'incredible' voice. These sisters and brothers did not only love my singing, they gave me a place to stay, food to eat, and clothes to keep me warm—for free. Still, they did not end there; they gave me love, a place in their hearts, and most of all funded my school fees.

The affirmation that Zondo and the other members of the performing group gain from acting, singing, and dancing in front of hundreds of clapping, cheering supporters is a key part of their transformation from hopelessness to a confident trust in the future. Before that, however, comes the hard work of collaborating with their mentors and with one another to create the plays that tell their stories, the hours of practice that hones their remarkable voices, the attention to all the small details that turn their native talent and energy into a polished evening of theater. On their return to South Africa, the skills and habits of mind that they learn in this process help them succeed in the more formal education and vocational training for careers that will lift themselves, their families, and their community out of desperate poverty.

The Bokamoso Youth Center is only one example of the many places all over the world that offer a place for young people as well as adults to open themselves to the kind of knowing that comes through participation in the arts. In Washington, DC, for example, arts organizations like ArtSpace and the Sitar Arts Center serve poor and at-risk children in low- or no-cost after-school and weekend programs in visual arts, creative writing, music, dance, and other forms of art.

ArtSpace is a mission of the New Community Church, located in the Shaw district of Washington. ArtSpace founder Rachel Dickerson has been heard to say that she wants the arts to be as common as basketball in the life of a city where athletes are idolized and pick-up games are easily found at every playground and schoolyard. At ArtSpace, experienced artists trade teaching and mentoring for low-cost studio space, help with marketing their work, and expanding their own skills. Understanding that art making is as much about building community as it is about individual expression, ArtSpace volunteers work with young people "to develop their artistic eye and individual talent and form a meaningful relationship between a youth and adult, a key to positive development of a young person."[22]

22. New Community ArtSpace, "Work with Us."

The Sitar Arts Center is located in a part of the city that is marked by great disparities in income, education, and opportunity. Similar in many ways to Artspace, but larger in scope, it opened in 2000 in the basement of a subsidized-housing apartment building. With a curriculum including music, dance, visual arts, drama and creative writing, all taught by volunteer artists and partnering arts organizations, the Center serves over 700 children from low-income households, who have little other opportunity to participate in the arts.[23] The Sitar Center sees its mission as that of empowering young people through the arts and believing "in the intrinsic ability of each individual to be creative, and that the development and discovery of one's creative gifts builds self-knowledge and self-love as well as respect and tolerance for the interests and gifts of others."[24]

This conviction that participation in the arts can help young people at risk become productive members of society was also at the heart of the Great Wall of Los Angeles, a project of the Social and Public Art Resource Center (SPARC). Through SPARC, artist Judy Baca employed over 500 youth and their families over the course of several summers, beginning in 1974. Together, Baca, the young people, and a team of artists, oral historians, ethnologists, scholars, and hundreds of community members created a gigantic mural known as The Great Wall of Los Angeles. Conceived as an invitation to interracial harmony, the Great Wall depicts the history of the ethnic peoples of California from prehistoric times through 1984, the year it was completed. The SPARC website says of it,

> The Great Wall was already the longest mural after the summer of 1976 when a team of 80 youths referred by the criminal justice department, ten artists and five historians collaborated under the direction of Chicana artist Judith Francisco Baca to paint 1,000 feet of California history from the days of dinosaurs to 1910 in the Tujunga Wash drainage canal in the San Fernando Valley. But Baca . . . with a history of large collaborative mural projects behind her, was not ready to stop at 1910. Mural Makers worked in the wash again in the summers of 1978, 1980, 1981 and 1983. Each year they added 350 feet and a decade of history seen from the viewpoint of California ethnic groups.[25]

The Great Wall was never just an art project, however. It was also intended to help participants learn to work with people from different cultural backgrounds and social locations. In addition to working directly on-site

23. Sitar Arts Center, "Sitar Arts Center Mission."
24. Ibid.
25. Social and Public Art Resource Center, "Great Wall of Los Angeles."

for four to eight hours a day under the supervision of professional artists, the young people received art instruction, attended lectures from historians specializing in ethnic history, did improvisational theater and team-building exercises, and acquired the important skill of learning to work together cooperatively in full awareness of their diversity. Today, at 2754 feet (about half a mile), the Great Wall attracts tourists as well as scholars from all over the world as an example of how art can help people see not only their ethnic and economic diversity but also their common humanity and heritage as a living community.

After the Great Wall was officially completed in 1984, Baca and SPARC turned their attention to other parts of the city. From 1988 to 2002, the Great Walls Unlimited: Neighborhood Pride project produced over 105 murals in many ethnic areas of Los Angeles, collaborating with community-based organizations, minority-owned businesses, and professional artists to train hundreds of youth apprentices. Similar projects exist in Philadelphia, Baltimore, and other cities as a way to channel the energies of at-risk young people and help them become productive members of their communities.

Art and Justice

John Oppenheim's poem, "Bread and Roses," with which this chapter began, spoke powerfully about the yearnings of people who were oppressed by a system in which employers could force them to work for long hours at low pay in dismal and dangerous conditions. The poem was written soon after the infamous Triangle Shirtwaist Factory fire in which 146 workers, mostly girls between the ages of thirteen and twenty-three, lost their lives because the doors to the ninth-floor factory floor in which they worked were locked, and the fire escape collapsed when they tried to use it. In a few, well-chosen words, Oppenheim contrasted the lives of the working-class "drudge" with that of the rich "idler," in the hope for an end to a social arrangement in which "ten toil where one reposes." Everyone, he said, needs to share not only work, but also "life's glories." Everyone should live in a world where they have enough bread to sustain their bodies and enough roses to sustain their spirits. Both bread and roses are necessary for a fully human life.[26]

A few weeks after the poem was published, the phrase "Bread and Roses" was seen on banners held by strikers at the Lawrence, Massachusetts textile mills. Set to music by Caroline Kohlsaat, "Bread and Roses" became an anthem for poor women who wanted not only living wages for their work as mill workers or seamstresses or household domestics, but to live and work

26. Oppenheim, "Bread and Roses," 214.

in decent conditions, with the small graces that make life worth living. A later musical setting, by Mimi Farina, became popular in the 1970s, with the rise of a new wave of feminist consciousness. It was recorded by Judy Collins, Ani DiFranco, John Denver, and several other well-known musicians, and sung often on picket lines, and at demonstrations, marches, and rallies for various causes. I cannot be sure, but I think I may have first heard it at a Take Back the Night demonstration in Los Angeles in 1979 or 1980, in which women marched together through the city streets protesting a culture in which leaving their homes after dark subjected them to the threat of harassment, rape, and murder. Today, I still weep just thinking about the song and all its rich history.

Indeed, of all the arts, music has been especially powerful in helping people maintain their courage in the face of seemingly insurmountable obstacles. During the earliest days of the Civil Rights era in the United States, spirituals and gospel were central. Later, songs that eventually became known as movement music or protest songs, like "We Shall Overcome" and "If I had a Hammer," were frequently used to help build group identity and solidarity. In their discussion of the role of music in the bus boycotts of 1954 and the subsequent growth of the movement for racial equality, Ron Eyerman and Andrew Jamison note that singing together was so important that song leaders filled the role that a chairperson might in other settings, bringing a group together, calling attention to common purpose, and establishing the opening of a meeting. They continue,

> As the movement developed so too did the music and its functions. The music continued to serve as a means of identification, but added other communicative functions as the boycott took its toll and patience waned. Music served as a source and sign of strength, solidarity, and commitment. It helped build bridges between class and status groups, between blacks and white supporters, and between rural and urban, northern and southern blacks. It also bridged the gap between leaders and followers, helping to reinforce the notion that all belonged to the same "beloved" community.[27]

This experience was reflected in the similar struggle against apartheid, which officially ended in South Africa in 1989. Nearly twenty years later, Bishop Desmond Tutu, who had been central to the Truth and Reconciliation process that followed the establishment of a new constitution and government, gave a talk called "Can We Forgive Our Enemy?" at the

---

27. Eyerman and Jamison, *Music and Social Movements*, 98.

Washington National Cathedral. In response to a question from the audience regarding the role of music in the struggle against apartheid, he said,

> Without it, I think we would not have made it in so many ways. There were times there were songs we sang when we were really low, when you heard of a massacre, 30–40 people have been killed over here, someone has died in detention. We had a wonderful piece that we used to sing, "What have we done?" And I'm thinking of the funeral of Steve Biko thirty years ago. Yes, when there were things that were ineffable. You couldn't put them into words. And then there were the incredible times too when we were inspired by what happened here, your Civil Rights movement, and we also sang "We Shall Overcome." It was something that lifted your spirits. Your heart soared. And in this wonderful way there were the connections across the seas. Yes. There was also music that could sometimes inflame people and their anger. But mostly it was music that consoled and strengthened and helped to wipe tears away.[28]

For those who worked to end apartheid in South Africa, as for those who worked to end Jim Crow in the United States, singing together, breathing together, joining their voices together into one voice helped them keep moving forward in the face of dogs, water cannons, tear gas, beatings, and bullets.

Music is not the only art form that helps people in their struggle for justice and freedom. Poets, novelists, screenwriters, and even dancers have created indelible experiences that stir people to action and console them in difficult times. In the visual arts, works like include Francisco Goya's painting from 1814, *The Third of May*, and Picasso's 1937 *Guernica* evoke a deep, visceral reaction against the violence exerted by an oppressor against helpless victims. In the Goya work, we see the brutality of an invading force in the form of well-dressed and well-armed soldiers aiming point blank at a group of unarmed protestors, one of whom kneels with arms upraised in surrender while witnesses cover their eyes in horror. Similarly, *Guernica* is a nightmare vision of the pain and fear suffered by both people and animals when the town was bombed by German forces in support of the fascist General Franco during the Spanish Civil War.

Works such as these continue to be invoked by those who work for peace and justice. In *The Art of Engagement: Visual Politics in California and Beyond*, the catalog for an exhibition of the same name, Peter Selz writes,

---

28. Tutu, "Can We Forgive Our Enemy?"

Art at its best, I would argue . . . may even be engaged in effecting social transformation. . . . Picasso himself was no formalist ideologue. "Painting," he announced at the end of World War II, "is not done to decorate apartments. It is an instrument for war for attack and defense against an enemy." And Berthold Brecht proclaimed, "Art is not a mirror held up to reality, but a hammer with which to shape it."[29]

Selz goes on to point out that, although art is a commodity that is bought mainly by wealthy people who do not want to be reminded of injustice and oppression, many artists continue to take risks as active participants in movements for social justice. In California, which has a large Mexican-American population whose roots extend to the period of early settlement in the eighteenth century, there is a strong tradition of public art that advocates for the rights of the oppressed and marginalized.

One of the earliest known examples is a project intended for historic Olvera Street, in the oldest part of downtown Los Angeles. In 1932, noted Mexican artist David Alfaro Siqueiros was commissioned to paint a series of murals, including one called *Tropical America*. The mural was intended to show an idyllic view of Native Americans working in tropical bliss. Instead, Selz continues,

Siqueiros, dedicating the work to the Mexican working class of Los Angeles, depicted a Mexican Indian strapped to a wooden cross with a triumphant American bald eagle above his head. The city whitewashed the mural, and soon thereafter Siqueiros . . . was expelled from the United States.[30]

Despite the destruction of the mural, Siqueiros influenced later generations of artists. In the late 1960s, in the midst of the civil rights movement, antiwar protests, and a strong counter-cultural impulse against the perceived materialism and shallowness of much of society, politically conscious members of the Mexican-American community began to call themselves Chicano/Chicana, re-appropriating a derogatory term as an act of defiance against what they saw as an oppressive and discriminatory majority culture. Artists like Judy Baca, whose Great Wall project is described above; Gilbert Lujan, Carlos Almaraz, Roberto de la Rocha, and Frank Romero, members of an artists' collective who worked together as Los Four; and Willie Herrón, Harry Gamboa, Gronk, and Pattsi Valdez, who collaborated under the name ASCO, identified with the Chicano art movement and were shaped by it.

29. Selz and San Jose Museum of Art., *Art of Engagement*, 29–30.
30. Ibid., 31.

These artists and many others addressed the impact of immigration, deportation, migrant work, poverty, violence, and ethnic tensions in murals and other works throughout the city, especially in the area east of downtown, colloquially known as "East Los."

In an interview made as part of a Smithsonian project to document the history of the visual arts in the United States, Willie Herrón talked about growing up in a poor family in the City Terrace area of Los Angeles in the 1950s and early 60s. Shunted between grandparents and various aunts and uncles after his parents' divorce, he taught himself to draw as a means of understanding his world. Talking about the connection between drawing and his realization that he was different from the other kids because his family spoke Spanish, he relates,

> I really didn't feel like . . . I belonged. And so with that type of foundation, I kind of felt like I had to create my own foundation. I had to create my own sense of belonging and begin to create my own history. And it came naturally. It wasn't anything that I studied at that time. Because I mean, I was in fourth, fifth grade and I was already thinking that that was necessary in order for me to feel like I was somebody and not feel like I didn't belong. Because I didn't think the feeling was right, for me to feel like I didn't belong. I wanted to feel like I fit, like I belonged, because I saw myself equal as everyone else.

When he was about eleven, Herrón was living with an uncle who had been stationed in Kentucky as a member of the military. Much to the surprise of everyone in his family, the boy won an award for his drawing. This, he says, helped him into a new self-awareness:

> Like I felt like I was on the right path because people I didn't know recognized what I was up to. And I felt that they saw inside of me and that's how they supported me, by saying, "His is the best." Then that teacher that I had that was teaching me French, that was teaching me English, that was teaching me geography, that was teaching me math, that was teaching me everything when I was in that one school . . . in Kentucky . . . I stood long enough to see all the seasons, I really felt like I crystallized what it was that I needed to do for the rest of my life. And that was to be an artist.[31]

Herrón goes on to describe his admiration for his grandfather and his uncles, who lived with great dignity despite the poverty, violence,

---

31. Herrón, "Oral History."

and discrimination that seemed inescapable. Herrón's 1972 *The Wall that Cracked Open* was painted near the site where his younger brother was beaten up and stabbed in the neck by local gang members. Marcos Sanchez-Tranquilino, in his essay "Murals del Movimiento: Chicano Murals and the Discourses of Art and Americanization," describes this piece:

> To provide a more relevant street culture dimension to the mural's content, he integrated his design of a gang-victimized bleeding young man, fighting youth, and crying grandmother with the graffiti already on the wall left by the young barrio calligraphers of the area. By incorporating the Chicano "graffiti" into an "artwork," Herrón initiated a critical rethinking of graffiti as solely signifying vandalism which in turn has led to a deeper understanding of the relationship between so-called Chicano graffiti and Chicano murals.[32]

While not quite convincingly illusionistic, the mural's depiction of the young man and his attackers breaking through the wall on which they are painted questions the separation between art and everyday life, as well as the alienation from the larger society felt by both the gang members and their victims. As Gusmano Cesaretti, an Italian photographer who has lived in East Los since 1970, notes,

> A Chicano kid grows up with walls of many kinds around him. When somebody is born into that situation, there are several things he can do. He can ignore the walls and sink into apathy. Or he can become violent and try to blow up the walls. But there is a third way, a way that people have used for centuries. And that is to perform a kind of ritual magic to neutralize the force of the walls by decorating them with signs, symbols, and art. Chicano street writers choose this third way.[33]

Many of the professional artists in the Chicano movement self-consciously saw themselves as the heirs of Siqueiros, dissolving the walls of racism and discrimination and exposing the evils of society with art. The less well-educated young people that Cesaretti refers to as "street writers" were largely unaware of this heritage but were equally moved to change the bleak environment in which they lived. While many of them defiantly covered the walls of the *barrios* of East Los with graffiti proclaiming their gang affiliation, others painted awkward, yet moving, images of Jesus and the Virgin

32. Sanchez-Tranquilino, "Murals Del Movimiento," 97.
33. Cesaretti, *Street Writers*, 61.

of Guadalupe as memorials to loved ones killed as a result of drugs and violence.

By the 1980s, the murals that had begun as protest art in the housing projects and slums of the *barrio* had become a source of pride for Los Angeles as a whole. Artists were invited by building owners and civic groups to paint murals on the sides of important buildings, freeway retaining walls, and other highly-visible sites. *Recuerdos de Ayer, Suenos del Manana* (*Memories of Yesterday, Dreams of Tomorrow*) was painted in 1981 by Judith Hernandez as part of the 1981 Los Angeles bicentennial celebrations.[34] In *Recuerdos*, a woman with her back turned to the viewer is seen in profile against a golden-rayed aureole above stylized images of palm trees, athletes, farm workers, and civic buildings. Her upraised hands hold a ribbon on which is inscribed the founding name of the city, "El Pueblo de Nuestra Senora la Reina de los Angeles" (The City of Our Lady the Queen of the Angels), associating her with the Virgin Mary, the Queen of Heaven. However, this woman wears a spangled white scarf similar to those worn by many Mexican-American women on their way to church, and has the straight black hair and brown-skinned features that immediately identify her with the native and *mestizo* people who are the original inhabitants of the city, as well as their patroness, the Virgin of Guadalupe. Moreover, the use of Spanish proclaims not only the Chicana identity of the artist, but the legitimacy of the prior claim of her people on the city and its surrounding areas. This implicit statement that "we were here first" is addressed as much to the dominant culture as it is to the Chicano community out of which this art arises.

In preparation for the 1984 Summer Olympics, which were held in Los Angeles, the local Olympics Organizing Committee commissioned a number of well-known local muralists to place murals along freeways and in other places that would be seen by large numbers of people. At that time, I was an apprentice in Frank Romero's studio, assisting him with a number of projects. One of these was *Going to the Olympics*, a 22' x 103' mural on a retaining wall of the Hollywood freeway near Olvera Street. In addition to work on that project and research for other planned murals, I also helped him curate a retrospective exhibition of some of the works by members of Los Four, ASCO, and other art collectives from the 1970s. In the course of my work in Frank's studio, I was privileged to meet several of the Chicano artists who were so important to *la lucha*, the struggle for equal rights for people of Hispanic descent. At that time, many of them had become successful and prosperous, but the issues of racism, economic and educational

34. Young and Levick, *The Big Picture: Murals of Los Angeles*, 35.

disparities, and lack of access to resources continued to be at the heart of their lives and work.[35]

Art and the Prophetic Word

Other artists are equally concerned about issues of justice, oppression, and marginalization, but express their concern in a more reflective mood. In one such work, the artist considers what Scripture has to say to us in our day about the obligation of those in power to care for those who are less fortunate. In Amos 8:4–6, the prophet is given a vision of a basket of summer fruit as a warning to those

> that trample on the needy, and bring ruin on the poor of the land,
> saying, "When will the new moon be over, so that we may sell grain,
> And the sabbath, so that we may offer wheat for sale?
> We will make the ephah small and the shekel big,
> and practice deceit with false balances,
> buying the poor for silver
> and the needy for a pair of sandals
> and selling the sweepings of the wheat."

God tells Amos that the sun will go down at noon, and the feasts of the people who cheat and oppress those in need will be turned into mourning. All their songs will become lamentations, the prophet warns, unless they change their ways.

In her visual commentary on this passage, the 2002 *Amos' Basket of Summer Fruit*, Texas artist Ginger Geyer has given us a vision of a somewhat tired-looking bushel basket filled with canned goods. The labels tell us that they are filled with Kadota figs, mandarin oranges, and slices of pineapple. Jammed among the cans is a small sign that looks like a postcard sized rendition of Caravaggio's *Supper at Emmaus*. On the back of the sign, the words "Food Drive" have been scribbled. Underneath it all, at the bottom of the basket, is a pair of work gloves.

What makes this work particularly powerful is that its meaning grows slowly in the viewer's consciousness. For one thing, it is life sized, and looks almost exactly like the things it depicts. Indeed, seen in a photograph, it is hard to distinguish the porcelain bushel basket and canned goods from their everyday models. What is even less obvious is that porcelain is a demanding

---

35. For a further discussion of the Olympic mural project, see my article, Sokolove Colman, "Going to the Olympics."

medium—Geyer sometimes refers to it as "the Queen of Clay"—not readily amenable to the kind of *trompe l'oeil* complexities that she demands of it.

Geyer not only compels porcelain to do her bidding, but also writes extensively about each work. About this piece, Geyer notes that canned fruit was probably not what Amos envisioned. Nor was he talking about a pretty fruit basket sitting on an elegant dining room table. As Geyer notes, some Hebrew scholars have suggested that the phrase "a basket of summer fruit" is a kind of rhyming pun on a word meaning "the end," turning an image of fecundity into a warning of disaster. On a wall label describing the piece when it was first exhibited, Geyer reminded viewers that Amos was a harsh prophet who lived in a time of decadence and materialism, when the rich oppressed the poor and many were starving. She goes on,

> So here we have nine cans, sealed and boiled, these fruits of the spirit, with no can opener. And yet, we have a hopeful sign jammed among the cans. It bears the Lord's Supper at Emmaus (Luke 24). Why? Peer into the basket—at the bottom is nestled a pair of worker's gloves. They are palms up, as if receiving the Eucharist. When firing the piece, the bottom of the basket had shattered. The only possible repair was something glazed in there to connect all the shards. The gloves do that. They resemble the worn out gloves that migrant workers wear . . .They saved the sculpture, and suggest that we are all being helped by hidden hands.[36]

Geyer's keen wit and powers of observation have been shaped and tested by the fire of her faith and her craft. But there are more layers of meaning here. First, as Geyer notes in her own exegesis of the piece, there is no can opener hidden among the preserved bounty, so the food depicted is tantalizingly unavailable. Then, one might note that the porcelain cans themselves are, in fact, only facsimiles, glazed with precious white gold rather than the common tin or aluminum that they mimic. Thus, whether looked at from the point of view of what is depicted or from that of the means of depiction, this fruit will feed no one. As if to underscore this point, it is unlikely that an artwork of this size and quality will ever grace the table of someone living on food stamps. Finally, turning to the simple calculus of how many solitary hours in the studio it takes to make art of this depth, complexity, and skill, Geyer, herself, was probably not spending much time collecting for the local food bank or serving up lunch at the local soup kitchen while she was involved in creating this meditation on wealth, poverty, and oppression.

36. Geyer, "Amos' Basket of Summer Fruit."

This sophisticated, subtle, yet powerful work of art, like the easel paintings done by many of the same Chicano artists who created the murals of East Los Angeles, or the many other works which address issues of justice, will never feed the hungry directly. What they do accomplish is to confront the viewer in much the same way that Amos' vision confronted the wealthy and powerful of his time. After all, the intended audience for such works is the privileged few who have not only more than enough food but also sufficient discretionary funds to buy art. And when a work of art is strong, when it comes from a place of deep knowing and speaks eloquently of the truth that is found in that deep place, it may open the hearts of those who experience it to new possibilities of generosity and compassion.

Art and Healing

The connections between art, spirituality, and healing are unquestioned in most non-Western societies. From Navajo sand paintings to Buddhist *mandalas* and *tankhas* to masks and songs and dances and effigies, the arts are intrinsic to healing rituals in many parts of the world. In the twentieth century, various psychosocial therapeutic models began to be augmented with visual art, music, dance, and other modes of creative expression to gain access to the thoughts and feelings of clients for whom talk therapies were insufficient. As the interconnection between the mind, body, and spirit becomes increasingly well understood in the scientific community, the potential of the arts to affect physical, as well as psychological, healing is being realized in more and more places. Hospitals turn their hallways into art galleries; senior centers recommend storytelling to help clients with dementia recover memories and reconnect with loved ones; and countless workshops, seminars, retreats, and conferences are offered for people to learn to use the arts in their own quest for healing.

In South Africa, artist Jane Solomon has been developing a process called body mapping to help people living with HIV/AIDS to reframe their personal narratives as a way towards new self-understanding. Working with clinical psychologist Jonathan Morgan under the auspices of the Regional Psychosocial Support Initiative (REPSSI), an international capacity-building organization, and the Canadian AIDS Treatment Information Exchange (CATIE), Solomon developed a facilitator's guide called "Living with X: A Body Mapping Journey in the time of HIV and AIDS." Solomon writes,

> Body mapping can be used in many different ways. It can be
> a tool for using art in a healing way. It is also good for helping
> people remember things from their lives. And it can help people

to find answers to the problems that face them today or may happen in the future. But most of all, body mapping is a good way of helping people to tell their life stories.[37]

The technique that Solomon·describes is a carefully planned series of experiences that begins with participants tracing one another's bodies on large sheets of paper; using guided meditation to devise symbols relating to their past and future; and painting, drawing, or using collage to put the symbols onto appropriate parts of the body map. Participants learn skills, including making prints from one's own hands or feet; making repetitive patterns; and drawing a self-portrait from observation. In the process, they also change their self-understanding from being defined by their disease to seeing themselves as the multi-faceted persons that they are. As Solomon puts it,

> When you see or hear the words "Living with X," you will probably be asking yourself "Who or what is X?" If you start to do some body mapping, you and others in your group will be the ones to answer this question for yourselves. For you, X might mean "love," "courage," "a particular person," or many other things.
>
> Instead of talking about someone who is "Living with AIDS," we talk about "Living with X." We have done this because we do not believe that having HIV or AIDS is the most important thing about a person. There are many other personal qualities that are more important, and we have called those things X. Different people will have different ideas about what X means.[38]

While Solomon developed this process to use with people living with HIV/AIDS, body mapping and other visualization techniques have also been used to help people with both mental and physical illnesses gain insight into their conditions and the relationship between the mind and the body.

Art and Death

A growing number of individuals and groups have been exploring ways that the arts, especially music, can help people towards a good death. A recent article in the online journal, *Evidence-Based Complementary and Alternative Medicine*, reviewed eleven empirical studies on the use of music

37. Solomon, "Living with X," 2.
38. Ibid.

therapy in hospice and palliative care. Six of these studies found significant improvement in patients' pain, physical comfort, fatigue and energy, anxiety and relaxation, time and duration of treatment, mood, spirituality and quality of life. The article defines music therapy as an established allied health profession in which,

> music therapists are Board Certified (MT–BC) by the Certification Board for Music Therapists (CBMT) upon the completion of at least an undergraduate degree in music therapy or its equivalent, a clinical internship (averaging 1040 hours), and successfully passing the CBMT examination. In hospice and palliative care, music therapists use methods such as song writing, improvisation, guided imagery and music, lyric analysis, singing, instrument playing and music therapy relaxation techniques to treat the many needs of patients and families receiving care. Needs often treated by music therapists in end-of-life care include the social (e.g. isolation, loneliness, boredom), emotional (e.g. depression, anxiety, anger, fear, frustration), cognitive (e.g. neurological impairments, disorientation, confusion), physical (e.g. pain, shortness of breath) and spiritual (e.g. lack of spiritual connection, need for spiritually-based rituals).[39]

Not everyone bringing music to the dying is a licensed music therapist, however. Family members, friends, and other visitors sometimes sing with or for a person who is ill, much as a mother will comfort a baby with a lullaby. It is said that the last sense to leave us is hearing, and there is some indication that even persons who are in a coma are able to hear what is said or sung in their presence. For some people, hymns may bring comfort; for others, chamber music may open a way into the mystery of life and death; for still others, folk music or rock-and-roll may bring back a measure of joy and laughter.

Jesse Palidofsky is a singer-songwriter, a graduate of the Earlham School of Religion, the Shalem Institute's Spiritual Guidance Program, and a certified chaplain with the Board of Professional Chaplains. For many years, he worked on the oncology ward at Children's Hospital. More recently, he has been serving as a hospice chaplain, as well as regularly bringing music to senior centers and retirement homes under the auspices of Arts for the Aging, and offering lectures and workshops on the relationship of music and healing for organizations like the National Hospice and Palliative Care Organization, the Maryland Hospice and Palliative Care Network, and the Association of Professional Chaplains annual conference.

39. Hilliard, "Music Therapy in Hospice."

In order to remain centered and open to the feelings evoked by his work with the dying, Palidofsky reflects thoughtfully on his experience in stories that reveal the power of music to help those who are dying, as well as the families they leave behind. He tells the story of Daniel, an eight-year-old with leukemia whose father, Joel, had been told by family members that the boy was sick because the family did not go to church.[40] Although the father was reluctant to let "the chaplain" come into the room, the guitar he always carried with him intrigued the little boy. When the boy and his sister laughed and sang along on a silly song about howling at the moon like a dog, the tension and fear that had filled the parents' hearts began to lessen.

After several visits, the father came to trust the musical chaplain, and, over time, the two started a father's group on the oncology unit. Palidofsky explains,

> The day-time oncology parents group, facilitated by a female social worker, is frequented almost exclusively by mothers. On the first Tuesday evenings of the month, Joel and I knock on doors on the Oncology and Bone Marrow Transplant units and invite fathers down to the 4 Yellow parents lounge for coffee and doughnuts and conversation. The Father's Group provides food for the starving. A core group of fathers attend regularly. Men who would not be caught dead in a men's support group or in a therapist's office hungrily show up to listen to stories of their brothers in the trenches, and to offer their own. None of this would have been possible without a silly little song in a moment of crisis opening the door to the possibility of relationship between Joel and myself.[41]

While the father's group did not use music or any other kind of art, the songs that Palidofsky offered on his rounds helped both the children and their parents experience him as a non-anxious presence, creating an opening for deeper conversation. He continues,

> To the untrained eye, it is easy to be confused and to see the chaplain's singing as mere entertainment. However . . . the chaplain's use of music has the unique ability to help create a non-anxious space, which is most basic to facilitating healing. Music is capable of doing this work in a way that simultaneously *circumvents* the tension or anxiety in order to finally *confront*

---

40. All names in the stories that follow have been changed.

41. Palidofsky, "Non-Anxious Presence."

the deeper feelings at work, when the time is right and the person chooses to engage at that level.[42]

Such engagement can help the dying as well as their loved ones. Often, a person who is facing death becomes withdrawn, refusing to communicate with loved ones, staring anxiously at a reality that only he or she can see. One such person was Ofelia, a Spanish-speaking woman in her late seventies who, her chart revealed, had no religious affiliation. Despite his inability to speak Spanish, Palidofsky wanted to help Ofelia and her daughter, Juana, and grandson, Arturo, who felt helpless at her apparent terror in the face of death. Palidofsky writes,

> Juana tells me that her mother is from Cuba. I know one song from Cuba. And yet it seems a bit absurd to offer it in this moment. I fear that I may be laughed out of the room—or, much worse, that I will only add to the great suffering of Juana and Arturo as they accompany their beloved through her final journey.

The one song is "Guantanamera," a love song, which he began singing in a soft, quiet voice, like a lullaby. At first, Ofelia remained unresponsive, immersed in her fearful visions. Eventually, however, she became calmer, and by the time Palidofsky reached the chorus, she began to sing along. He continues,

> Tears are freely splashing down Juana's face. Arturo's jaw has dropped through the floor. When we reach the second chorus, all four of us are belting it out together. . . . The spell is broken. When we finish the third verse and final chorus, Ofelia looks at Juana and speaks with great passion, delivering the first words she has said in three days. Arturo, Juana and Ofelia erupt into uproarious laughter.
>
> When the room settles down, I ask, "Juana, would you mind sharing with me what your mother just said?" Juana looks a little embarrassed, and shakes her head. "Oh, please, Juana, I would really like to know what your mother just said." She hesitates again. "It's really okay—whatever it is, please share with me."
>
> "She said, why does he have to sing it so slow and melancholy like a white man—why can't he pep it up and put some soul into it?"[43]

Everyone, even Ofelia, laughed, the terror banished. Over the next few days, Ofelia was able to be present to her daughter and grandson. When she

---

42. Ibid.

43. Palidofsky, "Ofelia."

died, Juana told the chaplain that her mother was much more at peace and that she and Arturo have been able to come to a sense of closure with Ofelia that would have been unthinkable only a few days before.

In this story, as in the story of Daniel and his father, music provides an opening into a deeper, more profound truth than the fear that so often accompanies serious illness and death. It doesn't really matter whether the music is sacred or secular, serious or funny, as long as it touches the heart of the person who is living and dying in fear. As Palidofsky reminds us, "Any piece of music can be spiritual. Any song can open the door to the Spirit of Healing, if it speaks to the deepest hunger of the person receiving it and if it is sung with the clear intention of loving connection to the Source of All Being."[44]

Art and Mourning

There is often a very thin line between art and ritual. In many societies, such as Japan or Mexico, it is customary to create shrines in the home which incorporate elements of both ritual and art. In the nineteenth-century United States, such shrines were common, and might include a daguerreotype of the deceased person, mourning lockets containing the person's hair woven into a wreath, embroidered or painted memorial pictures, and mourning scrapbooks or quilts. Creation of these private memorials, and many of the objects which they contain, was often therapeutic, a kind of hand-work or artistry that served to keep one busy while allowing healing outside of pre-scribed, and often insufficient, religious frameworks.[45]

In the public realm, bringing things to impromptu shrines similarly gives people something to do, a structure within which to act in the face of powerful forces and feelings that they cannot explain. Ever since it was completed, people have continued to lay flowers, military ID tags, and other items with personal meaning at the foot of the Viet Nam Memorial. Since then, it has become commonplace for people to pile up candles, flowers, stuffed animals, photographs, and other memorial objects at sites of public tragedies, such as the bombing of the Oklahoma City bombing in 1995, and the destruction of the World Trade Center in New York City on September 11, 2001. Other examples of the ambiguous border between art and ritual include,

> white, flower-adorned "ghost bikes" marking the spot where bicyclists have died in major U.S. cities; R.I.P. tags, bottles,

44. Palidofsky, "Joan."
45. Jorgensen-Earp and Lanzilotti, "Public Memory and Private Grief," 159.

balloons, stuffed animals and other mementos honoring murder victims on street corners in [urban] neighborhoods; small
backyard altars created with symbolic objects to memorialize a
friend's passing; the planting of trees and calling of names in
honor of transgendered individuals who have met violent deaths
in cities throughout the country; the participatory creation of
vast piles of shoes marking the loss of lives and limbs due to
landmines that has travelled to public spaces in European cities
like Paris to aid the international movement to ban land mines.
In each of these varied examples, the visual or poetic element
is used symbolically to enhance the experience of ritual—both
individually and collectively.[46]

In an article on a Service of Remembrance held at the Sidney Kimmel
Comprehensive Cancer Center at Johns Hopkins Hospital, Cinder Hypki
writes,

After 18 years of a community arts practice that has served many
community issues, I have begun to explore the potential of ritual
and the power of collaborative art making as a response to violence. In providing aesthetic and spiritual tools for transcending
loss, art offers a collective means for healing, celebrating the
lives of those lost and strengthening individual and community
resolve to keep living fully and working to prevent future violence. Poetry and visual art have become the tiles that I bring to
the collective mosaic of empowering change.[47]

The people remembered at this planned service, however, were not
victims of violence but rather cancer patients who had succumbed to their
disease in the previous year. Chaplain Rhonda Cooper and social worker
Louise Knight, who coauthored the article with Hypki, recognized that not
only the families, but the doctors, nurses, and other hospital personnel who
had become attached to patients in the course of long and intense treatment,
needed the opportunity to remember and to mourn. Realizing that an artist
might offer some skills and perspective that they might not otherwise be
able to access, they invited Hypki to collaborate with them in the design of
the service.

From the beginning, Cooper, Knight, and Hypki understood that
the spiritual nature of a Service of Remembrance was in tension with the
scientific, empirical nature of the institution that it was to serve. In addition, since the patients, families, and staff come from a variety of religious

46. Hypki, Cooper, and Knight, "Memorial Ritual and Art."
47. Ibid.

traditions, as well as none, the service had to respect many different ethnic, religious, and socioeconomic constituencies. The authors were clear that,

> By intent, the Cancer Center's Service would include ritual elements from various religious traditions, the substance of which would be sensitively and thoughtfully designed to uphold meaning-making and the feeling of transcendence, that which goes beyond the ordinary range of perception. The Service would also function as a worthy container of strong feelings related to loss. . . .
>
> The chaplain formulated the Service to include the elements of gathering and welcome, music, invocation, reflection, responsive reading and a time for the deceased to be recognized in a personalized way by the family members and staff. The chaplain also envisioned an opportunity for family members and staff to participate in creating an art piece, a place to "leave their mark," that would function as a transitional experience to move the participants from the world of the Cancer Center to their own homes following the Service.[48]

Over 300 people attended the service, which included an invitation for family members to call out the names of the deceased. Some held photographs, some merely stood, as those who had died were remembered as loved and valued individuals. As the service ended, everyone was given the opportunity to write a message—a wish, a prayer, a remembrance—on a strip of cloth, and weave that cloth into a sculpture that had been prepared to hold them. More than 250 people contributed to the sculpture by the end of the evening.

This was not some empty ritual. Nor was it meant to be high art in the strictest sense of the word. Rather, it was a means by which people could get in touch with their grief and share their memory with others through contributing to a common project with visual and tactile elements. Hypki reports that many people took out their cell phones and photographed the messages they had written and placed into the sculpture. She concludes,

> In effect, to take a photo and text it, e-mail it, post it on social networking sites, or save it, was to affirm: "I was here, I did this thing that was important to me and it was a part of something much larger that validates me and our collective coming together."[49]

48. Ibid.
49. Ibid.

Following the service, staff members expressed their gratitude at the opportunity to reconnect with the families of those whom they had served, and a Service of Remembrance, complete with the opportunity to contribute to a sculpture, has now become an expected annual event.

On reading the article describing this artful service, I found myself awash in tears, deep in my own memories of grief and loss. I contacted Hypki soon thereafter, and in a conversation with her and Cooper as they were planning the third iteration of the service, I asked what would become of the sculptures. On the one hand, the works were meant to be ephemeral, and were too large and fragile to store or exhibit. On the other hand, the strips of cloth with their heartfelt messages seemed somehow sacred, and could not simply be disposed of unceremoniously. Several weeks later, Hypki reported on what she calls "the second life" of the messages.

> Nurses and other staff began braiding the rope this spring, in anticipation of archiving them and freeing up the sculpture itself for this third Service. As I did the first year, they documented each strip by logging it in to a document for that purpose, and they braided three sets of braids which then became the strands for a larger braid about an inch thick and 9 feet long.[50]

Hypki, Cooper, and staff members have decided that the braids from each years' sculptures will be joined together in a continuous rope which will remain at the Kimmel Cancer Center as a witness to the ongoing life of this community of caring.

The Need for Art

William Carlos Williams once wrote,

> It is difficult
> to get the news from poems
> yet men die miserably every day
> for lack
> of what is found there.[51]

Poems, songs, stories, paintings, dances, and other forms of art are food for starving souls, feeding the imagination and freeing the heart from the images of war, poverty, disaster, and political nastiness that relentlessly fills the news. Seeing the transformations that can happen when people in

50. Hypki, "Re: Art and Mourning."
51. Williams, "Asphodel, That Greeny Flower."

situations of extreme difficulty are given the chance to participate in artistic experiences can change people in more privileged circumstances, as well.

One afternoon, a young woman sat in my office asking about art classes at the seminary. Trained as a lawyer, she told me that she had been working for a program that provides essential services—health care, legal aid, food, and shelter—to homeless people. She said that she believed passionately in the work that she was doing, but that she came to realize that the most important part of the program was not filling these practical, immediate needs, but rather the art experiences that were also made available to the clients. Given paint, clay, or other materials, and the time and space to explore what they could do, the people became more than the sum of what they lacked. They remembered who they were at the deepest, most spiritual and honest level, and became open to the truth of their shared humanity. Now, my visitor told me, she wanted to learn to make art herself, to find out how to tell her own deepest truth in art.

In this chapter, I have given only a few examples, a kind of sketch describing some of the ways that the arts give people a reason to live, the strength to carry on in the presence of terrible pain, or the ability to face death with dignity and peace. They are simply pointers, reminders of a reality that somehow we continually forget when we feel forced to choose between ministry and art, between bread and roses. This reality is that our bodies do not live long or well with hearts that are starving for meaning, for connection, for all the things that the arts do to help us live through the times of hardship and desperation.

We need to constantly remember, and to remind one another, that the need for art is not secondary, to be filled after people are adequately fed and housed, but rather is a primary part of what it means to be human. Art is not simply about making one's surroundings more attractive, or adding ornaments to an already satisfactory life. Nor is it merely a tool to help us through difficult times. Art is an important pathway towards knowing oneself, of communicating that knowledge to others, and becoming an integral part of the human community. Art fills a hunger that nothing else can fill; it opens doors that cannot be opened in any other way; it creates a channel for the truth that Jesus told us will make us free.

6.

Art in the Body of Christ

The place God calls you to is the place where your deep gladness and the world's deep hunger meet.

 —Frederick Buechner[1]

Don't ask yourself what the world needs. Ask what makes you come alive, and go do that, because what the world needs is people who have come alive.

 —Howard Thurman[2]

From the very beginning, the arts have had a tenuous place in the church. The church, as Paul tells us in 1 Corinthians 12:12–14, is not a building, or even an institution, but rather the living Body of Christ on earth. And that Body has always been ambivalent in its support for art and artists. Although frescos and mosaics have been found in some of the earliest known Christian buildings, and even, as in Ephesians 5:19 and elsewhere, Scripture exhorts us to sing psalms and hymns and spiritual songs, there is much evidence that many Christians have been suspicious of the power of the arts to work on the emotions and the minds of believers. Indeed, the second half of the very verse in Ephesians that mentions singing has been used to argue that we should not actually make music aloud, but rather keep the music that we make to the Holy One deep in our hearts. In the early church, painters and sculptors were often suspect because much of their work was done in service to other gods. Actors, too, were regarded with suspicion, because they pretended to be someone they were not. Indeed, all the arts were often

1. Buechner, *Wishful Thinking*, 95.
2. Bailie, *Violence Unveiled*, xv.

seen as so closely connected with matter and the body that their spiritual potential was constantly questioned.

The legacy of ancient Greek thought that divided evil matter from spiritual good has pervaded Christian arguments against the arts. Dissension about the proper role of painting and sculpture broke out with particular virulence during the iconoclastic controversies in the eighth and ninth centuries, and again in the sixteenth-century Protestant Reformation. Music, also, has come under suspicion at various times, most notably by Augustine who worried that his love of the tune made him ignore the holy words of the psalms,[3] and by Zwingli, who banned music in his churches for similar reasons. In recent years, the theological defense of the arts has been grounded—as it was by John of Damascus[4]—in the twin doctrines of the Incarnation and of the goodness of Creation, as well as in a growing recognition of a more unified understanding of matter and spirit inherent in Christianity's Jewish roots. In the past quarter-century, an increasing number of artists have begun to understand their work as a response to God's call on their lives; and an increasing number of churches have begun to re-evaluate the role of the arts in their worship, their congregational life, and their outward mission.

In this chapter, we will look at the relationships between the church, the arts, and the artists who are eager to share what they do and know with their brothers and sisters in Christ. In what way is a life in the arts a calling, a gift, a legitimate path of Christian service and witness? What kind of art is appropriate for worship? How else might the arts inform the life of the Body of Christ?

Art and Call

In the Bible, there are many examples of God calling an individual to some particular purpose or task. Moses sees a bush burning in the desert, and hears God telling him to bring the Israelites out of slavery in Exodus 3. In 1 Samuel 3, the boy Samuel hears God's voice calling his name, setting him apart as a prophet. In Isaiah 6:1–13, Isaiah has a vision of the Holy One seated on a throne, asking who should be sent to tell the people of God's judgment, and answers "Here I am. Send me!" And in the gospel accounts, Jesus calls Peter, James, John, and others by name, inviting them to follow him and be his disciples.

---

3. Augustine, *Confessions*, 235.

4. John of Damascus, *Defense of Icons*, 10–17 passim.

For more than a thousand years, the notion of vocation, or call, was usually restricted, applying specifically to those who joined religious orders or the priesthood. By 1520, however, Martin Luther was contesting this understanding, arguing that all Christians are called by God to a ministry of service, whatever their occupation. In contrast to the prevailing view of the church in his time, he argued,

> Therefore, just as Those [sic] who are now called "spiritual"— priests, bishops or popes—are neither different from other Christians nor superior to them, except that they are charged with the administration of the Word of God and the sacraments, which is their work and office, so it is with the temporal authorities, —they bear sword and rod with which to punish the evil and to protect the good. A cobbler, a smith, a farmer, each has the work and office of his trade, and yet they are all alike consecrated priests and bishops, and every one by means of his own work or office must benefit and serve every other, that in this way many kinds of work may be done.[5]

This understanding became widespread in Reformation thought, even though often resisted as a practical matter for its radical implications. The text of 1 Peter 2:9 "But you are a chosen race, a royal priesthood, a holy nation, God's own people, in order that you may declare to proclaim the mighty acts of him who called you out of darkness into his wonderful light," came to be summarized as the doctrine of the priesthood of all believers. This doctrine suggests that if all believers without exception are understood as priests, whatever work they do must therefore be understood and lived out as ministry.

Over time, *vocation*—which is simply the Latinate version of the Anglo-Saxon *calling*—began to take on a more general meaning in the secular world, becoming virtually synonymous with career or profession. Generally speaking, lawyers, doctors, and other professionals were understood to have vocations; tradespeople, manual laborers, and other low-status workers were not. Within the church, the language of call continued to be associated with an increasingly professionalized ordained ministry, with some extension towards missionaries, regardless of their ordination status. Despite an implicit or explicit belief in the doctrine of the priesthood of all believers, most of the denominations that grew out of the Reformation have continued to foster a sense that the clergy are called to their role in a way that others are not, with all the privilege and implications of sanctity such a notion of call implies.

5. Luther, "Letter to Christian Nobility."

In Protestant and, to a lesser extent, in Roman Catholic contexts, the language of call and ministry has come to include those who provide direct service to people who are poor, sick, or in some other kind of immediate need. In this understanding, call is also used to describe the work of social workers, doctors, nurses, and Peace Corps volunteers, as well as those who volunteer in soup kitchens and homeless shelters or mentor children at risk or tutor illiterate adults. This is still not Luther's sweeping, inclusive vision in which everyone could be seen as called to their specific labor, regardless of what kind of work they were doing, as long as they did it with integrity and for the good of others. It does, however, offer an understanding of call that is more expansive than simply joining a religious order or the ranks of the ordained. Whether or not a church explicitly subscribes to a doctrine of the priesthood of all believers, most teach that we are all called as Christians to participate in ministry in some way.

Unfortunately, with its emphasis on direct service to those in need, some descriptions of call often sound more like works righteousness—the notion that we are saved by our own good deeds rather than through God's grace—than a joyful response to God's invitation. In contrast, Frederick Buechner offers a different image, telling us that God calls us to meet the world's deep hunger with our own gladness. Howard Thurman, meanwhile, reminds us that we don't have to look around at all the needs of the world and decide which one we should address. Rather, we should simply do the thing that makes us feel truly alive, because it is the sense that life is worth living that the world needs more than anything else.

Both of these pieces of advice come as a challenge to people who are raised on the notion of self-sacrifice in the name of Christian service. But, we ask, what about our duty to feed the hungry, clothe the naked, and visit the sick and the imprisoned? What about simply doing what is right, what is needed for the greater good, regardless of one's own desires and well-being? For artists, these are difficult questions to answer, especially in a world of diminishing resources, increasingly unstable ecological conditions, and unrelenting war or poverty or both in so many parts of the world.

Nonetheless, many artists do experience their work as true vocation, a special calling from God, a way of life that does not stop at the close of the business day or depend on whether they are paid to do it. At the deepest level, Christian artists believe that practicing their art is exactly how they are called to live out the proper use of the divine gifts of creativity and talent. Like other ministries, the ministry of art requires serious commitment of time for education and practice. Even when the artist's inherent gift is undeniable, the first intimation that one is called to this demanding, challenging, astonishing way of life, the gift is only the beginning of the journey. Despite the gift, despite the sense of call, many artists continually ask themselves how they can spend their time painting/dancing/singing/composing/writing poems or participating in any other art form, when the world is filled with so much need.

Artist as Priest and Prophet

One answer to this dilemma is found in the widely held notion that artists possess the ability to make the invisible visible, to mediate between the sacred and the profane, to have special powers to discern the divine will. Both in the secular world and in the church, artists are often invested with a priestly mystique or understood as bearers of a prophetic vision. Where artists are seen as priests and prophets, it opens the pathway to affirming their work as a legitimate calling, a ministry that is as real and as necessary as that of preachers, teachers, and healers. While this may be a helpful way to think about art and artists, some caution is advisable lest art itself become an idol. Nevertheless, this is a pathway worth exploring.

In his widely admired work on theological aesthetics, *The Glory of the Lord*, Hans Urs von Balthasar quotes theologian Fritz Medicus as saying, "God needs prophets in order to make himself known, and all prophets are necessarily artists. What a prophet has to say can never be said in prose." However, Balthasar cautions, "if all prophets are artists, surely not all artists are prophets, although all of them may be in another, more general sense."[6] That Balthasar wants to simultaneously both affirm and deny the prophetic power of artists is not surprising, given the widespread ambivalence about the arts and artists both inside the church and in the wider society.

In his 1973 A. W. Mellon Lectures in the Fine Arts at the National Gallery of Art in Washington, DC, cultural historian Jacques Barzun examined contemporary ideas about art as a replacement for religion. Asking where such ideas come from, he writes,

> It has long been a commonplace of art criticism that the arts reach their greatest heights when they have the good fortune to serve a religion. It is almost a convention to feel awe-struck and worshipful before the art of the Gothic cathedrals, and to generalize from this example and that of the primitive tribes and lost civilizations, in which art and religion visibly sustained each other. Much ancient art served the gods and cults of the city, where hardly any distinction existed between religion and the state. In the very different conditions of the last 500 years, a

---

6. Balthasar, *Glory of the Lord*, 44–45.

longing for that simple unity has inspired the axiom about great
art and fervent faith.[7]

While the connections between art and spiritual life have been an un-
dercurrent in discussions of the arts at least since the time of the Greeks, it
became especially prominent in the thought of the Romantic poets of the
early nineteenth century. Indeed, for many of them, the connection between
artistic sensibility and divine inspiration was an essential part of their self-
understanding. Where previously artists might claim a special dispensation,
or genius, as the proof of their calling, now some of them, at least, would
assert that an artistic sensibility was the only true path to God. Thus, on an
1820 engraving depicting his sculpture of *Laocoön* and his sons in the grip
of the serpent, William Blake could assert,

> The Eternal Body of Man is The Imagination, that is, God him-
> self . . . It manifests in his Works of Art . . .
>
> A Poet, a Painter, a Musician, an Architect: the Man or Woman
> who is not one of these is not a Christian . . .
>
> The Whole Business of Man Is the Arts . . . Art is the Tree of
> Life . . .[8]

While asserting that only artists can be real Christians should be seen
as heretical to most faithful Christians, Blake's extravagant claims have ap-
pealed to many artists and their audiences. Barzun carefully documents
that as Western society became increasingly secular in the nineteenth and
twentieth centuries, art came to serve as a substitute religion for many
people who rejected institutional religion yet had strong spiritual yearnings.
Reviewing the various ways that artists thought of their role in society, he
refers to those who thought that artists should reject worldly concerns in
favor of a pure realm of art as "transcendental," and those who believed
that artists should lead society into a new world order as "revolutionary." By
1837, he notes,

> [W]e have the revolutionary artist and the transcendental art-
> ist fighting side by side. Their voices have rung in chorus ever
> since, because their common religious task is to repel the world,
> with or without the zeal to remake it. Except for brief interludes
> when science has been conspicuous and has seemed to promise
> intellectual and spiritual aid, the leading minds of western civili-
> zation have done their work in an "art epoch." Even now, despite
> the rebellion against high art, the present age as a whole assumes

7. Barzun, *Use and Abuse of Art*, 24–25.

8. Ibid., 35–36.

without question that [humanity's] loftiest mode of expression is art.[9]

Stressing the point that in a secular society, art is often seen as a substitute for organized religion, he continues,

> If art is a religion, it must become the moralizer of [humans] and monitor of life. The same holds true if art is the measure of social justice. Art inherits all the duties of the church. The artist is first prophet calling down heavenly vengeance, then priest dealing out anathemas and penances.[10]

Surveying the career of John Ruskin (1819–1900) as an example of artist as social reformer or revolutionary, he notes that Ruskin vilified those who did not agree with his judgments about various artists and art movements. Ruskin asserted that his vision was correct not only aesthetically and artistically, but also morally. Barzun describes Ruskin's prophetic fervor as he travelled throughout the British isles, admonishing the industrialists for the sorry state of their buildings and the objects that they manufactured. In Barzun's summary of Ruskin's critique,

> They were incapable of good architecture because they were not honest and noble; only a great people produces great art; art is the index of social health. But the English were money-mad, unjust, and spiritually rotten. So saying, Ruskin finally turned political economist and set up the guild of St. George to show how society must be recast if justice and art are to flourish.[11]

This notion of the priestly and prophetic role of art and artists is now so commonplace in Western society that it goes largely unquestioned, both in secular and Christian circles. In calling their 1988 volume, *Performer as Priest and Prophet: Restoring the Intuitive in Worship through Music and Dance*, dancer Judith Rock and composer Norman Mealy explicitly called on that understanding as they argued for a place for professional performances of dance and music in liturgical settings. Seeing trained, disciplined, theologically thoughtful performers as mediators of meaning, they write,

> Theology has to do with formally crafted communications to other people about what God might be like . . . By definition, these include communications about human beings in the created world, if we believe that human beings are made in the

9. Ibid., 38–39.
10. Ibid., 39.
11. Ibid., 40.

Creator's image . . . Rather than exploring dance and music as devotional practices, we are concerned here with these arts as formal architectures of meaning: architectures of meaning that communicate through our intuitive rather than our analytic faculties.[12]

For Rock and Mealy, as for many who think of artists as belonging to a kind of priesthood, the artist has the power to make visible the invisible, to make that which is known intuitively and experientially present to the conscious mind. Just as in many religions priests are understood as mediators between ordinary people and the divine, artists in our culture are presumed to mediate between their audience and the beatific vision.

A similar idea is found in Walter Brueggeman's understanding of the prophetic role of poets. In *Finally Comes the Poet: Daring Speech for Proclamation*, he writes of a prose-flattened world in which the living truth of the gospel is reduced into manageable facts or accommodated to social ideologies of either the right or the left. Suggesting that preachers have much to learn from the arts, he writes,

> The task and possibility of preaching is to open out the good news of the gospel with alternative modes of speech—speech that is dramatic, artistic, capable of inviting persons to join in another conversation, free of the reason of technique, unencumbered by ontologies that grow abstract, unembarrassed by concreteness. Such speech, when heard in freedom, assaults imagination and pushes out the presumed world in which most of us are trapped . . .To address the issue of a truth greatly reduced requires us to be *poets that speak against a prose world*.[13]

Brueggeman cautions that he is not speaking of poetry as consisting of rhyme, meter or rhythm, but rather as

> language that moves like Bob Gibson's fast ball, that jumps at the right moment, that breaks open old worlds with surprise, abrasion, and pace . . . Such preaching is not moral instruction or problem solving or doctrinal clarification. It is not good advice, nor is it romantic caressing, nor is it a soothing good humor. It is, rather, the ready, steady, surprising proposal that the real world in which God invites us to live is not the one made available by the rulers of this age.[14]

12. Rock and Mealy, *Performer as Priest and Prophet*, xiv.
13. Brueggeman, *Finally Comes the Poet*, 3; emphasis original.
14. Ibid.

Such speech, like much of the biblical text, both poetic and prophetic, anticipates and summons realities

> that live beyond the conventions of our day-to-day, take-for granted world . . . Those whom the ancient Israelites called prophets, the equally ancient Greeks called poets. The poet/ prophet is a voice that shatters settled reality and evokes new possibility in the listening assembly . . . The poetic speech of text and of sermon is a prophetic construal of a world beyond the one taken for granted.[15]

If for Brueggeman the preacher must be a poet, for many Christians as well as people in the secular world, poets and other artists fulfill the prophetic role more effectively than any preacher who stands in the pulpit on Sunday morning. And many artists, for their part, are eager to embrace the role of priest, prophet, or some combination of both, understanding themselves as called by the Holy One to the work of glorifying God, making the beatific vision that has been revealed to them present to others, or speaking truth to power through their art.

Liturgy and the Arts

Liturgy—the communal, corporate worship of the Body of Christ—is the most visible place where the arts and faith come together. While there are many denominational and local differences, organs, choirs, stained glass, vestments, pews, and steeples are just a few of the features that most people would associate with Christian worship. Even the most austere New England meeting houses tend to be carefully crafted, with thoughtful details and elegant proportions. From the neo-Gothic splendor of the Cathedral of St. John the Divine in New York City to the restrained elegance of Bigelow chapel on the campus of United Theological Seminary of the Twin Cities, art is often associated with the church in the guise of architecture. And whether a congregation meets in a building designed expressly for worship; a rented movie theater; an uninspired, blocky, cinderblock building; or someone's living room, there is usually singing. As advocates for the arts in the church continually remind us, from the prehistoric cave paintings onward, the arts have always been part of the communal expression of religion.

But if the arts are integral to worship, they are also frequently a battleground. During the iconoclastic controversies of the eighth and ninth centuries, and again during the Reformation, wars were fought, rulers were

15. Ibid., 4.

dethroned, and many people were killed over differing theological under-standings of the role of images in Christian worship. Today, there is merci-fully no actual bloodshed, but what is often termed "the worship wars" rend congregations over the relative merits of organs, choirs, and hymns sung from the pages of printed hymnals, on the one hand and drum sets, gui-tars, and praise music with lyrics presented electronically on screens, on the other. As Frank Burch Brown notes in *Good Taste, Bad Taste, and Christian Taste*, "Few things at present create more persistent conflict within Chris-tian congregations than differences over worship style, music, and media."[16]

One attempt to establish standards regarding the arts in the public worship of the church was the 1978 document, *Environment and Art in Catholic Worship*. Here, the National Conference of Catholic Bishops Com-mittee on Liturgy posited certain criteria for artworks to be used at Mass. Asserting that no particular style or period was superior to another, the bishops stressed the importance of both quality and appropriateness in any art used in worship. Quality, they wrote, is only perceived through contem-plation, which

> sees the hand stamp of the artist, the honesty and care that went into an object's making, the pleasing form and color and texture. Quality means love and care in the making of something, hon-esty and genuineness with any materials used, and the artist's special gift in producing a harmonious whole, a well-crafted work. This applies to music, architecture, sculpture, painting, pottery making, furniture making, as well as to dance, mime or drama—in other words, to any art form that might be employed in the liturgical environment or action.[17]

Along with the expectation that the arts used in worship be of a certain level of excellence, the bishops also insisted that even art work of the highest quality must also pass the test of appropriateness. They defined appropriate-ness in two ways. First, "it must be capable of bearing the weight of the mystery, awe, reverence, and wonder which the liturgical action expresses" and, second, "it must clearly serve (and not interrupt) ritual action which has its own structure, rhythm and movement."[18]

In their November 2000 meeting, the bishops approved a new docu-ment, *Built on Living Stones*, which described in greater detail certain as-pects of a church building and its furnishings, while reiterating the concern with quality and appropriateness regarding the arts used in worship. The

16. Brown, *Good Taste, Bad Taste*, 3.

17. National Conference of Catholic Bishops, *Environment and Art*, sec. 21.

18. Ibid.

ideas expressed in these documents have been highly influential, not just among Roman Catholics, but also among Protestants who are searching for ways to bring good, contemporary art into the worship environment.

But if quality—good art—is an important criterion for the art used in worship, the question of discerning that quality still remains. Where contemporary standards for good art outside the church stress the autonomy of art and artists, art for the church is asked to subordinate itself to liturgical needs. Likewise, artists who create works for the church often must subordinate their individual beliefs to express the collective faith of a congregation.

The tension between these ways of thinking about art is not easily resolved. When artists and congregations do not agree what criteria should prevail, the results can be divisive. A particularly problematic incident that exemplifies this is described by John Cook. Cook is, by training, an art historian. He served from 1992–2002 as the president of the Henry Luce Foundation, funding many initiatives regarding religion and the arts during his tenure. Some years earlier, he had become intimately involved in a controversy at St. Peter's Lutheran Church in Manhattan.

In 1984, abstract expressionist Willem de Kooning was invited to create an altarpiece for St. Peter's. The congregation was known for its commitment to high-quality, contemporary art, having earlier commissioned noted sculptor Louise Nevelson to create a small chapel. At the time of the events Cook describes, the congregation hosted frequent exhibitions, jazz concerts, theatrical performances, and other events that were well-attended and well-reviewed. So when the Art and Architecture Review Committee heard that de Kooning was interested in getting a commission to do a religious piece, it seemed a natural extension of the church's mission to invite him to create a triptych.

Unfortunately, for reasons that are difficult to discern, the Art and Architecture committee did not communicate very well with the rest of the congregation about its decision, and the Worship Committee took exception. Cook notes that the members of the committee who felt strongly that the commission should go forward pointed out how important the artist was in the world of the arts, how respected he was, the level of his mastery as an artist, and how noteworthy it would be in New York City for the church to own a de Kooning. He continues,

> [T]he arguments were between points of view rather than about a specific work of art, because nothing from the artist had been seen. The conflict was about ideas and process, not about an object of art. The process had caught a number of the members of the church by surprise. They had not been informed about

what was going on, and they felt as though something was being forced upon them. The committee had not acted on behalf of a fully informed constituency, with the approval and interest of that constituency. It allowed itself to appear as though it was doing something for the others, something that would be good for them. This unfortunately left the impression that they had an elevated level of good taste and aesthetic advantage, and should do what they were doing regardless of parish opinion.[19]

Although Cook does not say so directly, it appears that little or no discussion took place between the artist and the church about the church's theology and how the artist might help to embody that theological under-standing. It also seems that, once the commission was offered and accepted, there was no further contact between the artist and the church until the work was completed. Not surprisingly, when de Kooning delivered the work many members of the congregation objected both to the process and to the work that was ultimately presented. Since the intention was for the work to be installed in the main worship space, directly behind the altar, the Worship Committee was particularly concerned. In accord with the posi-tion outlined in *Environment and Art* that art in the worship environment should serve the liturgy rather than calling attention to itself, the committee registered a formal objection. Cook records the following excerpt from a document that noted liturgical scholar Gail Ramshaw wrote as chair of the Worship Committee:

> We in the Worship Committee agree with most liturgists that seldom in the history of Christendom has a church been im-proved as worship space by the addition of a great piece of art. In fact, the finer the art piece, the less likely that the art can serve the assembly in its attention to the liturgy.[20]

Cook sees Ramshaw's rejection of the piece as part of the long history of iconoclasm in the church. Having read some of Ramshaw's other writings in which she sensitively exegetes certain ancient artworks, I would suggest that she is not an iconoclast, but rather is defending the integrity of liturgy. When a large, imposing, evocative work of art enters a worship space, it tends to dominate the meanings and actions that can occur in its presence.

In response to this and other objections, Cook offers a careful reading of the actual painting as the artist's personal theological vision. He then ar-gues that just as the church values the contribution of individual preachers

19. Cook, "A Willem De Kooning Triptych," 61.
20. Ibid.

as well as the personal testimony of other church members, de Kooning's triptych should have a place in the midst of the worshipping community. Cook's position seems to be that the autonomy of the artist—or, at least, those artists who the art world considers important—should be paramount, regardless of the liturgical needs of the congregation. He writes,

> The church cannot properly afford to ignore the contribution of a culture's genuine artists. Their spirit is not the same as or exactly equivalent to any other type of human spirituality one could name. Artists are not necessarily any better than anyone else, but it is a matter of common observation that there are those artists who, with their medium, bring to bear in a world of material culture marvelous things that inform and enrich our lives and give us sources for life. And what it is that they have to offer us cannot be gained by any other measures. God's gift to artists is a range of gifts available to the world through artists. When the church, theological, liturgical, pastoral, and evangelical, ignores the best of what artists can show us, it ignores an essential aspect of the human spirit that is known best in and through artistic imaginations, objects, and forms. When we discover those moments when the life of the arts intersects divine revelation, and we see it for what it is, we shall understand when it is that art is theology.[21]

Despite the validity of Cook's impassioned defense of art as theology, it is not clear to me that a single artist's theological insight should be a permanent part of the worship environment any more than the same sermon should be preached or the same hymns be sung Sunday after Sunday. The great Medieval altarpieces, and even those of the Renaissance, for the most part did not distract from the liturgical action precisely because they were the expression of official church teaching. Similarly, icons, however fine, are not a distraction from the liturgy, but rather integral to it as visible expressions of the self-understanding of the Orthodox Church. De Kooning's work, on the other hand, was the self-expression of the individual artist. It was not made in consultation with the congregation nor was it intended to express the theological understandings of the church body for which it was made. As such, its permanent presence behind the altar could easily be a distraction from the purpose for which the congregation gathers, which is to worship God.

Unfortunately, none of the numerous articles, books, and worship resources published by the Roman Catholic Church, Protestant

---

21. Ibid., 73.

denominational bodies, or various experts can give definitive answers regarding the appropriateness of any given art work to any given worship setting. This always must be worked out case by case, hymn by hymn, Sunday by Sunday, as congregations learn what is and what is not possible with the musical, visual, cultural, and physical resources available to them. As I once heard someone say, what is appropriate at the cathedral just isn't going to work at Saint Joe's-by-the-Gas-Station.

Artists in Worship

The ongoing tension regarding quality in the arts is often posed in terms of excellence versus sincerity. David Taylor recounts a story of a woman in the church he attended as a child. She liked to sing, but each time she came forward, she would say, "I don't know how to read. I don't know how to sing. I don't know how to play. But for the glory of God!" Taylor continues,

> And that's precisely what we got: a poorly played, poorly sung musical piece that strained our ability to perceive any trace of God's glory. We loved her dearly, and there was no doubt that her heart was in the right place. But her actions betrayed a dismissive view of art that revealed something of her view about God. And, I submit, there is no evidence in Scripture that God pits the sincerity of our hearts over against the excellency of artmaking.[22]

There are countless stories of singers like the one in Taylor's story, or organists (or entire congregations) who only know a few hymns and refuse to learn others. Taylor argues that art like this gives one a distorted view not only of what art can be, but also of who God is.

On the other hand, too heavy an insistence on artistic excellence leaves no room for the untrained voices of the congregation, the drawings of children, the joyful participation of each member of the Body of Christ. As Taylor puts it, "Sometimes in the life of the church, aesthetic excellence will not be the most important. A different excellency will be needed." Sometimes, he says, we need

> to let our children dance before us. They will be anything but nuanced, and some kid will make faces at his mother while another dances to the beat in her own head.... Even as we witness unpolished dancing, *here in our corporate gathering* [emphasis in original], we will be reminded that our goal as Christians is

22. Taylor, "Dangers of Artmaking," 150.

not to be polished and impressive, but to be true. The children dancing before the God who in Jesus of Nazareth pulls the little ones into the middle of his preaching reminds us that we are all clumsy, unhinged humans. We too step on others' toes. We too need grace. So the kids' dance becomes not an interruption to the "serious" work of the pastor, but rather an occasion for the gospel to penetrate our hearts with truth.[23]

This kind of excellence is often ignored in congregations that equate the aesthetic experience with experiencing the presence of God. In such churches, a professionally proficient choir led by a paid, professional conductor and accompanied by a paid, professional organist sings so beautifully that no one else dares to join in. Or, if the local custom is praise and worship, the instruments and voices of the leaders are so highly amplified that the congregation cannot hear itself sing. I do not mean to imply that we should never pay musicians or other artists in the church, but rather that professional artists need to make sure that there is also room for full congregational participation. In too many churches, the kind of star system that so pervades the secular culture convinces the untrained and untalented to remain passive consumers, receiving in silent awe whatever the performers provide.

This tension between well-meaning but undisciplined art-making, on the one hand, and an aesthetic excellence that is more about the art and the artistry than about helping the congregation worship God together, on the other, raises the question of the appropriate role of artists in worship. If liturgy—worship—is the work of the people, must all music in worship be reduced to simple songs that everyone can sing, all dance be simple steps and arm-waving, all visual art be awkward banners made by the children? Is there a place for the highly trained, professional artist in congregational worship?

Judith Rock argues that there is, indeed, a place for professional performing artists in addition to direct, congregational participation. Concerned with what she sees as an emphasis among her colleagues on dance as self-expression and devotional practice, she writes,

> [T]here are several excellent books on congregational movement, but none that focuses exclusively on theatrical dance and its implications for the church. Though some advocates for dance in the church feel that professional theatrical dance

23. Ibid., 159.

creates barriers between people, rather than "building community," I believe that there is a place in the church for dance as performance.[24]

Noting wryly that Bach's *St. Matthew Passion* and Handel's *Messiah* do not seem to hinder the creation of community among churchgoers, she offers encouragement to artists who are concerned that performance as such detracts from congregational participation. Aware of the dangers of calling attention to themselves rather than to the glory of God, such artists want to differentiate between offering their art as a part of congregational worship and performing at a concert or recital. Rock, however, argues that performance is quite different from self-aggrandizement.

> The dancer as performer is one who subordinates the self to the art of dancing, serving choreographic and technical forms so that communication can take place through a disciplined, articulate body. The professional accomplishes more virtuosic feats of technique, but the responsible amateur brings no less commitment to the craft of dance at his or her chosen level. Technique is essential, because the point of performance is not self-expression, the giving of the self to the watchers; the point is the giving of the dance to the watchers. Neither in the theater nor in the church can one get by on sincerity.[25]

While Rock writes about dancers, her argument is equally applicable to musicians, actors, and any other artists who are concerned with issues of performance. To those who insist that performance, as such, is problematic in worship, she replies,

> If we cannot admit performance as a valid activity in worship, we have to conceive of the dancer as doing something else while we watch; and so we say that the dancer is not performing but praying. This perspective tends to privatize dance in the setting in which, of all others, dance ought to intend and achieve a strong relationship with the watching community. It is also denies the rich potential of dance as a performing art for the church, limiting the congregation's understanding of what they are seeing, and the artist's potential offerings to the community.[26]

Rock articulates a role for artists in worship that neither minimizes their commitment to technical and aesthetic excellence nor encourages an

24. Rock and Mealy, *Performer as Priest and Prophet*, xiii.

25. Ibid., 80.

26. Ibid., 91–92.

aestheticism that subordinates the needs of the worshipping community to the demands of art. For Rock, and for many artists who work within congregations, performance is a valid mode of proclaiming the word of God, of making the invisible realm of God palpably present through the physical matter with which they work. There is room both for the professional artist and for the untrained and untalented in the Body of Christ. Discerning the best way for both to offer their gifts is a matter for both prayer and conversation.

The Matter Matters

The arts are grounded in physical matter. Whether it is the ethereal sound of the column of air vibrating inside a Native American flute or the sensuous movements of a dancer's body as she leaps across the floor or the hard, polished, granite surface of the Vietnam Veteran's Memorial, every artwork is the result of human manipulation of the material world. Because of Christianity's historic distrust of the material, which is seen as antithetical to the spiritual, this grounding in matter is at the heart of Christianity's ambivalence about the arts.

From the time of John of Damascus onward, however, the paired doctrines of the Incarnation and of the goodness of Creation have been used to justify the church's embrace of the arts. In 730 CE, in response to those who equated the veneration of icons with idolatry, John of Damascus defended their use in his treatise, *On Holy Images*. John argued against the charge that because icons were mere matter they were unable to mediate a connection with the divine by asserting the unity of Christ's human and divine nature. Reminding his readers that, in the Incarnation, Christ did not take on flesh like a garment, but that His very flesh is divine and endures after its assumption, he shows that while it is impossible to depict the First Person of the Trinity, it is possible to depict the visible flesh of the invisible God. A few paragraphs later, after explaining that the Second Commandment against making graven images applied only to attempts to make images of the incorporeal and uncircumscribed God, he makes it clear that in venerating icons he does not worship matter, but rather the God of matter, who became matter for our sakes. He continues,

> I honour all matter besides, and venerate it. Through it, filled, as it were, with a divine power and grace, my salvation has come to me. Was not the thrice happy and thrice blessed wood of the Cross matter? Was not the sacred and holy mountain of Calvary matter? What of the life-giving rock, the Holy Sepulchre, the source of our resurrection: was it not matter? Is not the most

holy book of the Gospels matter? Is not the blessed table matter which gives us the Bread of Life? Are not the gold and silver matter, out of which crosses and altar-plate and chalices are made? And before all these things, is not the body and blood of our Lord matter? . . . Do not despise matter, for it is not despicable.[27]

For John of Damascus, not merely the image depicted, but also the very paint and wood out of which the image is made have a certain holiness. He insists that the materials with which the holy image is made are good because they are part of God's good creation and that, in the Incarnation, Christ demonstrates the intrinsic goodness of matter. Finally, just as Christ's divine and human natures are inseparable, so, too, is the holy image inseparable from the matter which bears it.

These ideas continue to inform those who argue for the importance of the arts to the life of the church. If matter is good, the materiality of art is an important part both of its symbolic and theological value. However, Jeremy Begbie laments that much of the discussion in theological and philosophical aesthetics has moved away from the actual material of art. He writes,

> In modern aesthetics, this shift away from the material has taken a myriad of forms. . . . One of the most prominent is a neo-Romantic focus on inner emotional dispositions, where the main task of art is seen as "expressing feelings." Another is . . . that an object of art is the externalisation of an inner vision idea in the mind or imagination of the artist. But whatever form it takes, remarkably persistent in Western aesthetics has been the tendency to subordinate the sensuous and material to the spiritual and immaterial.[28]

Not all theologians hold this view. In contrast, according to Begbie, Hans-Georg Gadamer argues that the material aspects of a work of art are integrally related to our experience of it.

> Gadamer insists that we do not react merely to the form of a work of art as opposed to its content; rather we respond to it as something which mediates meaning as a unity. Moreover, the experience of art leads not simply to self-awareness but to genuine knowledge. Art, to pick up Anthony Thiselton's paraphrase of Gadamer, "is not merely a matter of subjective consciousness, but of ontological disclosure." In this disclosure, *we*

27. John of Damascus, *Defense of Icons*, 16–17.
28. Begbie, *Voicing Creation's Praise*, 191–92.

are questioned—our self-understanding is revealed, illuminated and challenged.[29]

Whatever theologians and philosophers may say, artists know that form and content, material and idea, are inseparable. In the twentieth century, this awareness became more pronounced as artists experimented with new materials and new approaches. Richard Serra's massive, Cor-ten steel sculptures depend as much on our experience of the metal as an industrial material as they do on the contrast between their sheer weight and the delicate balance between the various elements. Claes Oldenburg's oversized replicas of everyday objects like electric fans and bathtubs depend on the fact that they are made of soft vinyl as well as their size for their humor and sly critique of consumer culture. Jackson Pollock's acclaimed drip paintings were, among other things, a refutation of the idea that a painting must be an illusion, a picture of something that is not actually present. Instead, they were an assertion that a painting is, at its essence, nothing but paint on canvas. Even a Conceptualist like Sol Lewitt was very specific about the materials and processes that were to be used to realize his ideas, carefully training his studio assistants to make manifest the concepts described in his sketches. For poets, the sound of a word is at least as important as its meaning. For musicians, the meaning and emotional charge of a composition changes when it is played on the piano rather than the guitar. A character in a play is known differently when embodied by different actors. In the arts, the matter always matters.

Indeed, rather than moving away from the material, many contemporary artists make the materials in which they work a significant element in the meaning of their work. Janine Antoni's *Lick and Lather*, consisting of several self-portrait busts made of chocolate and an equal number made of soap, is the quintessential melding of idea and substance. In an interview transcribed from the PBS television series *Art 21: Art in the Twenty-First Century*, Antoni describes making a mold of her head and shoulders, casting it in each of the materials, and then altering the chocolate ones by licking them and washing away some of the surface of the ones made from soap. Questioning the reasons why artists make self-portraits and why she, herself has done so, she says that the obvious response is to immortalize oneself. However, she continues,

> my materials are ephemeral, so I'm kind of trying to work against the grain of that. . . . And the other answer I gave myself about "Why make a self-portrait?" is this idea of creating a

29. Ibid., 199.

public image of yourself, an image that you were presenting to the world. And I guess my question was: is that an accurate description of the self? And are we more ourselves alone at home eating a meal or in the bathtub, these everyday activities? So, that's where I got the idea to work with the chocolate and the soap.[30]

Following this train of thought, the artist makes a conscious connection between the repetitive nature of eating and bathing, and more formal rituals. Speaking of the process of eating the chocolate and smoothing the sculptures made of soap, she says,

I was thinking about everyday rituals like eating and bathing but also other rituals. Certainly the Eucharist is about eating the body, so that also comes to mind. . . . It's interesting to think about cleaning and purity and just washing as kind of ritual and its bigger meaning. I think this idea of cleaning is associated with purity. I think I was thinking about purity in terms of woman, and that is a kind of idealized state, which of course is in contrast to the chocolate. . . . The brown and white . . . it comes from the material. So, I was not so much thinking of my self in a dark color and my self in a white color. I'm thinking of my self in chocolate and my self in soap. But there is something beautiful about the way that, in her purity, she disappears.[31]

Not all artists are as articulate or as deliberate about the relationship between the material properties of their works as Antoni is. Still, all are aware on some level of the ways that physical matter shapes their practice. Composers choose certain instruments, certain tonal qualities, to express particular musical ideas; actors change their voice and their gait to portray particular characters; poets choose words for their aural characteristics when spoken aloud or for their look on the page as much as for their meaning as language; potters choose stoneware or porcelain for the particular character each clay body brings to the finished product. An artwork is not a simplistic illustration of a free-floating intellectual proposition, but rather a concrete embodiment in which the matter in which it is incarnated matters both to the artist in the process of making and to the audience in receiving it.

30. Antoni, "Lick and Lather."
31. Ibid.

Icons and the Western Church

Icons have a special place in the conversation about the church and the arts. For devout, Orthodox Christians, an icon is much more than a picture, but rather Holy Scripture in a visual form. In the Orthodox understanding, an iconographer is like a scribe who carefully transcribes the text before him, always careful to avoid introducing any error. As the handwriting of one scribe differs from that of another, yet the sacred text remains the same, so some specifics of one icon of, for instance, Christ Pantocrator, may differ from another, while the proclamation that Christ is Lord of all remains unchanged. Like a sacrament, an icon is understood to participate in the reality to which it points. Icons are, it is said, windows or doorways through which eternity and everyday reality may meet. Unlike a contemporary artwork that is understood as the individualized expression of the artist, icons are the collective expression of the Body of Christ.

In Orthodox thought, an image is only an icon if it conforms to Orthodox teaching. Leonid Ouspensky, arguably the foremost authority on the theology of the icon, writes,

> The icon is not just a simple image, nor a decoration, nor even an illustration of Holy Scripture. It is something greater. It is an object of worship and an integral part of the liturgy. The Church sees in its holy image not simply one of the aspects of Orthodox teaching, but the expression of Orthodoxy in its totality, the expression of Orthodoxy as such. The icon is one of the manifestations of the holy Tradition of the Church, similar to the written and oral traditions. As we shall see in our study, the "icon," according to the teaching of the Church, corresponds entirely to the "word" of Scripture.[32]

For Ouspensky, it is inconceivable that an icon should be painted by anyone who is not a devout, participating member of the Orthodox church. Whatever art historians or other critics may say about style or quality, Ouspensky maintains that in the Church the only criterion by which to judge an icon is Orthodoxy. "Is an image Orthodox or not? Does it correspond to the teaching of the Church or not?"[33]

According to this definition, the only image that may properly be called an icon is one which is made for and used by those who are theologically Orthodox. However, for a variety of reasons, icons entered in a new way the communal imagination and practice of Western Christians, Protestants

32. Ouspensky, *Theology of the Icon*, 8.
33. Ibid., 12.

and Roman Catholics alike, in the latter part of the twentieth century. This change in perception opened new possibilities for iconography, but also raised some new questions regarding how icons might be used and understood for those whose theological understandings differ from Orthodoxy.

One of the people has been influential in the spread of icons beyond the Orthodox churches is Robert Lentz, a Franciscan friar with Orthodox roots. In the 1970s, Lentz studied traditional iconography at Holy Transfiguration Monastery in Brookline, Massachusetts. There, he learned to paint the standard icons of Christ, the Virgin, and Orthodox saints. Using what he learned from the traditional iconographers, and incorporating elements of the visual vocabularies of other cultures as well, over time he extended the tradition to portray the holy figures in surprising new ways. For example, his *Christ of Maryknoll*, painted for the Maryknoll missioners who serve poor and oppressed people all over the world, shows Christ looking like a Latin American farm peasant. His face is seen through a barbed wire fence, his bleeding hands pulling on the wires. Lentz writes,

> The icon does not make clear which side of the fence Christ is on. Is he imprisoned or are we? Through our cultural institutions and personal lives we all place barriers between ourselves and true happiness. We and our institutions also try to imprison Christ in various ways, to tame him and the dangerous memories he would bring us of our goals and ideals. The Christ of Maryknoll cannot be tamed.[34]

In his long career as an iconographer, Lentz has painted icons of many people who are not recognized as saints in either the Orthodox or the Roman Catholic tradition, but who have shaped our world in important ways. While these renditions of persons who are unlikely to ever be officially canonized, as well as his non-traditional renderings of Jesus, Mary, and other Biblical figures, would not be considered authentic icons according to Ouspensky's criteria, they are received as icons in many non-Orthodox settings. Whether Lentz is painting more traditional images as commissions in Roman Catholic and Protestant churches, or asking us to consider in what way Albert Einstein, the Oglala holy man Black Elk, or Johann Sebastian Bach might be considered a saint, he uses the visual language of icons to invite the viewer into contemplation and connection with the holy, eternal realm.

The example set by Lentz opened the way for many others. One whose work is widely known is Mark Dukes, whose image, *The Dancing Saints*, surrounds the rotunda at St. Gregory of Nyssa Episcopal Church in San Francisco. The seventy saints in the mural were chosen by members of the

---

34. Lentz and Gateley, *Christ in the Margins*, 11.

congregation, and include such figures as Malcolm X, Queen Elizabeth, Rumi, and Ella Fitzgerald. Another image by Dukes is seen on the east wall at Saint Gregory's behind the presider's chair. Said to be based on St. Gregory's Commentary on the Song of Songs, it depicts the marriage of Christ and the human soul.[35] In it, a dark-skinned woman, who may be meant to be the personification of Wisdom or may allude to the Holy Spirit, holds out her arms in blessing above Christ and his bride. Like some of the images painted by Lentz, many of those painted by Dukes would not be acceptable in an Orthodox setting. Nonetheless, both the congregation and the artist refer to these works as icons, and experience them as doorways opening into eternity.

Unlike Lentz, Dukes is not traditionally trained. Rather, he is an artist whose life took him on a quest through various religious traditions. In an interview several years ago, he spoke of coming to San Francisco to join a meditation group centered around the teachings of a Hindu guru. But, he says,

> I clearly felt in my heart that Jesus was my way. . . . Soon after that, I made a decision which I think God has blessed. I felt I want to do art again and I want it to be something that will glorify God. I decided "I am going to do icons.". . . I called up [a monastery] and said I want to do some icons for you. . . . I was there maybe six or seven months and I did two icons. Sister Vladimira taught me to do icons on ostrich eggs with scratch carving.[36]

Other than a few lessons with the otherwise unidentified Sister Vladimira and with another teacher at an art center in San Francisco, Dukes is essentially self-taught as an iconographer. He continues,

> I am not Eastern Orthodox, yet I feel I am doing something that is very Eastern Orthodox. I really feel the Spirit speaks in iconography and it speaks in me. . . . I didn't have a formal education in iconography. I felt God blessed me and gave me to understand iconography. The true teaching of icons is in the iconographic records themselves. Just looking at icons you see just what the iconographer is about. You may not know how they achieved a certain effect, like with egg tempera, but you can learn these things. The hardest thing is to have the spirit of

---

35. Barger, "The Light Within."
36. Ibid.

iconography. If you have the spirit of iconography then the rest
is just technical. I learned as I could.[37]

Like the icons made by Lentz and Dukes, the orthodoxy of icons
painted by Peter Pearson might be questioned, although he himself deeply
respects the Orthodox tradition. At one time a member of a Benedictine
community, Pearson now serves an Episcopal parish in Pennsylvania and
says that he has been studying iconography for nearly forty years. After
fifteen years of self-taught practice, he studied under a number of Russian
and Greek iconographers who are now working in the US, integrating the
techniques he learned from them into his own iconographic practice.[38]
While careful to observe the technical rules and canons of iconography,
some of his more recent icons address subjects that are outside of the Orthodox world, such as Saint Therese of Lisieux, Saint Francis of Assisi, Saint
Thomas à Becket, and the indigenous Mexican Juan Diego with his vision of
the Virgin of Guadalupe.

In addition to accepting numerous commissions from churches and
individuals, Pearson offers popular retreats and workshops, collectively
known as *A Brush with God*, at retreat centers and churches all over the
country. In the calm, Spirit-infused atmosphere that he fosters by beginning and ending each day with communal prayer, and by suggesting that
his students treat each brushstroke as an offering to God, Pearson shares
the techniques of icon painting with all comers, regardless of religious affiliation or previous artistic experience. Thanks to Pearson and a number
of other iconographers who teach workshops like his, what once had been
a closely held secret, open only to those willing and able to enter a long,
arduous, and often monastic apprenticeship, has become widely available to
anyone with the time and money to pay for a week, a weekend, or a series
of weekly lessons under the tutelage of someone who claims to know the
ancient ways.

Although most of those who have learned to make icons in this way
are not Orthodox, there has been very little discussion of what icons might
mean to Western Christians, especially Protestants. Two authors who have
tried to do so are Anglican Linette Martin and United Methodist Elder
Russel M. Hart. Martin, a professional journalist, embarked on a deep and
passionate study of iconography towards the end of her life. In her book,
Sacred Doorways, she set out the basic meanings of icons in a way that is
approachable for Anglicans like her as well as for other Protestants, but

37. Ibid. See also http://deacondukes.blogspot.com/2009/01/saint-gregorys-danc-
ing-saints-icon.html for photographs of the Dancing Saints.

38. Pearson, "Vitae."

essentially reiterating the Orthodox teachings.[39] In *The Icon Through Western Eyes*, Hart recounts his own journey learning to paint icons. Describing each of the traditional icons that he had worked with at the time of writing the book, he filters the Orthodox interpretation through his Protestant understanding. Reminding his readers that the pre-eminent art form for the Protestant church is preaching, Hart suggests that Protestants have a greater toleration for bad visual art than they do for bad proclamation of the Word. He writes,

> The Protestant West retains a suspicion of images which has been part of its very fabric since the time of the Reformation. This does not mean, however, that the artistic representations of Christ, other Biblical characters and church leaders are absent from Protestant houses of worship. But having no Tradition to follow, much "Protestant" art has followed the conventions of the age, and thus has a superficial character when it is new, and appears sentimental when conventions and taste change.[40]

While Hart argues for the visual as a means for receiving revealed truth, he makes no attempt to articulate a Protestant theology of icons beyond the simple assertion that Orthodoxy has something important to show us.

The problem with this formulation is that if icons are, as the Orthodox insist, the visual embodiment of Orthodox theology, importing them non-reflectively into Western worship and devotional life ignores the very real differences between Orthodox and Western theological understandings of both icons in particular and sacraments in general. This is particularly true for Protestants who, for the most part, doctrinally reject the very sacramentalism that is inherent in the Orthodox theology of the icon. For over five hundred years, many Protestant denominations have rejected the notion that Christ is physically present in the bread and wine of Holy Communion, positing instead that the eucharistic elements are mere aids to remembering the life, death, and resurrection of Jesus Christ. How, then, is it possible to reconcile this understanding with the Orthodox belief that the holy person is truly present through the mediation of the icon? Other questions may be raised by the more subtle, but still very real, differences between Roman Catholic and Orthodox beliefs.

In asking these questions, I am not suggesting that Western Christians reject the use of icons. Rather, I am hoping to open a conversation about what icons might mean for Western Christians, even if what they are found

---

39. Martin, *Sacred Doorways*, xv–xvii passim.

40. Hart, *The Icon Through Western Eyes*, 24.

to mean is not the same thing as what they mean to the Orthodox. For nearly a thousand years, the Orthodox have held the iconographic tradition in trust for the entire Church. As the rest of the Church reappropriates that trust, it must be done with thoughtfulness and care. Newly examined and carefully considered Roman Catholic and Protestant theologies of icons can enrich the understanding of all the members of Christ's Body, rather than assuming that what one branch has asserted, all must believe.

Art as Spiritual Discipline

However the theological issues raised by the use of icons outside of the Orthodox context are resolved, it is clear that icons may serve as a doorway through which the arts may enter more fully into the life of churches that are suspicious of the arts more generally. Whatever else icons may be, they are a form of art that takes Scripture and Christian life seriously. Both for those who learn to paint them, and for those who merely enjoy looking at them, they are an invitation to quiet, meditative prayer regardless of one's theological position about them.

Many years ago, when I began my own study of iconography, I was given a small piece of paper with the heading "Rules for the Icon Painter." I do not know the where this list came from originally, but since then, I have seen similar lists of rules, or spiritual practices, that differ in detail, but not in general outline. Whether these sets of practices derive from antiquity or are a modern invention based on what someone thought must have been the case, they are currently being passed on to students of iconography as if they were as ancient as the earliest icon or as authoritative as the Rule of Saint Benedict. However, for the purposes of such study, the origin does not really matter, as such lists are clearly in the spirit of both Orthodox iconography and more general Christian spirituality. This is the list as I received it:

1. Before starting work, make the sign of the Cross; pray in silence, and pardon your enemies.

2. Work with care on every detail of your icon, as if you were working in front of the Lord Himself.

3. During work, pray in order to strengthen yourself physically and spiritually; avoid above all useless words and keep silence.

4. Pray in particular to the Saint whose face you are painting. Keep your mind from distractions, and the Saint will be close to you.

5. When you have to choose a color, stretch out your hands interiorly to the Lord and ask his counsel.

6. Do not be jealous of your neighbor's work; his success is your success too.

7. When your icon is finished, thank God that His Mercy granted you the grace to paint the Holy images.

8. Have your icon blessed by putting it on the altar. Be the first to pray before it, before giving it to others

9. Never forget:

- The joy of spreading icons in the world.

- The joy of the work of icon painting

- The joy of giving the Saint the possibility to shine through his icon.

- The joy of being in union with the Saint whose face you are painting.

While many of these rules apply quite specifically to painting icons, their underlying spirit could be applied to any artistic endeavor, turning it into an explicitly spiritual practice. Indeed, many artists, Christian and otherwise, understand the studio as holy ground, a place where they are open to an experience of the divine. It is not a matter of media, but of intention. When musicians, dancers, poets, or actors begin to practice with the intention to offer their work and themselves to God, then the place where they work becomes a holy place and the creative process itself can become a devotional practice or spiritual discipline.

Many Christians are familiar with the concept of spiritual disciplines. Typically, these involve setting aside a certain portion of each day for reading Scripture, for prayer and meditation, and for self-examination in light of the Gospel. Other spiritual practices may include fasting, making retreats, reading devotional literature, journaling, tithing, service, confession, keeping the Sabbath, and many others. What is common to all of these is the sense that one is doing it in order to know and do the will of God, to practice being aware of the presence of God at all times.

For many artists, the creative process seems remarkably similar to the spiritual journey that the more traditional disciplines are meant to undergird. The initial insight or inspiration for a new artwork is often experienced as something akin to an epiphany, a vision, an experience of the immediate presence of God. This vision, however, is momentary, leaving the artist, like the spiritual pilgrim, to work out the details in fear and trembling.

This process of working out the details, trying first this and then that, making repetitive marks, learning a new piano part, memorizing lines, or whatever practice is applicable to the particular art form, can become at times dry, boring, and unpleasant. Like Teresa of Avila's spiritually arid periods, or the dark night of the soul described by John of the Cross, the long slog of bringing a new artwork from initial vision to fully developed, concrete reality is often so difficult or so tedious that there is the constant temptation to just give up, to believe that there is nothing worthwhile in the project. And, as in the spiritual journey, there are just enough consolations, just enough moments of new understanding or deep connection with the mystery that underlies everything, that the memory and promise of these gifts keep the artist going on even when the obstacles seem insurmountable.

It is because of this widespread recognition of the similarity between the artist's path and the spiritual journey that art-making has begun to be added to the list of the more classical spiritual disciplines. Consider, for example, the immense popularity of Julia Cameron's book, *The Artist's Way*. First published in 1992, it was a nonfiction best seller, and has been reprinted many times. The author, who was herself a struggling poet, novelist, and screenwriter, wrote out of her own experience of feeling blocked and of finding ways to free her creative powers. While Cameron was careful to keep her advice non-sectarian, she was clear about the connection between spirituality and creativity. She introduces herself like this:

> For a decade now, I have taught a spiritual workshop aimed at freeing people's creativity. I have taught artists and nonartists, painters and filmmakers and homemakers and lawyers—anyone interested in living more creatively through practicing the art of creative living. While using, teaching, and sharing tools I have found, devised, divined, and been handed, I have seen blocks dissolved and lives transformed by the simple process of engaging the Great Creator in discovering and recovering our creative powers.[41]

Cameron's techniques found an audience among all sorts of people who believed that there was something in the artist's way of life that could help them on their spiritual journey. Today, there are web sites, workbooks, and innumerable Artist's Way workshops through which people encourage one another to explore their creative potential.

Even before Cameron's book, Betty Edwards relied on then-recent discoveries about the differentiation of the brain's functions into left-brain logic and right-brain intuition to popularize her techniques for teaching drawing to both children and adults. Her 1979 volume, *Drawing on the Right Side of the Brain*, was followed soon thereafter with her equally well-received

41. Cameron, *Artist's Way*, xxi.

Drawing on the Artist Within. As with *The Artist's Way*, the *Drawing* books give people who are not artists a way to explore the creativity and freedom they had as children but had given up as they took on adult responsibilities. While Edwards did not make an explicit connection between art and spiritual life, her descriptions of the artist's way of seeing sound almost mystical.

> In drawing, there is always the sense that if you can just look closely enough, see deeply enough, some secret is going to be revealed to you, some insight into the nature of the world. Learning through drawing, therefore, can fill a lifetime, since such secrets lie at the bottom of a bottomless well, and the searcher never wishes the search to end. . . . By looking outward and seeing the world around you in the artist's mode of seeing, you gain insight into yourself. Conversely, by looking inward to find the artist within, you gain insight into the world outside yourself.[42]

Many of the techniques shared by Cameron and Edwards would be familiar to anyone who has gone to art school or done acting warm-ups or participated in creative writing workshops. Others were drawn from various forms of psychotherapeutic practice. Still others are virtually identical to traditional spiritual disciplines. Presenting them as exercises which would allow ordinary people to unleash their bound-up creativity proved immensely popular. Clearly, Cameron and Edwards have reached an audience that yearns to find its inner artist.

This audience is as present in churches, both Catholic and Protestant, as it is in the general population. In addition to the many Artists Way study groups and meditative drawing classes following the Edwards method based in congregations, books like Robert Wuthnow's *Creative Spirituality: The Way of the Artist*, Lois Huey-Heck and Jim Kalnin's *The Spirituality of Art*, Michael Sullivan's *Windows into the Soul: Art as Spiritual Expression*, and many others attest to the widespread conviction that art can be a pathway towards spiritual growth. As Robert Wuthnow puts it,

> [T]he perfection of art always involves discipline, and the practice of art thus becomes a model for understanding spiritual discipline as well. . . . Many artists speak of their work as a form of meditation. For some, the sheer rhythm of the daily routine brings them closer to the essence of their being. Writing all morning or practicing for the next musical performance requires mental and emotional toughness. For others, art is so much an expression of who they are that its quality depends on introspection, prayer, reading, listening, or finding other ways

42. Edwards, *Drawing on the Artist Within*, 231.

to reflect about life. Many artists emphasize the importance of staying with a single routine in order to learn it well. For spiritual dabblers, the insight these artists provide is that persistence and hard work may still be the best way to attain spiritual growth.[43]

With books like these, and an ever-growing number of arts ministries of varying descriptions all over the country, it is as if the church as a whole had suddenly woken up during a long, wordy service, noticed that it had been sitting still for a very long time, and, shaking its collective head in wonder, said, "There must be another way to get to know God."

There is a certain strangeness to this turn of events. In a culture that, both inside and outside the church, has historically had a profound distrust of the arts, it is very odd to think that sober-minded lawyers, physicians, scientists, and business executives, as well as their assistants, secretaries, bookkeepers, and receptionists, came to believe that artists held the secret path to the sacred. It becomes somewhat less odd, however, when one realizes how constricted and stressful each day, week, month, and year has become. For those who have achieved a certain amount of financial security and yet find their lives hollow and empty, and for those whose financial position is so precarious that any setback might send them toppling over the brink into poverty, artists seem to have a kind of freedom that they can only dream of.

For many, artists seem to know something important that is missing in their own lives. They find something both ennobling and salvific in creativity, whether it is drawing a picture or writing a poem or acting out a story from Scripture. So if they cannot become full-fledged artists, at least they can allow themselves to be creative, to spend time in a studio setting learning new techniques and playing with materials, to know themselves as made in the image of a creative God. Just as the regular practice of the classical spiritual disciplines can make a person more attuned to God's presence in everyday life, so, too, can the regular practice of any of the arts be a pathway towards knowing God, provided that one is predisposed to find God there.

The Good in Bad Art

One of the side effects of so many people using art as a spiritual discipline is the proliferation of bad art in the church. Not only are the children invited to dance in worship, but every person in the congregation who paints an awkward portrait of Jesus, writes a didactic drama, or composes a tuneless praise chorus often sees no difference between their offerings and that of serious artists like Judith Rock or T. S. Eliot. Like the woman in David Taylor's

43. Wuthnow, *Creative Spirituality*, 9–10.

story, who enjoyed singing but did it so poorly that the congregation merely endured it out of courtesy, the heartfelt but clumsy efforts of an art neophyte that are properly applauded at a retreat or weekend workshop usually cannot stand up to the scrutiny of colder eyes in a setting that separates the result from the context and process of its making.

These works do, however, have a place in the life of the Body of Christ. From time to time and for some well-understood purpose, that place might be worship or an all-church exhibition, but, more often, the more appropriate place for beginners to share their projects is in more protected settings. Initially, such a setting would be the class or workshop or small group in which the project is made. There, the artwork grows out of an immediate, shared experience.

One such experience occurred at a recent faculty retreat, where we were asked to reflect on our images of church. In a gesture familiar to many who have been on church retreats, visioning committees, or even some Bible studies, the dean put construction paper, markers, scissors, tape, and crayons on tables around the room where we had been meeting. She said that in the next fifteen minutes or so, we should make something that would be a visual representation of our idea of what church is or might be.

The response to this request was not surprising. Some people suddenly got deep into other conversations and ignored the whole thing. Others obediently sat around the tables, but stared at the materials with that deer-in-the-headlights look that people who don't think of themselves as artistic get when confronted with the demand to "be creative." The "artistic" ones dove in, happily playing with whatever caught their fancy. Sooner or later, most got in touch with their inner child, or, at least, considered what their own school-age children might do in the same situation. For some amount of timeless time, professors of systematic theology, biblical interpretation, pastoral care, and Christian formation began to scribble or cut or tear paper or draw more-or-less conventional symbols that conveyed, in some mysterious way, the ideas that had been circulating around the room in words all morning.

The results were visually predictable. My colleagues are accomplished scholars, much more accustomed to putting their ideas into words than into pictures. While some are dancers, musicians, or actors as well as theologians, none of the projects I saw that afternoon evidenced any engagement with the visual or conceptual discourse that fills galleries and museums of contemporary art. Like the children's art that they resemble both in material and in style, the things my colleagues made that afternoon were not particularly well-designed or well-crafted. They were, however, the products of sophisticated minds, and they carried more meaning than one might suspect at first glance.

At the end of the art-making session, we were invited to gather in groups of five or six to talk about what we had done. As each person shared his or her intention, the others listened closely, adding their own observations about what they saw in the colors, shapes, and symbols, and the relationships among these elements. A kind of passionate poetry emerged out of the conversation, in which a seemingly simple diagram stood for such complex notions as "the church is the place of struggle in the heart of God," or "the church is a spiral shell that draws us into a center where the divine voice may be heard." As people talked about their experience of drawing or tearing or cutting and pasting, it was clear that their ideas had changed in the process. New ideas had been engendered not by manipulating words, but by the physical manipulation of matter.

I do not want to say that this is the only, or the best, or even the most accessible way that art intersects with the church. It is, however, a tool, a method, one of many invitations into the truth that the Church already proclaims and that artists know in their hands and eyes and ears and bodies: that the Word of God is much, much more than words. In joining words to matter, these simple artworks became a sacrament, the outward and invisible sign of an inward and invisible grace. The question was not whether these artworks were good or bad in some objective, art-critical sense, but rather the recognition of the good way in which they contributed to building up the Body of Christ. [44]

Art and Sabbath

The artworks made by my faculty colleagues were in response to a specific question about the church. The presence of the arts in the church is often justified as a way to glorify God, as a means to proclaim the gospel, as a way to promote justice, or even as a path to self-knowledge. While all of these are worthwhile goals, the primary use of art is simply to be itself. Just as we are commanded to keep the Sabbath, not in order to be more productive, but to rest our bodies and our souls, to simply delight in the presence of God, so are we given the capacity and the yearning for art. In our results-driven world, we have to tell ourselves consciously to slow down, to pay attention, to listen for the God's voice. Like sitting on the front porch of a retreat lodge

---

44. Portions of this story have appeared on the author's blog *A Studio Incarnate*, as "Visions of Church" posted on August 23, 2011. The original version may be seen at http://luce-arts-and-religion.blogspot.com/2011/08/visions-of-church.html.

and staring at the tree line, or strolling along the seashore watching the waves go in and out, participation in the arts—whether as practitioner or as audience—has the potential to open us to a wider, deeper reality.

In a way, making art is like gardening. While some gardeners are serious about growing their own food, others simply rake and dig and pull weeds for the sake of a few, fleeting flowers in the springtime. Unlike artists, who so often feel conflicted about the value of their work, gardeners generally feel virtuous about their work regardless of whether the plants they tend produce food for the body or food for the soul. After all, they might say, they are keeping in touch with the earth and the natural world.

It is not coincidental that the Bible tells us that God planted a garden in Eden and placed the man and the woman in it, to tend it and care for it. However, a garden is not a wild place, the world in its natural state. A garden is planned, organized, the place of each plant considered for its relationship to its neighbors and the overall design in respect to the color of its leaves and flowers, the month in which it is expected to bloom, its maximum height, as well as its need for shade or full sunshine. Indeed, what is a flower garden but a living artwork, cultivated for no reason but the joy of the gardener and the delight of the chance passerby?

Like gardeners, artists take the raw material of the world and shape it into a form that gives it meaning. And, like gardeners who sweat and strain and sometimes even swear when digging out a stubborn weed or hitting rocks where they expect yielding earth, artists do not find every aspect of their work pleasurable. Sometimes, as in gardening, the work takes an unexpected toll on the body. Artist Audrey Flack writes of painting a large canvas in the middle of a blizzard. Isolated in her studio in East Hampton, with only her dog for company, she worked deep into the night. She continues,

> One frosty night, the night of the completion of the painting, I was standing on a scaffold, painting the drape at the top of the canvas. I must have lost all sense of time. The radio went off the air, the record player stopped, and I worked and worked in a state of total absorption. My right arm was stretched upright all that time, gripping a fine brush to control some delicate areas. Finally the last stroke was applied and the work completed. I stepped down from the scaffold and backed away to gain perspective and look at what I had done. With a sudden sense of shock and fright, I realized that I could not lower my right arm. It was locked into its upright painting position—rigid, frozen.[45]

45. Flack, *Art and Soul*, 53–54.

Flack's arm recovered as she walked around her studio, massaging the muscles into relaxation. Other times, it is not the body, but the artwork itself that resists even our best intentions, our most intense desire to control the outcome. Sometimes, no matter how hard we try, we cannot get an image to resolve, or a character to come to life, or a tune to really sing. As Flack cautions,

> Art can be: joyous, exciting, life-enhancing, fun-packed, insight-provoking, exalting.
>
> Art can be: terrifying, frenetic, devastating, deadening, life-draining, mean spirited, illusion-shattering.
>
> When art is mostly all of the first category, it means the go-ahead signal is on. When art is mainly all of the second category, it's time to go dancing.[46]

For Flack and for many others, sometimes art in another form is the respite from art as labor. But whether making art is labor or respite for the artist, the artwork itself often provides an opportunity for sabbath for someone else. After all, when it is time for the painter to go dancing, the musicians are working. Like people who build retreat centers, and those who continue to shape the landscape around them so that others can be at peace on their periodic retreats into silence, the artist who makes something for no other purpose than aesthetic contemplation is offering the possibility of an experience of delight, the shock of recognition, a moment of awakening to anyone who encounters it. If, as the theologians tell us, our ultimate purpose is to praise God and enjoy God forever, making opportunities for delight is not a frill, but a practice in delighting in the presence of God.

An Artful Body

As Paul tells us in 1 Corinthians 12, the Body of Christ is composed of eyes and ears, feet and noses, heads and bellies. Some are given gifts of wisdom, some of prophecy, some of speaking in different languages, and others of interpretation. Some are called to be apostles, others prophets, teachers, workers of miracles, or healers. And—although Paul does not say so directly—some are called to be artists, either as their primary professional identity or as part of their larger understanding of what it means for them to be fully human.

Buechner and Thurman challenge our easy assumptions about duty, self-sacrifice, honor, and doing what is right with the assertion that when

---

46. Ibid., 61.

we are truly in the will of God, doing the dutiful, honorable, righteous thing will, in fact, be joyful and vital. Conversely, when whatever we are doing does not, in its essence, bring us joy and vitality, then our doing does not add to the well-being of the world. Certainly, there will be times when we feel dejected, defeated, or simply worn out. This is as true of artists as it is of doctors or social workers or peace activists. As humans, none of us is able to live in exuberant joy every minute of every day. Sometimes the work goes badly, or we have an off day.

But the vital joy that is the true sign of call is not the same as simple happiness. Vital joy is the peace of God that passes all understanding, as Paul writes in Philippians 4:7. It is the deep assurance that, despite passing moods and setbacks, this is the true work for which God has prepared you. As Thurman says, this vitality, this excitement about life, is what the world needs more than anything else. When artists feel guilty about their true work, when they take on the world's lies that art is simply a nice frill to be added when everything else is taken care of, when they try to fill their time with works that are good but to which they are not really called, there is the danger that, whatever they do, they will do it grudgingly and with a bad attitude. This only adds anger and disappointment to the world instead of healing its brokenness.

When artists are affirmed in their call, they bring many gifts to the life of the church. Not the least of these gifts is the reminder of the goodness of God's creation. The arts are rooted in matter, in the unbreakable unity of body, mind, and spirit. The manipulation of matter, whether as brushes and paint, the singer's breath, or the dancer's body, teaches us something that we cannot know in any other way. The apprehension of matter in the arts reminds us that God called Creation "good" and, in the Incarnation, became fleshly matter for the healing of the world.

There is room in the Body of Christ for good art and bad, for professional artists and those with more enthusiasm than skill. There is a place for the arts in our public worship, and a place for the arts in our private devotion. There is a place for art that preaches, art that prays, art that teaches, art that heals. When the Body of Christ is artful, the arts can invite us into the presence of God.

7.

A Sanctified Art

Art is much less important than life, but what a poor life without it.
    —Robert Motherwell[1]

We are told in Genesis that we are made in the image and likeness of God. Among the many theories about what that might mean is the idea that, like God, we are creative beings. Some theologians have held that the Creator is entirely separate from the created order, and that God creates *ex nihilo*, out of nothing. Humans, on the other hand, necessarily begin with what God has already created. Thus, the creative activity of God and that of human beings are of entirely different orders, incommensurate with one another.

In *A Theological Approach to Art*, Roger Hazelton counters this notion. He points out that a close reading of the Genesis account reveals not so much God's absoluteness or self-containment of being, but rather God's action in creation. For God, as for humans, creation is a process. Hazelton writes,

> Creation does not happen all at once, nor is it entirely one complete and single act; God calls, forms, distinguishes, and names the multifarious world. Indeed, the more carefully we read and ponder the story told in Genesis, the more creation seems to take on the characteristics of a work of art.[2]

Indeed, once God created humans in the divine image, the human being was immediately invited to join God in the creative action by naming the animals and caring for the created order. Hazelton asserts that these tasks are the evidence that human beings are intended to be God's helpers in

1. Motherwell, *Collected Writings of Robert Motherwell*, 150.
2. Hazelton, *A Theological Approach to Art*, 53.

the ongoing work of creation. To be made in the image and likeness of God is to participate in the creative process.

Similarly, Alejandro García-Rivera sees a connection between the work of the artist and God's own creative freedom. Likening the artist's struggle to that of the monastic hermit, he writes,

> An artist's work ultimately becomes a sign of this relationship between God's creative freedom and the artist's human freedom. Just as the hermit struggles with his own freedom in order to receive a greater one, the artist also struggles with his or her own freedom in the presence of an awesome and absolute Divine Freedom. As such, the work of art reveals much about the artist's struggle with his or her own freedom. This struggle is given vision in the artist's personal style. It is for this reason that even in the 30,000-year-old paintings at Lascaux, one can sense the struggles and hopes of souls unknown to us but now expressed in the creative way those ancient artists depicted the animals that were so much a part of their way of life.[3]

As God's assistants, our own creative activity, especially when engaged in art making, is similar to that of God. As Hazelton notes, the Russian Orthodox theologian Nicholas Berdyaev interpreted the creation of humanity in God's own image to mean that a human being thereby becomes a creator too, called to free spontaneous activity in fulfillment of the Creator's inmost will. For Berdyaev, art is a creative breakthrough into a transfigured world.[4] If our creative potential is the evidence that we are made in the image and likeness of God, then the arts and the artists whose lives are given over to the creative process have something vital to say to the church.

At the beginning of this study, I argued that the church tends to think about art in ways that artists, even those who are themselves Christian, often find problematic and alienating. This alienation between the arts and the church is to the detriment of both. The church loses the specialized skills and knowledge that artists could bring to worship, to biblical study, and to congregational life; and artists lose connection between their lives in the arts and their Christian faith.

In order to help the church invite artists into a mutually beneficial conversation, I have offered some ways to think about art that are more in line with what artists actually experience and do. I have suggested that, since the experience of beauty is relational rather than absolute, the evaluation of art be disconnected from notions of beauty and grounded on more

---

3. García-Rivera, *Wounded Innocence*, 45.

4. Hazelton, *A Theological Approach to Art*, 57.

objective standards. I have shown that rather than a decorative extra to be added on when other needs are met, art is a real, human necessity, rooted in our need to understand our experiences as meaningful, and moving us towards justice and healing. I have also discussed several areas in which the arts may serve the church directly, as well as acting as a force for good in the wider world.

In this chapter, I return to the themes with which I began, offering some solutions to the problem of art and the church.

When we *instrumentalize* art, we see only its didactic possibilities. In making art an instrument towards some other end, we ignore its potential to open our hearts and our minds and tell artists that their work only has value when it is directly applicable to the projects of the church; however, when we take art on its own terms, rather than using it as an instrument towards some other end, we are able to understand the potential for *art as a means of grace*.

When we *commercialize* art, we think about its financial costs and benefits. In doing so, we disregard the intrinsic worth of art as a way of perceiving the world and tell artists that what they understand and care about has no value; however, when we attend to the creative processes that are intrinsic to the arts, rather than their financial costs and benefits, we are able to experience them as *a way of thinking and knowing*.

When we *demonize* art, we fear its power and the artists who understand how to wield it. Demonizing art leads us to refuse to consider that, like any human activity, the arts may be used for ill or for good; however, when we stop being afraid of the idolatrous uses to which some art has been put, we are able to *take the genuine power of art seriously*.

When we *trivialize* art, we relegate it to the status of childish pastime or therapeutic tool. When we think of art as a trivial pursuit, we forget that both talent and training undergird the real work of those who live out their calling as artists; however, when we recognize the commitment and discipline that serious art making requires, we can see *art as a legitimate calling*.

And when we *spiritualize* art, we divorce it from its sources in the concrete materiality of life. A spiritualized view of art asks artists to give us pious platitudes rather than the truth that connects us to God and to one another; however, when we recognize that the arts are grounded in our material brokenness as well as our finest spiritual aspirations, we recognize that the *arts may tell our deepest, most human truths*. It is only then that the arts may be sanctified to our use, and they in turn may become a sanctifying presence in our lives.

Art as a Means of Grace

Grace is the unmerited gift of God. In Matthew 5:45, Jesus says that God "makes the sun rise on the evil and on the good, and sends rain on the righteous and on the unrighteous." Similarly, Paul tells us in Romans 5:8 that the proof of God's love for us is "that while we still were sinners Christ died for us." There is nothing that we can add to grace, nothing that we can do to make God love us more than we are already loved.

Nevertheless, we are often unable or unwilling to receive the grace that God offers to us, to acknowledge that every breath is an astonishing, unearned gift. We continually fall into the heretical notion that we need to earn our salvation, that if we do enough good deeds God will repay us with good gifts. In a world where every encounter is seen as a means to some other end and we are constantly tempted to believe that we are saved by our good deeds rather than by grace, there is no place for things that cannot be turned into an instrument for some ulterior purpose.

Pastor and artist David Taylor argues that art, like worship, helps us to reject this instrumentalizing tendency. Worship is, to use his word, unuseful, and that is a very good thing. "We Christians," he says, "have a lot at stake in the unuseful. We stake our worship every Sunday on the belief that we do not need to convince God to be useful to us, and [God] does not require us to be useful to [God]." He continues,

> Art and worship stand together on the common ground of the unuseful. And this is why our attitude toward art ultimately has a great deal to do with our attitude toward worship. Much is at stake in whether we think that our worship is a free response to grace or an exercise in persuasion, an effort to get either God or people to do what we want them to do. If we have a utilitarian attitude toward art, if we require it to justify itself in terms of its usefulness to our ends, it is very likely that we will end up with the same attitude toward worship, and ultimately toward God.[5]

The arts, like worship, are ultimately unuseful, but not useless. The arts do not directly put food on the tables of those who have none, nor clothe naked bodies, nor even mend broken bones. Indeed, the arts are costly in time as well as money, often competing with other needs for resources that always seem too scarce. But, like worship, the arts need have no purpose except to bring us closer to God, to operate as a channel by which God's love is made real to us. They do this by stopping us in our tracks, inviting us to be still, to attend, to pay attention to what is immediately before us.

5. Taylor, *For the Beauty of the Church*, 40.

As invitations to live into the present moment in all its fullness, the arts can heal broken hearts, feed starving souls, and clothe the ineffable in garments of matter.

In their irreducible materiality, the arts call attention to the intrinsic goodness of creation. In their union of form and content, the arts remind us that Christ became flesh, inseparably uniting the divine and human natures. In their very unusefulness, the arts may be the best demonstration, the best analogy, for the way God showers grace on everyone, whether or not they realize it or deserve it. Indeed, "graceful" is a word often used to describe a thing artfully done or an artful way of moving in the world.

The church has a long history of instrumentalizing the arts, of putting them to didactic purpose, of overexplaining them rather than allowing them to simply be irreducibly themselves. When we invite the arts to enter fully into the life of the church, without any ulterior motive, they can do what they do best, which is move hearts and minds and bodies into new awareness of the physical, intellectual, and spiritual world in which we all live. When we allow the arts to be themselves, we will begin to see the arts as a means of grace.

Art as a Way of Knowing and Thinking

The tools of art are intuition, indirection, inference, allusion, metaphor. While every artwork has an inner logic, this logic is often hidden, of a different order than that of a discursive essay, an academic lecture, or a legal brief. The kind of knowing and thinking that the arts foster is usually not amenable to being summarized, listed, or quantified.

Artists may not be able to put it into words, but they know the precise tilt of a head or lift of an eyebrow that signifies a question, the ratio of red to green that makes a particular kind of brown, the kind of sound that will make an audience sit on the edge of their seats one moment and relax with a contented sigh the next. Artists think in color and form, in pitch and rhythm, in movement and gesture, in time and in space. As artists shape the material world into objects and experiences, they are continually learning about the limits and possibilities of muscles and matter, refining their ideas and their skills, and using what they have learned to affect what those who encounter their work think and feel.

This kind of knowing and thinking is not often valued, either by the church or by the wider world. Although the right brain/left brain division is not as strict as was once thought, the parts of the brain that uses discursive language to describe, to discuss, to argue, to persuade tends to ignore the kind of knowing and thinking that is at the heart of the arts. To the language and logic centers of the brain, the visualizing and noticing centers seem slow and stupid. As Betty Edwards says regarding learning to draw,

> Our problem is that the left brain is dominant *and* speedy and is very prone to rush in with words . . . even taking over jobs which it is not good at. The split brain studies indicated that the left brain likes to be the boss, so to speak, and prefers not to relinquish tasks to its dumb partner unless it really dislikes the job—either because the job takes too much time, is too detailed or slow or because the left brain is simply unable to accomplish the task.[6]

What is true of the division of responsibility in the brain tends to be replicated in social organizations, with those who are both logical and efficient tending to dominate the conversation and the value structure. The slower, more subtle methods and practices that are at the heart of the creative process tend to be discounted by those who are concerned with the bottom line. The kind of knowing that is held in muscle memory, in the body rather than in words, is hard to reconcile with profit-and-loss statements, cost-benefit analyses, and outcomes assessment.

This kind of knowing and thinking, however, is critical to the church, as well as to the wider society. Eugene Peterson writes about the importance of the arts to worship as a formative experience. Discussing the artists and craftspersons who made the various components of the Tent of Meeting described in Exodus, he writes,

> Worship has to do with a God whom no one has ever seen: "Let us worship God" is our standard rubric. But worship has to do simultaneously with all the stuff we see wherever we look: acacia wood, fabrics and skins, tent pegs and altars, tables and flagons. And this is to say nothing of all the workers in textiles, metal, and wood, weaving and smelting and casting. . . . bringing every detail and all the stuff of our lives into the sanctuary, where we are formed into salvation, detail by detail, day by day.[7]

The abundant artistry of the Tent of Meeting in the wilderness of Sinai, and later the Temple at Jerusalem, was not simply an exercise in excess. Rather, it was a way of using material splendor as an analog of God's own glory, a way for the community to experience God's extravagant abundance even in times and places that otherwise seemed bleak and empty. Similarly,

6. Edwards, *Drawing on the Right Side of the Brain*, 42.

7. Peterson, "The Pastor," 95.

both the great cathedrals and the little, country churches of the medieval period and the Renaissance were understood as a foretaste of heaven, a place where human beings whose homes were cold, dark, and poor could practice being in the light-filled, eternal presence of God. This presence was mediated through the arts, through music and mosaics, through paintings and statues, through stained glass and gold and silver vessels, nearly as much as it was through the equally material bread and wine of Eucharist.

The mediated presence of God is only one of the many kinds of knowing that comes through involvement in the arts. Through literature, drama, and the art of storytelling, we become aware of the humanity of people who are separated from us in time or place, learning what it feels like to live in the deserts of Northern Africa or the cold of the arctic tundra or the daily indignities of life on the streets of a big city. Through dance, we become aware of the tension between gravity and human energy, learning to attend to what it feels like to leap or spin or curl up into a tight ball. Through music we become aware of patterns of sound and silence, learning to attune ourselves to one another's rhythm and breath. The kind of knowing that comes through art making or being in the presence of art is different than that which is known through facts and statistics, but is no less important in the living out of our common humanity.

When the arts are experienced in all their sensuous physicality of color, form, rhythm, harmony, or whatever is proper to the particular form of art, they reveal truths that cannot be known in any other way. When we refuse to commercialize art, to see it only in terms of what it costs or what it can bring in, we counter the world's claims of scarcity with the proclamation of God's extravagant abundance. When we value the arts as a way of thinking and knowing, we value the created order that God proclaimed is good; we value knowing God through our bodies as well as our minds.

Taking the Power of Art Seriously

The tendency to demonize the arts is evidenced in the recurrent attempts to link violence among teenagers with watching certain movies or listening to certain kinds of music, to shut down exhibitions thought to promote anti-Christian ideas, or to stereotype artists as morally questionable and irresponsible. While such ideas tend to alienate artists, they are also confirmation of the very real power of art.

Power is, however, never one sided. If art has the potential to seduce us away from God, it also has the power to draw us closer to the divine. If art is able to glorify violence, it also can be the means of healing both personal and societal problems. Art, like any human activity, can be used for both evil and good.

The power of art, however, requires our cooperation, our attention for it to reach its full potential. While it is possible to ignore or even actively reject a work of art, allowing oneself to come into relationship with a painting or a play or a song is not unlike surrendering to the presence of God. As Alejandro García-Rivera writes about the Vietnam Memorial,

> The memorial's artistic power comes from its ability to bring presence to a broken relationship. Presence is the essential ingredient of the Wall's healing power. . . . Is the aesthetics of presence something that takes place in the psychological depths of the beholders? Or is the aesthetics of presence something that resides in the memorial itself? Does the healing process take place within the beholder? Or is it the art of the Wall itself that heals the beholder? Put this way, the insufficiency of the therapeutic explanation becomes self-evident. If healing takes place solely by the beholder's own powers, then the artistic contribution of the Wall becomes irrelevant. If the power to heal resides solely on the art of the Wall itself, then the aesthetic experience of the beholder becomes irrelevant.[8]

These are ultimately theological questions, similar to questions about the nature of beauty or the workings of grace. Garcia-Rivera continues,

> The healing aesthetics of the Vietnam Memorial restate the question in this manner. Does the healing presence of the Wall lie in its artistic contribution or in the aesthetic experience of the beholder? Put this way, the questions closely resemble the questions concerning the doctrine of justification. As such, they allow the theologian a certain insight not only into the nature of art but also into the nature of grace.[9]

Just as grace exists independently of whether we acknowledge it, but requires our cooperation in order for us to receive its full benefit, the power of art is only potential until we come into relationship with it. Like grace, an art work can affect us without our conscious or willing participation, merely by its presence. An insistent drum beat works itself into our consciousness whether we want it to, or even acknowledge it, or not. A sculpture in the middle of a courtyard conditions where we walk, whether or not we really look at it. But only when we open ourselves to receive what an art work has

8. García-Rivera, *Wounded Innocence*, 112.
9. Ibid.

to give, when we notice its shape and size and color, when we yield ourselves to receive its meaning, is its power fully realized.

Like the murals in the barrios of Los Angeles, the Vietnam Memorial has come to speak to and for the community for which it was made. In this case, the community includes not only those who fought in Viet Nam and their families, but an entire nation that was divided against itself over our involvement in that conflict. For a time, the Wall itself served as a symbol of that division, with some reviling it as an ugly gash in the earth rather than seeing it as a fitting memorial to the fallen. Over time, however, its simplicity and presence has increasingly invited public, communal mourning as people have made rubbings of the carved names of loved ones and laid tokens of their loss at its feet. Today, it has become a place of pilgrimage, an important stop for visitors to the nation's capital, where even people who are political enemies have been able to find common ground.

The arts have not only the potential to heal public divisions and invite people to express their grief, but also to move people to action, to change their minds, to help them to celebrate and to advocate for justice, to bring them to anger or laughter as well as tears. The arts help us to access our deepest emotions, to help us to see what we would rather ignore. When we take the power of art seriously, instead of just fearing its potential for idolatrous uses, it can help heal our wounds and open our hearts and minds.

Art as a Legitimate Calling

The tendency to trivialize the arts, to think of them as no more than a childish pastime, a hobby, or mere entertainment is widespread in the wider society as well as in the church. What artists know and do is devalued with comments like "my kid could do that." Once highly specialized jobs in graphic design and typography are disappearing, their projects increasingly assigned to administrative assistants or interns with no training in even basic visual skills, on the assumption that computer programs make it possible for anybody to design a poster or a brochure with only the push of a button. Even for the most successful artists, the hard work of learning and refining their craft, the endless hours of practice, the ongoing effort to reach perfection, is ignored, waved away with praise for their God-given talent as if that were all that is needed. Artists are either lionized as stars or completely disregarded, with no recognition or reward for those whose commitment to their art must be wedged in between the demands of day job, family, and civic life. As Hazelton puts it,

[A]rt is neither a job nor even a profession, but a true vocation. The doing of it claims the artist in a personally engrossing,
wholly committed way. In our society, to be sure, works of art
are usually done in the artist's spare time, despite other duties
and involvements. Only after one's reputation is established and
a market has been found in our economy can artists give their
entire attention and energy to their art. Until then, it is the rule
that works of art are created in the gaps of time and energy left
over after the means of livelihood have been won. And yet whatever may be the economic circumstances of the artist, between
[artists] and [their] art the relationship is typically one that is
intimate, permanent, and intensive. Whatever else [they] may
be or have to do, art is [their] "real work," as [they] will usually
insist.[10]

The artist's vocation is sometimes likened to that of priest, who mediates the divine presence to others or that of the prophets of ancient Israel,
who proclaimed God's words to those who oppressed widows and orphans
and trampled on the rights of the powerless. However, even to think of
artists in these ways may lead to misrepresenting what they do, if such
an understanding privileges the role of talent and inspiration rather than
recognizing the effort and intentionality that the artist's craft requires. The
widely prevalent understanding of biblical inspiration, in which the people
who wrote the Bible are thought of as merely transcribing words given to
them directly by God, misunderstands how inspiration works. The gifts of
talent and inspiration are a starting place, the impetus to begin a work of
art or to keep on going when the artist feels stuck or frustrated or hopeless, but the artist must still do the work of embodying the inspired idea.
The interplay between work and inspiration is as complex as that between
the power of an artwork and the aesthetic experience of the audience. As
Hazelton points out,

To be inspired is not merely to be used by a blind automatic
process but to be caught up and carried along by a creative impulse or suggestion which is then developed or elaborated in the
finished work. . . . The notion given currency by the Romantic
poets that inspiration unconsciously produces works of art cannot stand up under careful scrutiny of the works themselves.
Anyone who has studied the rough draft of a poem by Word-
sworth or the notebooks of Leonardo da Vinci knows better.
Yet the view that consciously controlled art can generate an
inspiration is equally unsound. . . . To be sure . . . much skill and

10. Hazelton, *A Theological Approach to Art*, 92–93.

perseverance are necessary, for we do not call a great work of art a masterpiece without reason. All the same, inspiration is the one thing needful if such work is to be brought into existence. Without it, labor is useless and study is vain.[11]

Making art, whether writing a novel, composing a concerto, or combining images and type in a way that is simultaneously aesthetically pleasing and readable, is real work. It involves the manipulation of both matter and ideas, speaking to bodies and to spirits as well as to the mind. To do this work well requires much time as well as money for canvas and paint or a piano or a guitar, a studio or theater or rehearsal hall, and, often, the cooperation—paid or unpaid—of other artists, such as actors, musicians, or dancers.

For those who are called as artists, as for those who are called to other vocations, their work is often enjoyable, but it also can be difficult, burdensome, and costly. This reality is often lost on those for whom art is a hobby, pastime, or therapy. When we begin to see art as a legitimate calling, rather than just a trivial pursuit to be taken out in moments of leisure, or a therapeutic tool requiring no training or expertise, we will enrich the life of the church and help artists connect their artistic vision with an authentic Christian faith.

The Arts Tell Difficult Truths

There is an old joke about the person who is too spiritual to be any earthly good. Similarly, expecting the arts to depict the glory of God while ignoring the brokenness of creation is to make the arts so spiritual that they cannot address the earthly realities of sin, heartbreak, and death. While the abundant grace and glory of God is one important truth that the arts are able to embody, there are other truths that are equally important for artists to tell, and for Christians to receive.

Many years ago, the Dadian Gallery sponsored a juried art exhibition entitled *Expressions of Faith and a Marginalized Existence*. As the curator of the gallery, I assisted in the selection process conducted by two other well-respected artists and curators. During the process of looking at all the submissions, all of us were in general agreement about which works should be selected to be in the show. At the end of the session, the other jurors chose one work that I found particularly problematic. While I agreed that it both had aesthetic merit and fit the stated topic, I knew it was too big to fit into the gallery along with all the other works that we had selected. The

11. Ibid., 119–20.

jurors insisted, however, and the next day I installed the show, putting the disputed piece in the seminary's board room, which was the only space that could accommodate its size.

The painting in question was called *The Last Supper*, and consisted of nine panels. The central panel, six feet tall, was an extreme close-up view of a face with contorted features. Its mouth was open in a scream of rage or despair, and its skin was a bilious shade of green. On either side, smaller panels depicted various vignettes of human brokenness—a person holding a needle, injecting drugs; a prostitute soliciting a customer; someone in a drunken stupor; a casket ready for a victim of violence. The final two panels were slightly larger, as if enclosing the others in parentheses or an embrace. The one on the far right showed a loaf of ordinary sliced bread, spilling out of its wrapper into the street. On the far left, a bottle of wine, partially hidden by a brown paper bag, poured its contents into the gutter.

The piece was painted in an expressionistic style, reminiscent of the lurid movie posters of the 1940s. Its size, its style, and its subject matter made it difficult to ignore, especially in a room where the faculty met each month for their deliberations. So I was not terribly surprised when, after it had been up for a while, some faculty members challenged me to defend the work. Describing it as ugly and disturbing, they asked what was good about it.

As their questions revealed, these faculty members expected art to be beautiful, or at least decorative. They did not want a screaming, green Jesus looming over their shoulders, reminding them of the lost and broken people that were otherwise invisible in that gracious meeting room. While their own classroom discussions often stressed God's preferential option for the poor, and they would not have been surprised or upset to hear stories like those depicted in the painting preached from the pulpit a few yards away, the visual images confronted them in a way that was at odds with their understanding of the purpose of art.

This *Last Supper* was no comforting image of Jesus calmly at table with his disciples, but rather an imaginative depiction of God's distress when people reject and misuse the good gifts that have been offered to them. It was not about the glories of Holy Communion or even Christ's sacrifice on our behalf, but rather about the waste of human life and the isolation of those who do not understand the healing power of the bread and cup shared within the Body of Christ. The artist intended to upset the viewers, and succeeded in that intention.

To those who reject art works like this, ones that are ugly or that tell uncomfortable truths, Hazelton responds with the reminder that artists need to be free to work with any subject matter, any situation, any truth, just as preachers and teachers are free to speak of judgment and sin as well as glory. He notes, "When an artist gives fair warning that [this] truth is going to hurt, portrays human nastiness with compassion, or mingles biting scorn with sympathy, [the] work is strangely analogous to the words of judgment and reconciliation spoken together in Christian faith."[12]

When people experience existential despair, become indignant at injustice, suffer physical pain, or grieve their losses, such events often become the impetus for works of art. As Hazelton puts it,

> [O]ne can only see what is there to be seen, can only disclose to others what has been disclosed to [one]. There is in principle no reason why moral indignation or spiritual despair may not serve as creative stimuli quite as effectively as do experiences of serenity and positive assurance. Moreover, is it not true that we often learn best what something means by taking a hard look at its opposite? The person who has felt the sharp edge of injustice is the one who knows what justice really is. [The one] who has been dealt with unmercifully cries out most earnestly for true mercy. Is there any form of radical protest which is not also at bottom an affirmation? Let it be granted that a work of art should be judged and responded to on its own terms, aesthetically, but those whose complacency has never been disturbed by the artist can scarcely even know what [artists are] about.[13]

I should note that the painting stayed in place for the entire run of the show, and also that the faculty members who objected to the painting described above would be unlikely to do so today. The questions that troublesome *Last Supper* engendered were part of an ongoing conversation about the arts that began long before I arrived at the seminary, and continues to permeate our life together, many years later. In the course of that conversation, the faculty has learned that art has many moods and many purposes. Today, I can say with assurance that our faculty would agree that, like good preaching, good art should both comfort the afflicted and afflict the comfortable. Rooted in the material world of sight, sound, and movement, the arts speak through our bodily senses to change our hearts and our minds. When we bring the arts down to earth, recognizing their ability to help us connect with matter, to tell our deepest, most human truths as well as to reveal the invisible mystery of God's presence, they teach us something important about what it means that Christ is fully human and fully divine.

12. Ibid., 111.
13. Ibid., 110–11.

A Sanctified and Sanctifying Art

To sanctify an object or an activity is to set it aside for divine purposes, to purify it, to make it holy. Similarly, a person is said to be sanctified when he or she lives in close alignment with God's will. While denominations differ in their definitions of complete sanctification, as well as whether it is even possible for a person to attain such a state of perfection while living a mortal life, Christians generally recognize that some individuals are more attuned to God than others.

Art is one of the tools that human beings have been given to aid in the process of sanctification. In order to do that, we must think clearly about what art is, the role of artists in the community, and how the arts affect those who participate in them, both as makers and as audience. For art to be both sanctified and sanctifying, we must first recognize the possibility that it can be a means of grace; accept that it is a way of thinking and knowing that has genuine power to heal the broken places in the world; and acknowledge that artists are called by God to tell our deepest, most human truths by manipulating matter in ways that speak to our minds and hearts through our bodily senses.

All of these things, however, can only be accomplished when both artists and the church view art not as a solitary activity, but rather as a communal process. As Jeremy Begbie puts it, the creativity that is at the heart of the arts must "be set in a *corporate* context, for the inner logic of the Gospel compels us to affirm that self-fulfillment is discovered only in relationship."[14] He continues,

> If it is true, as I have indicated, that art carries ethical and cognitive dimensions, then questions of an artist's obligation to a given community simply cannot be side-stepped, (nor, by implication, can issues of constraint and censorship). Part of this obligation will be a sensitivity to the shared values and assumptions of [one's] social setting (insofar as there *are* shared values and assumptions). An artist's very vocabulary depends on communities of interest, on established precedents and particular conventions of appraisal. These cannot be ignored, even if they are to be modified and in part rejected.[15]

Even beyond this acknowledgment of shared values and conventions, a willingness to work collaboratively is an important dimension of the obligation of artists toward the community to which they address their work.

14. Begbie, *Voicing Creation's Praise*, 180; emphasis original.
15. Ibid., 220–21.

In the popular imagination, as well as in their own training and experience, artists are largely thought of as solitary beings, working out their private visions without regard for the needs and desires of anyone else. This image is largely a legacy of the Romantic era, in which the idea of individual genius raised those thought to possess it to a nearly divine status. For most of human history, however, artists made music that bound communities with song and dance; told the communal stories dramatically and passionately; and made objects that helped communities work, play, and worship together. They made art that addressed their communities in ways that the community could comprehend, and in return they received both economic and spiritual support.

Today, many artists are relearning how to work collaboratively and communally, sharing their vision and their skills within communities and congregations that, without them, become sterile and boring. While artists will always need time, space, and other resources to pursue their inward vision, some artists are discovering that working in collaboration with others brings forth new ideas, new approaches, new excellencies that would never emerge in the solitude of the private studio. Such collaborative efforts may take a variety of forms, depending in part on the differing demands of artistic methods and materials. What they have in common, however, is a resemblance to the eternal Perichoresis—the never-ending dance—of the Holy Trinity, in which each person equally and fully participates without any sense of greater or lesser importance. In the collaborative dance, each partner leads and follows at different times, creating together an intricate pattern of mutual trust and support. Like members of a jazz ensemble, each elaborating the theme in turn, artists working collaboratively with other artists and with the church make no attempt to dominate or oppress one another or reject their gift, but rather share leadership and inspiration freely and fluidly.

When the church works collaboratively with the artists in its midst, the church will rediscover the power of symbolic language that is inherent in the arts. When those who understand both the potential and the limitations of the arts are given the opportunity to bring their skills and knowledge into genuine conversation with the other members of the Body of Christ, the arts will assume their rightful task of telling the truth about human life and the life of God. Art, like any human endeavor, can be used both for good and for ill. A sanctified and sanctifying art is one that helps each person, the entire Body of Christ, and ultimately all of Creation move towards the wholeness and goodness that God intends.

Bibliography

Adams, Doug. *Dance as Religious Studies*. Eugene, OR: Wipf and Stock, 2001.

Antoni, Janine. "Lick and Lather: An Interview with Janine Antoni." Interviews with artists. *Art21*, 2003. http://www.art21.org/texts/janine-antoni/interview-janine-antoni-lick-and-lather.

Aquinas, Thomas. *Summa Theologica*. 1947. http://www.sacred-texts.com/chr/aquinas/summa/sum194.htm.

"Asteroids, Stars, and the Love of God: Two Vatican Astronomers and Their Faith." *Speaking of Faith with Krista Tippet*. American Public Media (April 1, 2010). http://www.onbeing.org/program/asteroids-stars-and-love-god/transcript/2416.

Augustine. *The Confessions of St. Augustine*. Translated by E. B. Pusey. New York: E. P. Dutton, 1907.

Bailie, Gil. *Violence Unveiled: Humanity at the Crossroads*. New York: Crossroad, 1995.

Balthasar, Hans Urs von. *The Glory of the Lord: A Theological Aesthetics*. Edited by Joseph Fessio and John Riches. 7 vols. San Francisco: Ignatius, 1983–1991.

Barger, Michael. "The Light Within: An Interview with Mark Dukes." *God's Friends* 6/3 (January 1997) n.p. http://godsfriends.org/Vol6/No3/Light_Within.html.

Barnett Newman Foundation. "Chronology." *Barnett Newman Foundation*, n.d. http://www.barnettnewman.org/chronology.php.

Barr, Alfred. *Picasso: Fifty Years of His Art 1895–1945*. New York: Museum of Modern Art, 1946.

Barzun, Jacques. *The Use and Abuse of Art*. Bollingen Series 35. Princeton, NJ: Princeton University Press, 1974.

Bayles, David. *Art and Fear: Observations on the Perils (and Rewards) of Artmaking*. Santa Barbara, CA: Capra, 1993.

Begbie, Jeremy. *Voicing Creation's Praise: Towards a Theology of the Arts*. Edinburgh: T. & T. Clark, 1991.

Bell, Clive. *Art*. New York: Frederick A. Stokes, 1913. Kindle electronic edition.

Benezra, Neal, and Olga M. Viso, eds. *Regarding Beauty: A View of the Late Twentieth Century*. Washington, DC: Smithsonian Institution Hirshhorn Museum and Sculpture Garden, 1999.

Bernard of Clairvaux. "Bernard of Clairvaux: Apology." *Internet History Sourcebooks Project*. n.d. http://www.fordham.edu/halsall/source/bernard1.asp.

Birch, Bruce. "The Arts, Midrash, and Biblical Teaching." In *Arts, Theology, and the Church: New Intersections*, edited by Kimberly Vrudny and Wilson Yates, 105–25. Cleveland: Pilgrim, 2005.

Bokamoso Youth Foundation. "Bokamoso Youth Foundation." n.d. http://www.bokamosoyouth.org/centre/index.php.

Boyle, Katherine. "D.C. Area Homeless Women to Tell 'Life Stories' in Kennedy Center Performance." *The Washington Post*. Washingtonpost.com, April 29, 2012. http://www.washingtonpost.com/lifestyle/style/dc-area-homeless-women-to-tell-life-stories-in-kennedy-center-performance/2012/04/29/gIQAbdxUqT_story.html.

Brown, Frank Burch. *Good Taste, Bad Taste, and Christian Taste: Aesthetics in Religious Life*. Oxford: Oxford University Press, 2003.

Brueggeman, Walter. *Finally Comes the Poet: Daring Speech for Proclamation*. Minneapolis: Fortress, 1989.

Buechner, Frederick. *Wishful Thinking: A Seeker's ABC*. Rev. and exp. San Francisco: HarperSanFrancisco, 1993.

Cage, John. "4'33'." Edition Peters, 1952. http://www.sheetmusicplus.com/title/4-33/1008430#.

Cameron, Julia. *The Artist's Way: A Spiritual Path to Higher Creativity*. 10th anniversary. New York: J. P. Tarcher/Putnam, 2002.

Cesaretti, Gusmano. *Street Writers: A Guided Tour of Chicano Graffiti*. Los Angeles: Acrobat, 1975.

Cook, John W. "A Willem De Kooning Triptych." *Theological Education* 31/1 (Autumn 1994) 59–73.

Dahlin, Cynthia. "Sermon for Sunday, May 8, 2011." *Seekers Church Sermons* (May 8, 2011). http://www.seekerschurch.org/index.php?option=com_content&view=article&id=1188:a-sermon-by-cynthia-dahlin&catid=18:sermons-blog&Itemid=79.

Danto, Arthur C. *The Abuse of Beauty: Aesthetics and the Concept of Art*. Chicago: Open Court, 2003.

———. *After the End of Art: Contemporary Art and the Pale of History*. Princeton, NJ: Princeton University Press, 1997.

———. *The Transfiguration of the Commonplace: A Philosophy of Art*. Cambridge, MA: Harvard University Press, 1981.

Dickerman, Leah, et al. *Dada: Zurich, Berlin, Hanover, Cologne, New York, Paris*. Washington, DC: The National Gallery of Art and D.A.P., 2005.

Dissanayake, Ellen. *Art and Intimacy: How the Arts Began*. Seattle: University of Washington Press, 2000.

Dyrness, William. *Reformed Theology and Visual Culture: The Protestant Imagination from Calvin to Edwards*. Cambridge: Cambridge University Press, 2004.

Edwards, Betty. *Drawing on the Artist Within: A Guide to Innovation, Invention, Imagination, and Creativity*. New York: Simon and Schuster, 1986.

———. *Drawing on the Right Side of the Brain: A Course in Enhancing Creativity and Artistic Confidence*. Revised. Los Angeles: J. P. Tarcher, 1979.

Elkins, Heather Murray. *Holy Stuff of Life: Stories, Poems, and Prayers about Human Things*. Cleveland: Pilgrim, 2006.

Elkins, James. *On the Strange Place of Religion in Contemporary Art*. New York: Routledge, 2004.

Eyerman, Ron, and Andrew Jamison. *Music and Social Movements: Mobilizing Traditions in the Twentieth Century*. Cambridge: Cambridge University Press, 1998.

Flack, Audrey. *Art and Soul: Notes on Creating*. 1st ed. New York: Dutton, 1986.

García-Rivera, Alejandro. *A Wounded Innocence : Sketches for a Theology of Art*. Collegeville, MN: Liturgical, 2003.

Geyer, Ginger Henry. "Amos' Basket of Summer Fruit." Exhibition label, 2002. http://www.gingergeyer.com/art_stories/stories/amos_basket.html.

Harris, David. *Street Corner Majesty*. Bloomington, IN: Authorhouse, 2009.

Hart, Russel. *The Icon Through Western Eyes*. Springfield, IL: Templegate, 1991.

Hazelton, Roger. *A Theological Approach to Art*. Nashville: Abingdon, 1967.

Herrón, Willie. "Oral History Interview with Willie Herrón." Oral Histories Archives of American Art, Smithsonian Institution (February 5, 2000). http://www.aaa.si.edu/collections/interviews/oral-history-interview-willie-herrn-12847.

Hilliard, Russell E. "Music Therapy in Hospice and Palliative Care: A Review of the Empirical Data." *Evidence-Based Complementary and Alternative Medicine* 2/2 (June 2005) 173–78.

Hypki, Cinder. "Re: Art and Mourning." Private correspondence to author, May 28, 2012.

Hypki, Cinder, Rhonda Cooper, and Louise Knight. "Memorial Ritual and Art: A Case Study and Exploration of the Potential for Healing." *MICA (Maryland Institute College of Art) Community Arts Journal* 3 (Fall 2011) n.p. http://www.mica.edu/Research_at_MICA/Research_in_Community_Arts/Community_Arts_Journal/Writing_Group_Texts/Memorial_Ritual_and_Art.html.

John of Damascus. *In Defense of Icons*. Translated by Mary H. Allies. London: Thomas Baker, 1898. http://www.fordham.edu/halsall/source/johndam-icons.asp.

Jorgensen-Earp, Cheryl R., and Lori A. Lanzilotti. "Public Memory and Private Grief: The Construction of Shrines at the Sites of Public Tragedy." *Quarterly Journal of Speech* 84/2 (May 1998) 150–70.

Kalnin, Jim. "Art as Sacerdos." In *The Spirituality of Art*, edited by Lois Huey-Heck and Jim Kalnin, 33–59. Kelowna, BC: Northstone, 2006.

Keats, John. *Ode on a Grecian Urn*. Poem, 1819.

Kiesler, Frederick. "Second Manifesto of Correalism." *Art International* 9/2 (March 1965) 16–17. Reprinted in *Theories and Documents of Contemporary Art: A Sourcebook of Artists' Writings*, edited by Kristine Stiles and Peter Selz, 510–11. Berkeley: University of California Press, 1996.

Langer, Susanne. *Problems of Art: Ten Philosophical Lectures*. New York: Scribner, 1957.

Leaver, Robin. "Liturgical Music as Corporate Song I: Hymnody in Reformation Churches." In *Liturgy and Music: Lifetime Learning*, edited by Robin Leaver and Joyce Ann Zimmerman, 281–307. Collegeville, MN: Liturgical, 1998.

Lehrer, Jonah. "Musical Language." *WNYC Radiolab*, September 24, 2007. http://www.radiolab.org/2007/sep/24/.

Lentz, Robert, and Edwina Gateley. *Christ in the Margins*. Maryknoll, NY: Orbis, 2003.

Lerner, Alan. *The Street Where I Live*. New York: Norton, 1980.

Leviton, Daniel. *This Is Your Brain on Music: The Science of a Human Obsession*. New York: Plume/Penguin, 2006.

Lewis, C. S. *An Experiment in Criticism*. 2012 reissue. Cambridge: Cambridge University Press, 1961.

Luther, Martin. "An Open Letter to the Christian Nobility of the German Nation concerning the Reform of the Christian Estate." Wittenberg, 1520. Electronic Text Center, University of Virginia Library. http://etext.lib.virginia.edu/etcbin/toccer-new2?id=LutNobi.xml&images=images/modeng&data=/texts/english/modeng/parsed&tag=public&part=1&division=div1.

Martin, Linette. *Sacred Doorways: A Beginner's Guide to Icons.* Brewster, MA: Paraclete, 2002.

McDannell, Colleen. *Material Christianity: Religion and Popular Culture in America.* New Haven: Yale University Press, 1995.

Milspaw, Yvonne. "Protestant Home Shrines: Icon and Image." *New York Folklore* 12/3–4 (1986) 119.

Motherwell, Robert. *The Collected Writings of Robert Motherwell.* Edited by Stephanie Terenzio. New ed. Documents of Twentieth-Century Art. Berkeley: University of California Press, 1999.

Muller, Melissa, and Reinhard Piechocki. *Alice's Piano: The Life of Alice Herz-Sommer.* St. Martin's, 2012.

National Conference of Catholic Bishops. *Environment and Art in Catholic Worship.* Washington, DC: National Conference of Catholic Bishops, 1978.

New Community ArtSpace. "Work with Us." *ArtSpace DC,* n.d. http://www.artspacedc.org/mission.

Newman, Barnett. "The Sublime Is Now." In *Barnett Newman: Selected Writings and Interviews,* edited by John O'Neill, 331. New York: Knopf, 1990.

Nicolosi, Barbara. "The Artist: What Exactly Is an Artist, and How Do We Shepherd Them?" In *For the Beauty of the Church: Casting a Vision for the Arts,* edited by W. David O. Taylor. Grand Rapids: Baker, 2010.

O'Connor, Elizabeth. *Servant Leaders, Servant Structures.* Washington, DC: Servant Leadership School, 1991. http://www.theoblogical.org/dlature/itseminary/wischris/Ch1arts.html.

O'Connor, Flannery. *Mystery and Manners: Occasional Prose.* Edited by Sally Fitzgerald and Robert Fitzgerald. New York: Farrar Straus and Giroux, 1970.

Oppenheim, James. "Bread and Roses." *American Magazine* 73 (December 1911) 214.

Ouspensky, Léonide. *Theology of the Icon.* Vol. 1. Translated by Anthony Gythiel. Crestwood, NY: St. Vladimir's Seminary Press, 1992.

Palidofsky, Jesse. "Joan." Unpublished manuscript. Silver Spring, MD: 2011.

———. "Non-Anxious Presence: The Story of Daniel." Unpublished manuscript. Silver Spring, MD: 2011.

———. "Ofelia." Unpublished manuscript. Silver Spring, MD: 2011.

Pearson, Peter. "Vitae." *Peter Pearson Iconogapher,* n.d. http://www.nb.net/~pearson/vitae.htm.

Peterson, Eugene. "The Pastor: How Artists Shape Pastoral Identity." In *For the Beauty of the Church: Casting a Vision for the Arts,* edited by W. David O. Taylor, 83–102. Grand Rapids: Baker, 2010.

Picasso, Pablo. "Picasso Speaks: Statement to Marius De Zayas." *The Arts* (May 1923) 315–26.

Reinhardt, Ad. "25 Lines of Words on Art: Statement." *It Is* 1 (Spring 1958) 42. Reprinted in *Theories and Documents of Contemporary Art: A Sourcebook of Artists' Writings,* edited by Kristine Stiles and Peter Selz, 90–91. Berkeley: University of California Press, 1996.

Rock, Judith, and Norman Mealy. *Performer as Priest and Prophet: Restoring the Intuitive in Worship Through Music and Dance.* San Francisco: Harper and Row, 1988.

Sanchez-Tranquilino, Marcos. "Murals Del Movimiento: Chicano Murals and the Discourses of Art and Americanization." In *Signs From the Heart: California*

Chicano Murals, edited by Eva Sperling Cockcroft and Holly Barnet-Sanchez, 84–101. Albuquerque: University of New Mexico Press, 1993.

Scarry, Elaine. *On Beauty and Being Just*. Princeton, NJ: Princeton University Press, 1999.

Selz, Peter, and San Jose Museum of Art. *Art of Engagement: Visual Politics in California and Beyond*. Berkeley: University of California Press, 2005.

Siedell, Daniel. *God in the Gallery: A Christian Embrace of Modern Art*. Grand Rapids: Baker Academic, 2008.

Sitar Arts Center. "Sitar Arts Center Mission." *Sitar Arts Center*, n.d. http://www.sitarartscenter.org/beliefs.

Social and Public Art Resource Center. "Great Wall of Los Angeles." *SPARC Murals*, n.d. http://www.sparcmurals.org:16080/sparcone/index.php?option=com_content&task=view&id=21&Itemid=53.

Sokolove Colman, Deborah. "Going to the Olympics: A Muralist's Journal." *Images and Issues* 5/1 (August 1984) 18–19.

Solomon, Jane. "Living with X: A Body Mapping Journey in the Time of HIV and AIDS. Facilitator's Guide." Edited by Jonathan Morgan. REPSSI, 2007. https://sites.google.com/site/bodymaps/history.

Stiles, Kristine, and Peter Selz, eds. *Theories and Documents of Contemporary Art: A Sourcebook of Artists' Writings*. Berkeley: University of California Press, 1996.

Suger. "De Administratione." In *Abbot Suger on the Abbey Church of St. Denis and Its Art Treasures*, translated by Erwin Panofsky. 2nd ed. Princeton, NJ: Princeton University Press, 1979.

Sullivan, Michael. *Windows into the Soul: Art as Spiritual Expression*. Harrisburg, PA: Morehouse, 2006. Kindle electronic edition.

Taylor, W. David O. "The Dangers: What Are the Dangers of Artmaking in the Church?" In *For the Beauty of the Church: Casting a Vision for the Arts*, edited by W. David O. Taylor, 145–64. Grand Rapids: Baker, 2010.

Taylor, W. David O., ed. *For the Beauty of the Church: Casting a Vision for the Arts*. Grand Rapids: Baker, 2010.

Tobin, Richard. "The Canon of Polykleitos." *American Journal of Archaeology* 79/4 (October 1975) 307–21.

Tolstoy, Leo. *What Is Art?* Translated by Richard Pevear and Larissa Volokhonsky. New York: Penguin, 1898.

Tutu, Desmond. "Can We Forgive Our Enemy?" *Washington National Cathedral: Sunday Forum Transcript*, November 11, 2007. http://www.nationalcathedral.org/learn/forumTexts/SF071111T.shtml.

"Two Vatican Astronomers: A Twitterscript." On Being Blog (February 25, 2010) http://blog.onbeing.org/post/411480037/two-vatican-astronomers-a-twitterscript.

United States Holocaust Memorial Museum. "Theresienstadt." n.d. http://www.ushmm.org/wlc/en/article.php?ModuleId=10005424.

Williams, William Carlos. "Asphodel, That Greeny Flower." In *Journey to Love*. New York: Random House, 1955.

Winner, Ellen, and Lois Hetland. "Art for Our Sake." *The Boston Globe*, September 2, 2007. http://www.boston.com/news/globe/ideas/articles/2007/09/02/art_for_our_sake/?page=full.

Winton-Henry, Cynthia, and Phil Porter. "InterPlay." n.d. http://www.interplay.org/.

Witvliet, John D. "Series Preface." In *Inclusive Yet Discerning: Navigating Worship Artfully*, by Frank Burch Brown, viii–xi. Calvin Institute of Christian Worship Liturgical Studies Series. Grand Rapids: Eerdmans, 2009. Kindle electronic edition.

Wolterstorff, Nicholas. *Art in Action: Toward a Christian Aesthetic*. Grand Rapids: Eerdmans, 1980.

World ORT. "Music in the Nazi Concentration Camps." *Music and the Holocaust*, n.d. http://holocaustmusic.ort.org/places/camps/.

Wuthnow, Robert. *Creative Spirituality: The Way of the Artist*. Berkeley: University of California Press, 2001.

Young, Stanley, and Melba Levick. *The Big Picture: Murals of Los Angeles*. New York: New York Graphic Society, 1988.

Index